Death in Briar Bottom

Death in Briar Bottom

THE TRUE STORY OF HIPPIES,
MOUNTAIN LAWMEN, AND
THE SEARCH FOR JUSTICE
IN THE EARLY 1970s

Timothy Silver

THE UNIVERSITY OF NORTH CAROLINA PRESS

Chapel Hill

Designed by Jamison Cockerham
Set in Scala, Warnock, Unit Gothic, and Sentinel
by codeMantra

Cover art: The Clearwater campers and friends at the Bungalows
in Florida in April 1972, three months before the events in
Briar Bottom. Photograph by Roger D. Altland.

Manufactured in the United States of America

LIBRARY OF CONGRESS CATALOGING-IN-PUBLICATION DATA
Names: Silver, Timothy, 1955– author.
Title: Death in Briar Bottom : the true story of hippies, mountain
lawmen, and the search for justice in the early 1970s / Timothy Silver.
Description: Chapel Hill : The University of North Carolina Press, 2024. |
Includes bibliographical references and index.
Identifiers: LCCN 2024029883 | ISBN 9781469682860
(cloth ; alk. paper) | ISBN 9781469682877 (epub) | ISBN 9781469682884 (pdf)
Subjects: LCSH: Altland, Stanley, –1972—Death and burial. |
Police brutality—North Carolina—Yancey County—History—20th century. |
Counterculture—United States—History—20th century. | Hippies—Public
opinion. | Yancey County (N.C.)—Social conditions—20th century. |
Clearwater (Fla.)—Social conditions—20th century. |
BISAC: TRUE CRIME / Historical | BIOGRAPHY & AUTOBIOGRAPHY /
Personal Memoirs | LCGFT: True crime stories. | Biographies.
Classification: LCC HV7936.P725 S55 20024 |
DDC 363.2/3209756873—dc23/eng/20240725
LC record available at https://lccn.loc.gov/2024029883

Who breaks a Butterfly
upon a Wheel?

ALEXANDER POPE,
"EPISTLE TO DR ARBUTHNOT,"
1735

CONTENTS

ILLUSTRATIONS

Death in
Briar Bottom

PROLOGUE

I Thought They Were Going to Shoot Us All

By 10:30 on that summer night in 1972, the party at the remote woodland campsite had run out of steam. Beer cans littered the ground. Garbage bins overflowed with discarded food, greasy paper plates, plastic cups, and other refuse. Every now and then, the faint stench of overused pit toilets drifted across the clearing. About half of the twenty-five men and women staying there had gone to bed, but those awake were in good spirits. They were young, ranging in age from sixteen to twenty-six, and all but one came from central Florida, around Clearwater.

Two days of hard driving had brought them here, to Yancey County, deep in the North Carolina mountains, a place so different from their hometown that it seemed like another planet. Surrounded by some the highest peaks in eastern America, their seven vehicles (six cars and a Volkswagen van) sat parked in a grassy field, flanked on all sides by tall hemlocks, yellow birches, large leafy oaks, and giant poplars. The South Toe River, a clear, cold, boulder-strewn stream, flowed right past their campsite.[1] Local people called the place Briar Bottom.

Campsite occupied by the Clearwater group in 1972.
Courtesy of the National Archives and Records
Administration, College Park, MD.

It was the week of July 4, pinnacle of the tourist season, and it had been tough to find a place to stay. Fortunately, they made a new friend at a local store who told them about Briar Bottom and agreed to meet them there. The Florida kids had to drive their vehicles across a shallow ford in the river, unload in the field, and carry their gear into the woods to make camp. Even then, they were not alone. Several families, a couple of college students, and three men from Orlando, Florida, had already parked vans in the meadow or set up tents among the trees along the river. But the place was beautiful, everything they had hoped for when they left Clearwater, and they settled in for the night.[2]

That afternoon, three of the guys drove to Asheville and returned with seventeen six-packs of Budweiser and two bottles of Jack Daniels. They already had a stash of marijuana and some mild hallucinogens, all brought from home in anticipation of the week's activities. Once the alcohol arrived, someone set a couple of speakers atop the van and cranked up a tape player. Out in the open field, kids danced and flirted, shouting or singing along when a favorite tune came up on the tape deck. In a group that large, people tended to hang around those they knew best, congregating in small clusters, talking, laughing, smoking, drinking—just getting off on the beer, the dope, the mountains, and each other.

Stanley Altland, the twenty-year-old who had organized the trip, enjoyed a good outdoor party as much as anyone, but he took it easy that night. He drank a couple of beers and had a hit or two off the joints his friends passed around, but mostly he just wandered about, chatting with the others. He ate supper with David Satterwhite, the boy from North Carolina who had guided them to Briar Bottom. An experienced camper, Satterwhite had his own van, a motorcycle, and a big white dog. Stan also spent time with Kim Burns, a tall, attractive eighteen-year-old woman from Clearwater he had begun dating a few weeks earlier.

Altland had shoulder-length blonde hair, a scruffy beard, and wore round, wire-rimmed glasses to correct severe astigmatism. He frequently dressed in bib overalls and old work boots purchased from secondhand stores. Most of the Clearwater kids thought he was the walking definition of "cool," a much-coveted youth descriptor in 1972. For Stan, being cool was more than a matter of style. He believed that young people like him—those others derisively labeled "hippies"—were pointing the way to a better world. Back home, he and his business partners had recently opened Clearwater's first health-food store. Stan hoped it would one day become a "true community center" and a vehicle for "cultural, economic, and political change." He invited local artists, craftspeople, and filmmakers to display their work there. His friends loved the place.[3]

An hour or so after dark, Altland walked over to the VW van to talk with his pal Phil Lokey. Phil also wore wire-rimmed "hippie" glasses and had a beard and long dark hair that he often pulled back behind his ears. He and Stan had once been roommates, but several months earlier, Phil had moved to the Bungalows, a string of rundown, two-bedroom dwellings on the outskirts of Clearwater. The Bungalows had a well-deserved reputation as a hippie hangout, where the tenants threw raucous weekend parties. Several other residents had joined the outing to North Carolina, including Kevin Shea, Max Johnson, Ron Olson, and Gary Graham, four more twenty-year-olds with well-worn clothes and shoulder-length locks. Eighteen-year-old Sue Cello, who described herself as "a Catholic school girl with a mouth to match," had also come along.

Over the course of the evening, Kevin Shea partook liberally of the beer and pot, found a stick, and announced that he was off to the woods to hunt rattlesnakes. Max Johnson and several women left for a night hike up a nearby hillside, carrying a bottle of Jack Daniels. Sue Cello joined a few others around a small campfire at the edge of the woods. Ron Olson and Gary Graham headed for their tents.

It was that kind of mellow, do-your-own-thing night. Most of those present thought it better to get too stoned than too drunk, much cooler to toke up with friends around the fire than end up puking in the bushes or sitting alone in a car sorting out the kaleidoscopic images brought on by heavier drugs. But if hard drinking or stoned snake-hunting happened to be your trip, no one would stand in your way. On July 3, 1972, the prevailing party ethic—to the extent that one existed—might well be summed up by that famous line from Bob Dylan, "Either be groovy or leave, man."[4]

By 11:00, temperatures dipped into the low sixties at Briar Bottom, sending more campers to their tents and sleeping bags. Heavy dew covered the ground, and anyone who strayed from the fire could see their breath in the thick, humid air. Filmy clouds drifted across a half moon.[5] Stan Altland left the van and found a place to stretch out under a small tree. Kim Burns decided to join him, at least for a while if the bugs were not too bad. Phil Lokey walked out to his car to retrieve his bedroll.

Eight or nine others lingered around the campfire. They had turned off the music and were talking quietly, sipping beer and smoking cigarettes. Sue Cello was still there, along with David Satterwhite and his dog. Donald Porter, whom everyone called "Poonie," was at the firepit, too. A twenty-six-year-old Vietnam veteran recently turned beach hippie, he was a regular at Bungalow parties. With his long hair pulled into a ponytail that stretched well down his back, Poonie was the likeable "old man" of the group.

Just as a few of those at the fire began to doze, two of the girls glimpsed some flickering lights on the other side of the river, near the ford. Headlights from vehicles on the access road? Maybe some late-arriving campers looking for a site. They would have fun negotiating that rocky streambed in the dark. Max Johnson was too sleepy to care. Returning from the night hike, he spread a sleeping bag on the ground and crawled inside. Somewhere nearby, Kevin Shea, still in search of venomous reptiles, howled like a wolf.

As Phil Lokey walked back from his car, he saw two pickup trucks with their headlights off drive quickly across the river and pull into the parking area. Seven men jumped out. Even in the dark, Phil could tell they were heavily armed. They moved through the trees "like a SWAT team," and he heard them racking shotguns as they advanced on the Clearwater campsite. "What the hell . . . ?" For a second, Lokey thought maybe he should make a break for it, just run as fast as he could into the forest. But he could not make himself move.

At the campfire, Satterwhite's dog growled, waking its sleeping owner. Without warning, five of the armed men came out of the woods and surrounded the group at the firepit. Caught completely off guard, the half-inebriated, half-stoned, drowsy campers tried to make sense of the abrupt turn of events. It seemed crazy, dreamlike, surreal. The men looked to be in their thirties or forties, with short hair, dressed mostly in civilian clothes. One, who wore yellowish-brown attire, appeared to be in charge. He mumbled something like "What's the problem?" or "Do you have a problem?" or "What's the trouble here?" No one could be sure exactly what he said. But one thing was certain. The men all had pistols and three of them wielded short-barreled, 12-gauge shotguns.

Without identifying themselves, the armed visitors fanned out around the camp, turning on flashlights, beating on tents, kicking at those asleep on the ground, and poking them with nightsticks. The good vibes from earlier in the evening instantly evaporated. Max Johnson and several others crawled from their sleeping bags, weak-kneed, shaking uncontrollably from the late-night chill and sudden anxiety. As one of the group later recalled, "We were scared to death. We didn't know what was happening, but we figured some kind of bad shit was about to go down."

Thirty yards away, the other two men, both carrying sawed-off shotguns, confronted Phil Lokey. They said nothing, but as Phil noted, "you didn't have to be a genius to tell they were cops of some sort, and we were about to get busted." He asked the man closest to him, "Sir, could you please tell me what's going on?" He grabbed Lokey, slapped handcuffs on him, and said, "I'll tell you exactly what's going on." Then he stuck his shotgun in Phil's back and marched him toward the campfire.[6]

Unbeknownst to the campers, the men rousting them were—at least for that night—duly sworn agents of the Yancey County Sheriff's Department. Sheriff Kermit Banks, the man in buff-colored clothing, led the raiding party.[7] The posse included his brother Robert, four deputies, and a town cop from Burnsville, the Yancey County seat.[8] On the sheriff's orders, the lawmen began rounding up all the campers so that they could be searched. Robert Banks shoved Poonie Porter against a big tree. Two deputies found Kevin Shea at the edge of the woods. They took his snake stick and made him stand next to Porter.

A moment later, someone kicked Kim Burns "in the back of the neck."[9] She and Stan Altland scrambled to their feet to see what was going on. Stan put his hands in the air and urged everyone else to do likewise, imploring his friends to "just be cool" and "do what they say." Then he appealed to the cops, "Hey, man, we're harmless. We don't want to hassle with you." It made no difference. Using nightsticks to keep the campers in line, the lawmen began frisking both men and women, collecting pocketknives, key chains, even hairpins. They asked repeatedly about drugs but found nothing except a bottle of prescription medicine one of the women had in her pocket. They took it.

Waiting to be searched, Phil Lokey glanced back toward the fire and saw Sheriff Banks in a heated argument with David Satterwhite. From twenty feet away, Lokey could not hear what either man said, but he could tell that "Banks was really pissed off, mad as hell." Apparently when the sheriff asked Satterwhite to get up so he could be searched, the young man did not move. Instead, he insisted that he had done nothing wrong and added, "My dad and I camp here all the time."[10]

According to Satterwhite, Banks told him to "put that God damned dog up" or he would shoot it. The young man tethered the canine to a tree and pointedly asked, "Don't I have any rights?" Banks allegedly responded "No, you don't" and turned his shotgun on the youth. Satterwhite then asked the sheriff "to please put that gun away" and twice pushed the weapon aside.[11] Phil Lokey strained to get a better view. He could not believe that this skinny North Carolina teenager would argue with an angry sheriff holding a loaded 12-gauge. At that point a deputy struck Phil with a shotgun and told him to "stand up straight." The same officer frisked Stan Altland and Kim Burns and sent them over to stand near Poonie Porter and Kevin Shea.

What happened next would be disputed for years, but according to the eyewitnesses from Clearwater, Sheriff Banks stuck his shotgun in Satterwhite's stomach and told him to get up against the big tree. Perhaps thinking the young man did not move fast enough, the sheriff reportedly raised the gun and, with a slashing motion, struck Satterwhite on his left arm with the butt of the weapon. The 12-gauge went off with a deafening roar, echoing across the quiet campground like a thunderclap.[12]

As the campers tell it, Stan Altland was standing eighteen feet away when nine pellets of double-aught buckshot, each as large as a .32 caliber bullet and capable of penetrating a car door, slammed into the left side of his chest and neck. The impact lifted him off his feet and sent him flying backward.[13] Unable to regain his footing, he gasped and stammered "Oh my God! Somebody help me!" as he slumped to the ground. Two women near Stan felt his blood splatter onto their clothes. Others screamed, "Jesus! No!

No! No!" as Poonie Porter and Max Johnson rushed to Altland's side. Porter tore off Stan's shirt, wadded it into a ball, and held it tightly on the wound, trying to stanch the blood now streaming onto the ground.

Poonie had seen plenty of gunshot victims in Vietnam, and he could tell Stan was badly hurt. About "a third of his neck and chest had been blown away." Stan tried to speak, but only gurgled and coughed up blood. Kim Burns dropped to one knee and held his hand. Sue Cello stood nearby, screaming and crying. Poonie put his head to Altland's chest and listened for a heartbeat. He heard nothing. Stan's eyes flickered briefly and became fixed in his head. Three bystanders saw smoke rising from the sheriff's gun as he pulled another shell from his pocket and reloaded his weapon.[14]

Apparently in shock, the deputies all stared in silence as Altland's blood pooled on a patch of dark-green moss beneath the tree. As Lokey described it, "The cops just flipped out. They had no idea what to do." After what seemed like three minutes, the sheriff told Poonie, Max, and the others to get away from Stan. Banks instructed all the campers to sit down, telling them that Altland would get no help until they did. Still handcuffed, Phil thought, "They were going to shoot us all and bury us in the woods. I thought I was dead." He fought off a wave of nausea and felt faint, but as he started to pass out, he fell against another camper and never lost consciousness. Instead, he watched helplessly as Stan lay on the ground for what seemed like another fifteen minutes, blood seeping ever more slowly from what was left of his chest and neck.

Finally, a Forest Service ranger who had been waiting near the river ford drove up in one of the pickup trucks. Banks and three of his men wrapped Altland in a blanket, dragged him across the ground, and dumped him into the truck bed. The remaining campers, who just minutes earlier had been asleep or relaxing around the fire, looked on in horror as the vehicle rolled away with their friend. Sue Cello could no longer contain herself. Red-faced, wiping away tears, she screamed at the lawmen, "You shot him! Fuck you, you bastards!" Kim Burns and several others just wailed in utter despair. Poonie Porter later called it "the sickest scene I've seen since Vietnam."[15] No one who witnessed it would ever be the same.

1

Absolution and Obsession

Two days after that shotgun went off in Briar Bottom, I woke mid-morning at my home in Raleigh, some 240 miles away. That summer, at age seventeen, I worked the afternoon shift at a local A&P supermarket and usually spent my mornings lounging around the house, reading the *Raleigh News and Observer*. Since I rarely stirred before 10:00 a.m., my father always went through the newspaper first and then put the pages back together for me. But on that day, he left the *Observer* open to page 8, where I could not help but notice a bold headline: "Florida Youth Slain at Yancey Campsite." Wondering why the paper had been left in such unaccustomed disarray, I started reading. Five paragraphs in, a single line stopped me cold. Stan Altland and his friends had gone on "an outing to camp in the mountains and later attend a Rolling Stones concert in Charlotte."[1]

A couple of months earlier, when I learned that the Rolling Stones were coming to Charlotte, I had begged my parents to let me go. I had promised to pay all my expenses, including a hotel room for the night. The parental verdict was a resounding no. I was crushed. For weeks I had imagined what it would be like to be on the road with a couple of friends, windows down, music blaring, worried about nothing except getting to the concert on time.

Instead, with the big event now a day away, I sat at home in a deep adolescent funk, anticipating nothing more than another afternoon of bagging groceries and mopping floors. My father knew all that when he left the *News and Observer* open that morning. He wanted to make sure that I saw what happened to those kids from Clearwater. He could not know that their story would become so deeply entwined with my own.

Since 1967, we had lived in south Raleigh, where my dad served as pastor at a midsized Southern Baptist church. Like others who came of age in those years, I had seen the nation absorb one devastating shock after another: assassinations of Martin Luther King and Robert Kennedy, race riots, and the violence that accompanied mandatory school integration. Alabama governor George Wallace ran for president in 1968 and 1972, promising that if he got elected, Black children would never go to school with whites. His message had a lot of appeal in our neighborhood. The closest high school was predominantly Black, but the district had been gerrymandered so that my friends and I attended a mostly white county school. Lots of parents grew increasingly nervous as Raleigh's Black residents moved out from downtown and ever closer to our segregated enclave. A man down the street had a 1960 Cadillac covered with Wallace's "Stand Up for America" stickers.

On top of all that, there was Vietnam. Richard Nixon had vowed to end the war by turning the whole enterprise over to the South Vietnamese. But in 1971, Daniel Ellsberg leaked the Pentagon Papers, classified government documents that revealed how US presidents had taken the country deeper into the conflict, knowing all the while that prospects for victory were bleak. For some reason, Nixon still seemed to think he could win and ordered yet another American offensive in early 1972. Antiwar protests erupted across the nation. Bank heists, shootouts, and random bombings became commonplace as radical groups like the Black Panthers and Weathermen tried to foment worldwide revolution.

On some level, I understood that the demonstrations and violence stemmed from deep rifts between young and old, urban and rural, Black and white, over basic notions of right and wrong in American society. Today's media calls those battles culture wars, but no one used that phrase in the early seventies. Few people at my high school talked much about current events either. Thanks to a couple of student teachers, I had read Eldridge Cleaver's *Soul on Ice* and Alex Haley's *The Autobiography of Malcolm X*. I liked to think of myself as sympathetic to civil rights and Black Power. But

I did not rush into the streets to rail against injustice or protest American aggression in Vietnam. As self-absorbed as any teenager, I spent my time hanging out with friends.

That summer, we often gathered at the Cardinal Theatre near the North Hills shopping mall, where weekend late shows, beginning at 11:30 p.m., catered to disaffected youth. Second-run antiestablishment films like *Easy Rider*, *Vanishing Point*, and *Strawberry Statement* drew kids from across the city. All those movies had a similar theme: peaceful young people harassed by local rednecks, cops, or campus police. With a bit of forethought, you could get a girl to stash a quart of Colt 45 malt liquor or Boone's Farm Strawberry Hill wine in her shoulder bag before entering the theater. When the lights went out, the drinking started, usually with multiple moviegoers sipping from the same container. Sneaking in pot was riskier, but not impossible, and occasionally a whiff of burning marijuana filtered through the darkness.

House parties hosted by teens with absent parents were also good places to meet friends that summer. Beer and wine flowed freely. Kids smoked joints in their cars or found some out-of-the-way spot where they could take a hit off someone's bong. Couples retreated to back seats and back bedrooms, favored venues for what remained of the sexual revolution. We all lived in fear of being found out by parents or police. Drug laws had loosened a bit, but simple possession of marijuana could still land a first-time offender in jail. The drinking age for beer and wine was eighteen, meaning that a lot of us imbibed illegally. But we knew the places that sold alcohol without checking ID, and self-styled outlaw status was part of the attraction.

As a preacher's kid, I had to be especially careful. What passed for normal teenage misbehavior in other households could quickly set the congregational tongues wagging and might cost my dad his job. Not that the all-white Baptist faithful were paragons of Christian virtue. When my father delivered a sermon mildly critical of racism and violence, we got hang-up calls in the middle of the night. Sometimes, an angry voice spat out "N—— lover!" before the line went dead. Such incidents only fueled my growing distaste for hypocrisy and pretense, both of which seemed to be everywhere that summer.

Like a generation of young people before us, we took refuge in rock and roll. But we no longer harbored any illusions that peace, love, and music could change the world. Despite all the protests, the war showed no signs of ending. San Francisco's Haight-Ashbury neighborhood, once the epicenter of countercultural flower power, had collapsed into drug-saturated ruin.[2] The Beatles, who had proclaimed "All you need is love," were defunct, torn apart by jealousy, infighting, and John Lennon's affinity for opiates. Jimi Hendrix, Janis Joplin, and Jim Morrison were dead, victims of heroin and barbiturates. Woodstock might have promised a better world a-comin', but that rock-inspired, drug-infused utopia had yet to show up.

My crowd preferred solo artists like Joe Cocker, whose soulful take on the Beatles' "With a Little Help from My Friends" provided a fitting anthem for everyday life. We liked Leon Russell, who understood that we were all "Stranger[s] in a Strange Land," and Neil Young, who "felt like getting high" and excoriated the South for its long history of bigotry and racism. At house parties, blues-based hard rock from bands like Led Zeppelin and the Allman Brothers pulsed from oversized speakers. Those artists usually ignored politics in favor of lengthy guitar solos, screaming vocals, and a hypnotic backbeat. Nevertheless, hard rock became part of our identity, a way to set ourselves apart from supposedly less sophisticated listeners who preferred the Top 40. Hard rock had a certain sameness that made it immediately recognizable. The Who said it best: "Don't raise your eye / It's only teenage wasteland."

Black artists had also grown cynical about prospects for change. In 1970, Curtis Mayfield, who had once written hopeful tunes like "Keep on Pushing" and "People Get Ready" (both favored by the civil rights movement) recorded a new song called "(Don't Worry) If There's a Hell Below, We're All Going to Go." It seemed like a perfect assessment of the status quo. A year later, Marvin Gaye released *What's Going On*. He intended the title as a statement, not a question. The album's lead track insisted that "war is not the answer" and bluntly asked, "Who are they to judge us simply 'cause our hair is long?'" Other songs on the album chronicled the sad plight of heroin addicts "flying high in the friendly sky," warned of polluted oceans with "fish full of mercury," and recounted the suffering of the urban poor. Like everyone else, Gaye could only say that it all "make[s] me wanna holler [and] throw up both my hands."

No musicians, Black or white, captured the cynicism and amorphous angst of the early seventies better than the Rolling Stones. With music rooted in Delta blues, American country, and early rock, mixed with a hint of gospel, the shaggy-haired Englishmen had always promoted themselves as the bad boys of rock and roll. Although the Beatles sold more records in the late sixties, Mick Jagger and his mates flourished with countryfied hits like "Honky Tonk Women" and electric rockers like "Street Fighting Man," the unofficial theme song of American antiwar protesters. The band's 1969 song "Gimme Shelter" fit nicely with apocalyptic visions of the future, predicting that war, rape, and murder were "just a shot away."[3]

The Stones had street cred, too. Founding member Brian Jones drowned in a swimming pool after swallowing a handful of amphetamines and quaaludes washed down with half a bottle of whiskey. The coroner called it "death by misadventure." Jagger and guitarist Keith Richards had both been busted for drugs, the latter more than once. Mick briefly dabbled in Satanism, something that only enhanced his antiestablishment image.[4]

The band's last trip to the States in 1969 had ended with the disastrous Altamont concert, in front of 300,000 volatile freaks awash in alcohol and acid. Four people died on-site, including Meredith Hunter, a Black man stabbed to death by Hells Angels right in front of the stage. After that, Nixon put Jagger on the White House's "enemies list," and the FBI tried to infiltrate the band's inner circle. None of that mattered to the Stones. They flew back to England with a fat suitcase full of cash and, ignoring the bad press, proceeded to make a movie about the ill-fated Altamont concert. Titled *Gimme Shelter*, it became both a critical success and a box office hit, not to mention a perennial favorite at Cardinal Theatre late shows. As far as anyone could tell, the Rolling Stones just did not give a shit, and among disenchanted youth—in Raleigh, Clearwater, and across America—that made the band unspeakably cool.[5]

When I read that *News and Observer* article, I knew that those kids from Florida had turned a pilgrimage to see the Stones into a weeklong party. They were on the road, camping out, away from parental authority and the trappings of an oppressive, moribund society. I could easily picture them sitting around a campfire, a little buzzed from the alcohol and pot, full of anticipation, laughing, talking about which songs the Stones might play. They were living the dream—my dream—until the county sheriff showed up and turned it into a nightmare.

That evening, at the dinner table, when talk turned to the shooting, my parents—in that understated, "we know best" voice that teenagers loathe— said simply, "This is what we worried about when you wanted to go to that concert. You just never know what might happen." For them, the story provided absolution. For me, it became an obsession. I could turn my back on Vietnam; I could ignore hypocrisy and racism. I could drop the needle on a record or plug in a tape and drown out all the political turmoil. But I could never forget those Florida kids who saw their road trip to see the Rolling Stones go so horribly wrong.

My family moved later that summer, and I spent my senior year at a new high school in Burlington, North Carolina. I found another job bagging groceries and continued to live the paranoid double life of preacher's kid turned hippie. I went to college and graduate school and enjoyed a long career teaching American history at Appalachian State, the largest university in western North Carolina. An avid outdoorsman, I visited Yancey County often, backpacking through the high mountains and fly-fishing on the South Toe River. I frequently camped with friends in Briar Bottom and eventually wrote a book about the surrounding region.[6]

In time, I thought less about July 3, 1972, but more than once over the course of my academic career, I promised myself that one day I would put my historian's skills to use and investigate the incident. Sometime in 2020, shortly before I retired from university life, I googled "Shooting Briar Bottom Yancey County, NC 1972." The search turned up a couple of newspaper articles, including the one my father had shown me almost fifty years earlier when I worked at the A&P.

A bit more reading soon revealed that Stan Altland's death was not an isolated local incident. Events like Kent State and the FBI's relentless pursuit of Black activists like Angela Davis made national news, but out of the spotlight, in small towns and rural areas across America, local police and sheriffs came down hard on young people for even minor infractions of the law. That tactic had long been used to suppress Black and Latino people and other American minorities. Amid the upheaval of the late sixties and early seventies, law enforcement turned it on white kids, especially those with a countercultural bent.

In April 1971, authorities in Ruidoso, New Mexico, a state famous for hippie communes, arrested a transient longhair named Paul Green. For months he had lived in Ruidoso with his girlfriend, technically a violation of obscure 125-year-old state and town laws against "lewd cohabitation." According to the state statute, a first offense warranted only a verbal warning, but the local judge sentenced Green under the town ordinance, throwing him in jail for thirty days and fining him one hundred dollars. Two weeks earlier, Green had accidentally cut his foot with an axe and, at the time of his arrest, walked with a cane. When prosecutors allowed him to leave his jail cell to call an attorney, Green, with stitches in his foot, allegedly tried to run. An officer fired two quick "warning shots," one of which hit Green in the head.

Investigators charged the lawman with voluntary manslaughter, but he went free after local people raised money for his defense. According to one reporter, Green's death marked "the beginning of a rash of crime-connected youth killings."[7] New Mexico's "epidemic of hippie lynchings" included a teenage girl gunned down by a shopkeeper for passing a bad check and a drug user shot and killed after being taken into custody by local law enforcement. In some New Mexico communities, townsfolk delighted in bombing hippie vehicles, especially the multicolored vans driven by commune members.[8]

Two months after Green's death, a young man named Guy Gaughnor disappeared from Nederland, Colorado, a tiny town near the Continental Divide. A wandering longhaired eccentric, Gaughnor lived in a makeshift teepee and walked around carrying a toy cap pistol. His friends nicknamed him "Deputy Dawg," after a TV cartoon character. The local authorities described Gaughnor as "a huge pain," and his clothing as "hippie, dirty, and stinking." In July 1971, the town marshal, an Air Force veteran named Lenner LeRoy Forbes, got a call about Gaughnor causing trouble in a bar. Forbes had once suggested that the easiest way to deal with Colorado's "hippie problem" was "to shoot the bastards," and that is precisely what he did to Gaughnor.[9] A month later, Deputy Dawg's decomposed body turned up in a remote area of a nearby county.

Suspicion centered on Forbes, but he went unpunished. As one resident put it, the hippie's death "was good riddance to bad rubbish."[10] The case remained unsolved for twenty-six years until the marshal, suffering from a stroke and confined to a nursing home, had an attack of conscience. As he told it, Deputy Dawg had assaulted him and lunged for his pistol. In the ensuing scuffle, Forbes shot the young man in the head. Reporting on the belated confession in 1997, the *New York Times* noted that in the early seventies "thousands of young Americans were adrift" and "deaths of hippies were often sketchily explained."[11] The number of those harassed, thrown in jail, and killed by rural law enforcement is anybody's guess.

I recognized that the incident at Briar Bottom offered a chance to probe one of those sketchily explained hippie deaths; it provided a case study in the violence between lawmen and young people that occurred in small communities across America. Getting at the evidence would be a challenge. After fifty years, some of those involved were dead; arrest records and court documents had been destroyed or stashed away in various archives with restricted access.

I also knew that mountain people could be wary of strangers asking questions. Yancey County residents still refer to anyone not born there as being "from off," an epithet that suggests outsiders, including nosy writers like me, should be kept at arm's length, at least until they prove they can be trusted.

But Briar Bottom was still there, with much easier access and immensely improved facilities. Thanks to the internet, I could peruse newspapers from across the country and track down anyone with a viable street address. I discovered that Kermit Banks and his brother Robert still lived near Burnsville where Kermit's son, Gary, now served as sheriff. I eventually found addresses for about half of the young people who made the trip from Clearwater to Yancey County that summer.

Strangely enough, in a world of social media, smartphones, email, and instant messaging, my efforts to contact eyewitnesses began with writing old-fashioned letters asking if they might talk with me. I stood at my mailbox a long time holding the first two stamped envelopes. At that point, I knew none of the people involved. In Yancey County, where I had made some friends over the years, I would look like an outsider stirring up unpleasant memories. Why court needless trouble? Why not just settle into retirement and leave the whole thing alone? I took a deep breath, slipped the letters into the mailbox, and raised the flag.

For almost a month, nothing happened. I read a few more newspaper accounts and thought again about abandoning the whole enterprise. Then, while out on my daily bike ride, my cell phone rang. It was Donald "Jay" Barrett, another member of the Clearwater group who had a shotgun leveled at his chest on that fateful night in 1972. A few days later, I had a long conversation with Linda Putney Mancini, a Clearwater camper who, like me, was only seventeen at the time. I also spoke with Stan Altland's younger brother, Roger. All three had vivid memories of the killing and its aftermath.

With a historian's penchant for accuracy and balance, I wrote Kermit Banks, Robert Banks, Kermit's son Gary, and Robert's son, Seth. I offered to meet any or all of them in person, talk by phone, or send written questions that they could answer at their leisure. Gary Banks left a phone message saying that the sheriff's office had no records dating back past 1991. He did not answer a follow-up letter. Seth Banks's secretary called to tell me that it all happened "before his time." I never heard from Kermit or Robert.

As I talked with others from Clearwater, I became convinced that theirs was a story I had to tell. Valuable as it might be to historians as a case study, the killing in Briar Bottom has important implications for modern Americans mired in their own culture wars. It serves as a warning of just how easily someone can die when we assume the worst about those we perceive as enemies. The protracted legal battles that followed the incident speak to the unchecked power of law enforcement and to the inequities in American justice, issues that still make headlines every day. Considering the tenor of our times, Stan Altland's death and its aftermath are as relevant now as in 1972.

For me, though, it remained a deeply personal story. I could not shake the notion that something similar might easily have happened to me or my friends. We feared being caught by parents, not getting blown away by a load of buckshot at some isolated spot in the dead of night. Long-haired kids got killed in the movies—in *Easy Rider* and *Vanishing Point* at the Cardinal Theatre late shows—not in real life, not while camping in the North Carolina mountains, and not while on a once-in-a-lifetime road trip to see the Rolling Stones. For the group from Florida, a lot of innocence died that night in Briar Bottom. They spent a half century trying to figure out what went wrong and why. In a way, so did I. Fifty years later, I again went looking for answers. To borrow a well-worn line from the Grateful Dead, I had no idea "what a long, strange trip" it would be. But I knew where it had to begin.

2

The Law Was the Law

"You can't get there from here." It is the punchline from an old joke about a stranger asking for directions, and I think of it every time I drive from my home in Boone to Burnsville. It is only about fifty miles, fewer as the crow flies, but the trip takes an hour and a half. And that assumes that Three Mile Road, a twisting ribbon of asphalt that winds down the side of the Blue Ridge, has not been washed out by a flash flood, blocked by a rockslide, or shut down by an eighteen-wheeler that failed to make one of the hairpin curves. The drive used to take even longer, but now Three Mile eventually connects to US 19E, a mostly straight, partly-four-lane thoroughfare that whisks travelers into Yancey County, Burnsville, and beyond.

Once you hit that highway, it is easy to forget you are on a mountain road. The landscape rolls past at sixty miles an hour, and about all you can see are churches with names like "Temple," "Bethel," and "New Beginnings," old mines, gravel quarries, modest houses, and auto repair shops. Burnsville, like the rest of America, now has chain restaurants, gourmet coffee shops, and craft breweries that charge twelve dollars for a pale ale. But on this day in early October, just as I cross the county line, a wild turkey, wings spread in a full glide, swoops low across the superhighway. I take it as a good omen. Maybe I can recover something of the region's past, even after fifty years.

According to the federal census, Yancey County had a year-round population of only 13,000 in 1972, roughly the same number of people that showed up for the Stones concert in Charlotte that July. Population density hovered around forty people per square mile, with some 3,000 residents living in and around Burnsville, and the other 10,000 scattered about in various townships and unincorporated communities.[1] The region had a mixed economy that blended manufacturing, mining, and farming. Glen Raven Textiles, a leading producer of nylon hosiery and synthetic fabrics, operated a plant in Burnsville. Nearby mines yielded mica and feldspar. Burley tobacco, livestock, apples, various grains, and produce dominated the agricultural side. The population was overwhelmingly white. Only 176 African Americans lived in Yancey in 1972.[2]

The county had two high schools, Cane River and East Yancey, each with a senior class of sixty to eighty students. After legal action by the NAACP in 1960, Yancey had been the first North Carolina county to integrate its public schools. Before that, the school board sent Black students to Asheville.[3] But with so few African Americans in residence, integration had little practical effect. Cane River's sports teams retained the name "Rebels," and the yearbook kept its title, *The Confederate*, both of which referenced Yancey's secessionist leanings in the Civil War. If that bothered the few African American students, no one noticed.[4]

All of that is important, but to understand what happened in Briar Bottom, I need something not found in statistics and documents. I want to know how the local community defined itself and its relationship to the wider world.[5] My plan is to show up unannounced at country stores and gas stations and talk casually with residents. My first stop is an establishment not far from Briar Bottom. It has been here since the mid-1950s and is where the kids from Clearwater met David Satterwhite.

The place has been rebuilt and remodeled several times since then, but the original structure is still standing, with its walls crumbling and roof caved in, on the same site. Inside the new store, a large Confederate battle flag—the infamous "rebel flag"—covers an entire wall, just above a pool table. I note lots of military and motorcycle paraphernalia for sale, along with a multitude of patriotic bumper stickers, some of which reference guns. I get cash from the ATM, buy a soft drink, and try to chat up the clerk.

We talk for only a minute or two before he wants to know where I live. "Boone." He asks what I do for a living "over there." Sensing the need to be careful, I explain that I "used to teach history." Apparently, subtlety is not my

**Remains of the original country store where members
of the Clearwater group met David Satterwhite.**
Photo by the author.

strong suit because he says, "I can tell you're an educated man; you're not a liberal, are you?" I describe myself as "middle of the road." The last thing I want to do is talk politics.

I ask if he grew up in Yancey County, and he explains that his family has run this store since it first opened. I proffer what I hope is a leading question: "Guess you've seen a lot of changes over the years?" He does not respond to my query and instead tells me that he does not have cable television and that he restricts his kids' time on the internet. "It's just a mess out there," he concludes. I desperately want to ask about the 1972 killing, but at this point, simply do not have the nerve. I make some small talk about camping and fishing. He says little and finally, after a long silence, picks up his cell phone, my cue to exit the premises. Whatever his reasons, he is not about to talk at length with someone from off—or at least not with me.

Thoroughly discouraged, I drive on to Briar Bottom, where I camp alone while waiting for friends to arrive. It is a weekday, and the place is quiet. Lying in my tent, with the rainfly off, I stare into the clear October night, wondering what to do next. Today's encounter seemed to confirm every unfavorable stereotype I have heard about Appalachian people: that they are reticent, defensive, conservative, and suspicious of outsiders.

Having taught at Appalachian State for almost four decades, I know not to trust that impression. Some of my university colleagues have spent years proving that, despite Appalachia's reputation for feuds and moonshining, it was no more insular or violent than the rest of the country. They also argue that the region was less isolated and more diverse than most visitors think.[6] Appalachia and its people have not been static, nor have they been cut off from the political and cultural currents that shaped the rest of the country. Various industries came and went; individuals migrated in and out of the region for all sorts of reasons; opinions changed and diverged with the times.[7] Maybe the store clerk was having a bad day or my questions seemed overly intrusive. I vow that the next time I set out to talk with local people, I will bring along someone who can help.

It takes patience, several phone calls, and maybe twenty emails, but seven months later, on a May morning full of sunshine and birdsong, I find myself driving up the South Toe River valley with Danny McIntosh. Trim and fit in his mid-sixties, wearing blue jeans and a plaid shirt, Danny speaks in the slow twangy dialect common to the region. He has lived in Yancey County all his life and has been mayor of Burnsville, chief of the fire department, a deputy sheriff, county magistrate, and county tax administrator and assessor. He knows the place as well as anyone. We met through a mutual acquaintance and have had lunch a couple of times.

Danny takes me to a different country store and introduces me to its proprietor, another lifetime Yancey resident. The decor here is less intimidating, just some photos of local hunters with bear and deer, and the conversation flows freely. This storeowner and his granddaughter (who tracks inventory on a digital spreadsheet and orders new stock over the internet) are friendly and open with me and the customers who come and go. The proprietor tells a hiker from out of town to "c'mon in and spend three or four hundred dollars!" They do not seem to care that we are from off.

Danny asks the owner about his military service. He tells us he volunteered for the army right out of high school and notes that "there was a lot of respect for the military back then." He did a tour in Vietnam, where he spent most of his time driving for an officer, but still managed to step on a punji stick. It took seventeen stitches to close the wound. He got back to the States just before the war became such a divisive political issue and encountered no antiwar sentiment in Yancey or anywhere else. "Came home and went to work on the store; laid the floorboards myself in 1966." Since then, he has been open for business all day, every day, starting at 6:00 a.m., closing only for an occasional blizzard and a few days during the COVID-19 pandemic.

The storeowner worked for a while as a postman in Yancey County. "I knew everyone on my route," he says, "and they looked forward to seeing me every day." He shows me a poem he wrote about finding dead opossums on the road while he delivered the mail. It is good: descriptive, witty, with nice meter, dark humor, and interesting turns of phrase. I laugh out loud, compliment his writing, and we swap a few stories about fishing and golf. He is proud of his store, his place in the community, and likes meeting people who stop by. All in all, a pleasant experience, and nothing like my first country-store encounter. Apparently, having Danny along makes a difference. Nevertheless, when I work up the courage to ask about the killing at Briar Bottom, the proprietor says he knows nothing about it and "never had any trouble" with Sheriff Banks.

Outside, Danny is chatting with a man in a pickup truck. Of course, Danny knows him; he knows everybody. The man used to be a highway patrolman in Yancey, potentially a good source for me. Leaning against one of the gas pumps, I introduce myself and note that "my people" are from Mitchell County, but that I am still an outsider, even in Boone where I have lived for forty years. He laughs, explaining that "mountain people have always been a little clannish." I ask if he ran into many hippies when he patrolled the county in the early seventies. "We didn't call them hippies," he says. "We called 'em 'longhairs' and I only knew two locally." Eventually, we get around to what happened in Briar Bottom. "What I remember, or just what I've heard," he explains, is that "the boy who got shot up there was the ringleader of that bunch." Without prompting, he adds, "The problem with a lot of young people today is that they don't respect anything. Back then, the law was the law. You had to respect it. It wasn't like it is now." With that, he climbs into his truck and drives away.

Danny and I go into Burnsville for lunch. My favorite barbecue joint, Pig & Grits, is closed, so we end up not far from the county courthouse, in an upscale place called the Garden Deli. Danny works the room like the local politician he is, shaking hands, chatting with patrons, introducing me to his friends. He knows everyone by name, and they call him "Mr. Mayor." He graduated from Cane River High in 1974 and after we order, he tells me about growing up in Yancey.

Radio reception was hit or miss in the early seventies. On the AM dial, local listeners could get 570 out of Asheville and WEMB from Erwin, Tennessee, for news and weather. Beginning in the mid-sixties, Burnsville got its own country station, WKYK. If conditions were right, young people could hear rock music on WJSO from Jonesborough, Tennessee. Danny and others had access to records and eight-track tapes from various sources, including older siblings, but he does not remember listening to a lot of rock and roll: "I don't think I had a rock tape the whole time I was in high school." He does not mention Black music, but later conversations with county residents revealed an appreciation for Motown among some local youth.

Danny had a 1964 Chevy Impala Super Sport and when he got his driver's license, he joined his friends on weekends as they "cruised the Robo," a route around Burnsville named for a recently installed automatic car wash. As he explains, the "town was congested with young people every Friday and Saturday night and on Sunday from about 3:00 p.m. to 10:00 p.m., especially in summer when a group of us gathered on the front porch of Johnson's Store." Sometimes they headed out to the movies, but mostly they just "cruised and hung around," trying to figure out "who was with who and what sort of romantic relationships might be forming." High school athletic events, school dances, and hunting and fishing on the county's 30,000 acres of National Forest lands, were also popular activities in the early seventies. Danny and nearly everyone else I talked with in Yancey County noted that church functions, especially meetings of Baptist and Methodist youth groups on Sunday nights, provided opportunities for local kids to get together.

Yancey was a dry county then, but Danny recalls teens buying beer, liquor, or moonshine from local bootleggers at exorbitant prices. Marijuana came into the high schools in the late sixties, along with rumors of harder drugs, but he knew no one who experimented with anything stronger than pot. As in suburbia, underage drinking and dope-smoking took place out of the public eye. In summer, the local stoners might be found at a bonfire out on someone's farm or some other secluded spot. Yancey also had plenty of isolated stretches of deserted pavement to facilitate drag racing, another common pursuit among males with muscle cars. Dodging the authorities could prove difficult. Sometimes local deputies or town cops took first-time offenders home to their parents, promising to "lock them up" if they got caught drinking or racing again. Danny sips iced tea and smiles, "Like the man said, the law was the law."

I note that the county now has a solid reputation as a conservative Republican stronghold. Danny is quick to point out that it has not always been that way. In the 1950s and '60s, most county residents voted for Democratic presidential candidates—Adlai Stevenson in 1956, John Kennedy (by a narrow margin) in 1960, and Lyndon Johnson in 1964. The shift came in 1968, just as in the rest of America, when the nation and its "liberal consensus" fell apart over Vietnam, integration, the youth revolt, and other divisive issues. That year, Nixon carried Yancey County by a slim 233 votes over Democrat Hubert Humphrey. George Wallace got 752 votes, roughly 14 percent of all ballots cast. The county went solidly for Nixon in 1972, with the Republican capturing 57 percent of the vote.[8]

The conservative backlash that put Nixon in office drew support from some of Yancey County's most influential families and largest landowners, as well as transplanted retirees and other newcomers seeking a quieter rural life. Danny is walking testament to the political shift, a native-born lifelong Democrat now living in a Republican county. He is not alone. Local elections are still hotly contested, and Danny got to be Burnsville's mayor, as he puts it, "by just being friendly and not trying to hoodwink folks."

What about the polarizing events of the early seventies? How did local people react? "Well, the antiwar stuff wasn't in our faces every day. You could only get two TV channels, WATE out of Knoxville and WBTV from Charlotte. Later, we got WLOS from Asheville." Newspaper delivery from Charlotte and Asheville could be sporadic too. Danny remembers the Black students at Cane Creek but does not recall "any trouble" over integration. I suggest that Wallace's relatively strong showing in 1968 indicates some sympathy for his segregationist leanings. Maybe so, Danny says, but he thinks that Wallace's support, like Nixon's, came mostly from certain county elites. For proof, he suggests I have a look at the local newspaper for those years, a weekly called the *Yancey Record*, edited by Ed and Carolyn Yuziuk.

Originally from Fort Lauderdale, Florida, the Yuziuks bought property in Yancey in 1968. A year later, they moved to Burnsville and took over the *Record*. As Ed Yuziuk explained at the time, they were "impressed by the friendliness and helpfulness of the people," and in search of a wholesome, small-town atmosphere in which to raise their children.[9] The *Record* is exactly what one would expect in a local newspaper. It chronicles births, weddings, deaths, public meetings, and the activities of 4-H clubs, theater groups, churches, and Boy Scout troops. At election time, local political news takes over the front page, with ads for various candidates running in the back sections alongside the grocery coupons.

When it came to national issues, the *Record* leaned heavily toward hard-right Republican commentary. Well before Jesse Helms ran for Senate, the *Record* published and promoted his Viewpoint column. One of those, from July 1970 (two months after the Kent State killings), featured Helms railing against college students who "skip classes, or duck exams, or dodge the draft." He went on to compare those who opposed the Vietnam War to the Hitler Youth who brought the Nazis to power in Germany. It was way past time to rein in those kids "who had jumped the tracks," even if, as Helms, believed, they were in the minority.[10]

Tom Anderson, a fiery syndicated columnist and proud member of the John Birch Society, also appeared regularly on the *Record*'s opinion page. In one of his Straight Talk editorials, published in 1970, Anderson ridiculed the hit Broadway musical *Hair* for glorifying "marijuana, LSD, and sexual promiscuity" as "the 'in' things for young people to sample." According to Anderson, *Hair* appealed only to godless city folk who had long ago abandoned any pretense of morality.[11] Another syndicated favorite, Marilyn Manion, used her column to disparage college students protesting the war and ridicule their support from "liberal elites," declaring on one occasion that the generation gap was nothing more than media hype.[12]

In 1971, a letter to the editors suggested that a recent high school assembly led by a religious group might have violated separation of church and state. The Yuziuks immediately printed a flurry of rebuttals from readers who saw nothing wrong with a little evangelism in a public place. One respondent pointedly explained, "If the right to give religious training had been left in the school curriculum, there would be less time to experiment with dope."[13]

In May 1972, just two months before the incident at Briar Bottom, the valedictorian at Cane River High lamented that George Wallace could not run for president "without being in fear of getting shot or killed." The speaker went on to disparage those who "demonstrate, protest, burn and destroy" and who refer to law enforcement as "pigs, coppers, or the fuzz." He concluded by urging his fellow graduates to "go out and build up our great America for it is the greatest nation in the world."[14] The *Record* published the speech in its entirety.

It does not take me long to discover—just as Danny said—that plenty of Yancey people did not share those views in 1972. One place has long been recognized as a source of alternative thought: the Celo community. The folks who live there hold leases to, but do not own, the land on which they live. They govern themselves by consensus, with decisions made in monthly Quaker-style meetings. Celo was the brainchild of Arthur Morgan, a city planner born in Cincinnati. He founded the community during the Great Depression, when it appeared that American capitalism had failed. Celo has endured for three quarters of a century as a liberal experiment in right living, an example of how to get along and prosper with other human beings in the modern world. It currently has a long waiting list of prospective residents.[15]

A fixture of Celo is its alternative school for junior high students, the Arthur Morgan School, and more than one Yancey resident told me that kids who went there were "really different." They came to the public high schools with long hair and "very liberal ideas." According to one woman who attended East Yancey at the time, the Celo kids had few problems with other students, but sometimes ran afoul of administrators, including a principal who "called in a Celo boy" for having a bag of dope. It turned out to be "oregano or basil or something," but as marijuana found its way into the county schools, some officials believed Celo might have been the source of the contraband. If the county residents who spoke with me can be believed, similar suspicions linger to this day, mostly among conservative civic leaders and law enforcement.

By the early seventies, other small bands of former city-dwellers had drifted into Yancey County. They were some of more than a million well-educated, mostly white, middle-class Americans who went "back to the land." It was the revival of an old American idea, the belief that if things got too hectic, you could leave the city, move into the woods, and retreat to a more authentic existence. You could raise your own food, maintain your own shelter, and generally have done with urban life and consumer culture.[16]

About a dozen or so of those true believers established a small commune not far from Burnsville in 1970. Known as the Sunshine Company, it consisted of expatriates from Detroit, along with assorted friends, casual acquaintances, and other "unattached freaks." Their leader got a loan from a Yancey physician and moved the group onto ten acres of hilly farmland with a rundown house and barn. Like a lot of others who left cities in those days, the Sunshine Company found life on the land harder than they anticipated. They lived without indoor plumbing and bathed in a nearby river. They struggled to grow crops using organic methods, sometimes planting the wrong varieties of tomatoes and green beans. Their plans to finance the experiment by selling handmade leather goods and pottery fell apart, and they had trouble making payments on their loan. Still, the group lived together in a house full of books and records (a stereo was one modern convenience they did not reject), enjoyed occasional "marijuana treats," and for a while at least, seemed content.[17]

In September 1970, the *Detroit Free Press* published a front-page story on the back-to-the-landers. The writer complimented both county and commune, noting that most of the local people had welcomed their long-haired neighbors and even assisted with various chores, including plowing and spring planting.[18] That kind of tolerant "bemused and helpful" reaction seems to have been the norm in Appalachia and similar regions that attracted vagabond hippies.[19] Like most rural folk, a lot of Yancey people could warm up to anyone who shared their affinity for work on the land.

The commune encountered far more resistance from retirees, politicians, and recent emigres concerned with maintaining the status quo. They saw hippie culture as an impediment to economic growth and an unpleasant reminder of city life.[20] When another article by the same Detroit reporter suggested that communes were popping up "like mushrooms" in western North Carolina and that hippies might soon "elbow hillbillies" off the land, the Yuziuks struck back with a blistering editorial in the *Yancey Record*. Their county (which they claimed after only a year of permanent residence) was "no hippie heaven" and never would be. Neither Celo nor any of the local craft guilds were part of the "hippie movement," and there had been no great migration of freaks to the region. A hippie invasion, the Yuziuks insisted, would "be real cause for alarm," and the hairy reprobates would quickly be "tarred and feathered and chased out of the mountains."[21]

Nine months after my visit to that first country store, I had a much more nuanced view of Yancey County. I now marveled at how much this supposedly out-of-the-way, insular place *resembled* the rest of America in 1972. In the county, as in the nation, a slim majority of residents had recently embraced conservative ideology and were suspicious of longhairs and their liberal-leaning neighbors. Others, including a lot of those born in the county, had no problem with the Celo residents, back-to-the-landers, hippies, or anyone else who found fault with the establishment. Some local kids drank beer, smoked dope, and tried to avoid the ever-watchful eye of law enforcement, not unlike my friends in Raleigh and Burlington.

Any differences I noticed stemmed from Yancey's smaller population and rural character. With so few Blacks in residence, school integration appeared to be less of an issue than in urban areas. Overt resistance to the Vietnam War also seemed less evident, perhaps because television, radio, movies, pop music, and other trappings of urban culture had less influence on local youth. From what I could tell, plenty of county kids went to church regularly and, even in 1972, did not share my cynicism about religion.

Like the friendly storeowner, many of those I spoke with either did not remember much about what happened at Briar Bottom or did not want to talk about it. As one local woman put it, "That whole thing got swept under the rug a long time ago." Nor did they want to go on the record about Sheriff Kermit Banks. Still, I listened to what they had to say and tried to sort fact from gossip as I pieced together what I could about the nature of Yancey County law enforcement in 1972.

In 1938, with the county in the throes of the Great Depression, Yancey voters entrusted the sheriff's office to Kermit Banks's father, Donald Banks, who at age twenty-two was the youngest sheriff in North Carolina. After completing his first term, Donald lost to a rival in 1942 and three years later got elected to the state senate, where he served from 1945 to 1947. In 1958, he came back for another stint as sheriff, before losing again in 1962 (more evidence of political diversity and contested local elections). Four years after that, Donald Banks won the office a third time and held it until he died unexpectedly of a heart attack in August 1969.

Conservative county officials immediately appointed Kermit Banks to finish out his father's term. Born in 1940, Kermit had grown up around the sheriff's office and the county jail, where his mother cooked for the staff and inmates. He became a skilled mechanic and operated a local garage before going to work full-time for his father in 1966. At that point, Kermit had no formal training in law enforcement. He learned on the job, working his way up to first deputy, the position he held when Donald died.[22]

That kind of naked nepotism was nothing new in western North Carolina. Two brothers, E. Y. and Zeno Ponder, ran Madison County for thirty-five years. E. Y. served as sheriff, while Zeno became chairman of the board of elections. Anyone who wanted anything in Madison County had to go through the Ponders.[23] In my home county, Watauga, a small cadre of families controlled things during the same period, handing down offices from father to son, to in-laws, to cousins. With Kermit's appointment, the Banks family effectively took charge of law enforcement in Yancey County and became powerful players in local politics.

From the moment he took over from his father, Kermit liked to call himself a "twenty-four-hour sheriff." As a teenager, he had cruised the county's backroads, honing his high-speed driving skills. As sheriff, he drove a 1967 Chevy sedan, outfitted with a 427-cubic-inch V-8, and took great pride in his ability to chase down fleeing suspects, especially on twisting mountain roads. He sometimes patrolled local highways late at night, looking for malfeasance. Some in Yancey liked it that way. One eighty-one-year-old woman noted in 2010, "I certainly sleep better when there's a Banks in the sheriff's office."[24]

Kermit's 1970 campaign ads featured a photo of him in a suit and tie, with a crewcut and thin smile, touting his honesty, experience, and membership in Cane River Baptist Church. Running as a Republican and borrowing a phrase from Nixon's campaign, Banks promised to maintain "law and order" through "vigorous, impartial, courteous enforcement." Even with his family connections and support from the Yuziuks and others like them, Banks won the 1970 election by only 300 votes.[25]

By 1972, the new sheriff had enrolled part-time at a community college where he completed courses on civil procedure, police science, and narcotics.[26] He surrounded himself with a crew of loyal deputies, all of whom were well known to local people and well positioned to keep tabs on county residents. Chief Deputy Erwin Higgins had operated a small grocery in Burnsville. A second full-time deputy, Bill Arrowood, had worked for Kermit's father. Kermit's brother, Robert Banks, who served as a "special deputy," had graduated from Cane River High and attended Mars Hill College.[27]

Because no one from the sheriff's office will talk with me, I end up at the county courthouse, poring over sparse trial records, trying to get a handle on local crime in the early 1970s. In addition to learning that a lot of people named Silver (some of them my relatives) were at odds with the law, I come away with the impression that property crimes, especially trespassing, robbery, petty theft, and vandalism, dominated the court docket. Occasionally local authorities investigated a murder, perhaps resulting from an argument over a property boundary or passions ignited by a cheating spouse. Public drunkenness seems to have been common, though in a county notorious

Sheriff Kermit Banks, ca. 1972, in a photo published in the *Native Stone*.
Courtesy of the Special Collections Research
Center at Appalachian State University.

for bootlegging and illegal shot houses, I find relatively few indictments for illegal liquor manufacture or sales. I cannot help but wonder if that reflects a tendency of law enforcement to look the other way.

In July 1971, Richard Nixon issued his now infamous directive declaring yet another "war on drugs." Recent revelations from John Ehrlichman, one of Nixon's closest advisors, suggest that the president planned to use drug laws against his political opponents, including Black people and young dissidents. As Ehrlichman put it, "We knew we couldn't make it illegal either to be against the war or [to be] Black, but by getting the public to associate hippies with marijuana and Blacks with heroin, and then criminalizing both heavily, we could disrupt those communities." Nixon could "vilify them night after night on the evening news."[28]

Whether Kermit Banks shared those objectives or not, he led a similar crackdown in Yancey County. As the sheriff remarked, "Drug use is, without doubt, becoming a way of life for some young people. . . . And so think about these things—my friends, we are all in this together. As adults, it is up to us to head this thing off in our community."[29] According to my sources, the sheriff was as good as his word. He had few qualms about locking up longhairs caught with dope. He took pleasure in busting out-of-towners who grew marijuana and occasionally posed for pictures with giant pot plants confiscated in raids by his deputies—photos that often turned up in the *Record*.[30] The law might be the law, but by 1972, it was well on its way to becoming the law according to Kermit Banks. And that did not bode well for anyone who might not share his values or those of his supporters.

Meanwhile, some 700 miles away, twenty-four kids grew up in a starkly different big-city environment. They were rebellious, free-spirited, and prone to thumb their noses at authority. They ignored almost any law that stood in the way of a good time. In the deeply divided nation, they personified everything that Kermit Banks detested. On a warm July night, he and his deputies tried to chase those young people out of a public campground at gunpoint. To understand why, I needed to leave Yancey County and take another, much longer excursion, deep into the suburban wilds of central Florida.

3

Weekend Hippies

Two hours and fifteen minutes out of Boone, rolling down a South Carolina interstate, the landscape is drearily flat—marked by stubby pine trees and broom sedge, fire ant mounds, and road-killed carcasses of white-tailed deer. It was snowing when I pulled out of my driveway, but now temperatures hover in the mid-forties under an ashen sky. Billboards advertising personal-injury lawyers mingle with bright-orange and yellow banners urging me to confess my sins. Everywhere, construction crews are clearing away woods to make room for more traffic, road signs, gas stations, and convenience stores. It makes for a depressing drive, and it does not help to know that I am traveling on November 14, Stan Altland's birthday.

I need to stay overnight along the way, and I opt for a generic hotel in Brunswick, Georgia. A few years ago, in a nearby suburb, Ahmaud Arbery, a Black man who made the mistake of jogging through a white neighborhood, also fell victim to a 12-gauge shotgun. His killers initially told a local prosecutor that they shot Arbery while trying to make a citizen's arrest. Only after a cell phone video of the killing surfaced did district attorneys charge and convict the three white men of murder and a hate crime.[1] Eating dinner alone in a Brunswick "ale house," I think about how close Arbery's killers came to

33

getting away with murder and idly wonder what might have happened if cell phones been available the night Stan Altland died.

By the next morning, my mood improves with the warming temperatures. I drive another five hours across north-central Florida—pleasant country, marked by lofty pines and lush pasturelands where white birds, called cattle egrets, mingle with fat livestock. Stopping for gas, I check the altimeter on my watch and note that I have been driving steadily downhill, losing about 3,200 feet in elevation since I left Boone. When I get to my hotel in Oldsmar, a town of 13,000 residents adjacent to Clearwater, I am a mere seven feet above sea level, 6,677 feet lower than the highest point in Yancey County. The thermometer stands at 82 degrees.

Oldsmar is named for its founder, R. E. Olds, an early innovator in the automobile industry.[2] He would be proud of the place today. Oldsmar and the nearby communities are the epitome of auto-inspired suburban sprawl, a labyrinth of congested highways, chain restaurants, strip malls, and gated subdivisions. I am completely disoriented; I cannot tell where Oldsmar ends and Clearwater, Dunedin, Palm Harbor, Safety Harbor, Clearwater Beach, or half a dozen other cities begin.

All those municipalities lie in Pinellas County, situated on a flat peninsula between Tampa Bay and the Gulf of Mexico.[3] Clearwater is the county seat; St. Petersburg is the largest city. Having a nodding familiarity with Florida history, I can fill in major episodes from the county's past: contact between the Indigenous cultures and Spanish explorers; the Seminole Wars that drove many of the remaining natives out of the region; the slow growth of citrus, cattle, and fishing industries, including a lucrative sponge-diving enterprise in Tarpon Springs; the Florida land boom and bust of the 1920s; the advent of air-conditioning and post–World War II population increase, all followed by suburbanization, tourism, and the ongoing influx of retirees.

Roger Altland, Stan's younger brother, picks me up at the hotel, and we meet Linda Mancini at a nearby restaurant. They immediately talk about how much Clearwater has changed over the last half century. In 1972, Pinellas County had 592,000 residents. Today, with just under a million people crammed into 280 square miles, it is the most densely populated county in Florida. Clearwater, where the population hovered around 56,000 in 1972, is now home to more than 116,000, with an average density of 3,500 people per square mile.[4] Much of the Clearwater that Roger, Linda, and their friends knew in the seventies has been swallowed up by condos and big-box retail, but they promise to show me what is left.

Our first stop is Philippe Park, located in Safety Harbor. Named for Odet Philippe, a nineteenth-century settler who helped introduce grapefruit trees into the region, the park's major attraction is a large temple mound originally built by Indigenous people. From the top, you can look out on the calm waters of Safety Harbor.[5] In 1972, Roger, Linda, and their friends gathered here for picnics and touch football. Roger recalls, "We brought food, kegs of beer, and maybe a little dope. Sometimes we tossed a frisbee around. There might be twenty or more of us on a weekend. The park was more open then. It was just a fun, laid-back place for kids to enjoy. No one hassled us."

We drive a short distance and take a modern causeway out to Clearwater Beach and Pier 60, another old haunt. Pink and aqua hotels, T-shirt shops, and restaurants dominate the landscape. Brick sidewalks, dressing rooms, and an arched entryway invite sightseers onto the pier, a concrete structure that stretches well out into the Gulf. Vendors offering jewelry, balloons, shirts, and assorted souvenirs set up displays, hoping to profit from the crowds gathering for a city-sponsored event called "Sunsets at Pier 60." As the online advertisements say, it is a "family-friendly site." Or as Sue Cello would later note, a place that "reeks of tourists."[6]

It was not always so. In 1972, driving to Clearwater Beach meant negotiating a balky drawbridge that could leave traffic backed up for miles. Pier 60 had few of its present conveniences. It was merely an extension of an old municipal structure that had been there for decades.[7] The pier could get busy, especially on weekends, but Linda remembers it as "just the coolest place where lots of hippie kids hung out. You could just sit around, read the paper, maybe drink a beer, and see your friends." Teenagers rarely ventured onto the pier itself. The twenty-somethings ruled that sacred space. "Poonie [Porter] used to go out there," Linda explains, "but we stayed on the beach or in the parking lot."

Pier 60 also had a reputation as a good place to buy pot, so much so that the Clearwater Beach police eventually erected some concrete-and-glass towers near the pier to spy on suspicious transactions. Much like the youth of Yancey County, Linda, Roger, and their friends cruised a regular route between the pier and a nearby Steak 'n Shake, just to check out the vibe, see who might be around, and get a lead on where they could find a party.

Back across the causeway in Clearwater, the mood shifts as we wind through a residential district and turn onto Tioga Avenue. "That was Stan's house," Roger says, pointing to a small, tan structure near the corner. "Our mom helped him buy it. We closed in the garage while I lived with him. Phil Lokey lived with us there for a while, too."

Originally from Minnesota, Roger and Stan moved to Key West and then Clearwater after their parents divorced. Roger went to Clearwater High, while Stan, still a few credits shy of graduation after his time in the Keys, attended night school and got his diploma in 1970. "Stan was really smart," Roger explains, but "we were all a little unconventional, him more than the rest of us." The conversation lags for a moment. When Roger picks it up again, I hear new emotion in his voice. "Stanley was way ahead of his time. He was into eating healthy and taking care of himself long before that became a thing. At that house, we lived on rice, fruit, and fresh vegetables. Sometimes we'd go through a fifty-pound bag of carrots in a single week." He pauses again. "I haven't eaten much meat since the seventies."

A short distance from Tioga Drive, we pull up at 1428 Gulf to Bay Boulevard beside what is now a Mexican restaurant and grocery. In 1972, the building housed Alternative Vittles, Stan's health-food store. Roger shows me a photo of the sign that used to be out front, advertising the "Juice Bar" and "Information Center." Stan made no apologies for what some saw as the store's hippie values. "We can't help being political," he wrote in a press release about the grand opening. "Politics affects the food we eat, the water we drink, and the very air we breathe. We believe it is time to return the control of the government to the people." Stan and his business partners promised to keep prices as low as possible and suggested that customers bring their own shopping bags "to save the trees."[8]

The store had odd hours and young people often sat around at night, just talking. A visitor in 1972 described a typical scene: "At a big table made from a large cable roll are several long-haired young men, reading, talking, discussing what young people discuss today. *The Last Whole Earth Catalogue* is there and so are cookbooks about vegetable juices, bread, living off the land and organic gardening."[9]

That summer, a lot of the table talk centered on the Vietnam War, especially since the young men who gathered there worried about the military draft. Each year representatives from the US Selective Service placed 366 blue plastic capsules (one for each day of the year, including February 29) in a giant glass receptacle and drew them by hand at random. The earlier an eligible draftee's birthday got pulled, the better the chances that he would be called for service and go to Vietnam.[10]

**Original sign for Alternative Vittles, Stan Altland's
health-food store in Clearwater.**
Courtesy of Roger Altland.

"A lot of guys we knew were really afraid of getting drafted," Linda Mancini recalls. "After the lotteries, some of us would go down to Pier 60 together and read the paper to see who had a low number." Stan Altland was one of the unlucky few; the year he became eligible, his birthdate was in the eleventh capsule pulled by Selective Service. Predictably, he got the notice to report to Jacksonville for an army physical, but his astigmatism kept him out of the military and away from the war.[11]

In mid-May 1972, Nixon stepped up bombing of North Vietnam to levels not seen since 1968 and authorized the mining of Haiphong Harbor to restrict the flow of supplies to the enemy. College campuses exploded in anger. Some of the largest protests erupted in Florida. In two days, police arrested more than 400 student demonstrators at the state's universities. Things got so tense that the president of the University of Florida worried that "the tragedy of Kent State can be in the making here."[12]

Stan Altland had long been a staunch opponent of the war, but unlike most of his peers, he tried to do something to stop it. Using his contacts at the health-food store, he helped organize a "bicycle protest" against Nixon's actions. An avid cyclist and proud owner of an expensive Peugeot road bike, Stan convinced Sue Cello and eighteen other like-minded young people to join him on May 11 along US 19, one of the busiest highways in the area.

Horns blared and traffic slowed to a crawl as the protesters pedaled single file down the middle of the road, holding up homemade signs with antiwar messages. Cello's sign read "Drop Nixon on Hanoi."[13]

Clearwater police followed the riders until they reached the end of their route, then arrested Altland and two other organizers for "obstructing traffic." When an officer asked Stan if he had any weapons, he replied, "No sir, I'm a nonviolent person." The policeman responded, "Yeah, I'll bet." As Stan posted bail, a second cop scoffed, "Where did you get that money, pushing drugs?" The police arrested another girl for littering when the sign blew off her bike. She was also cited for riding "no hands" style, apparently a willful and malicious violation of a critical city ordinance.[14]

Vietnam was not the only issue dividing Floridians in 1972. As in most southern states, the Supreme Court's ruling in favor of busing white students to predominantly Black schools met harsh resistance from white parents. African Americans made up roughly 10 percent of central Florida's population, and much like my neighbors in Raleigh, many white residents hoped George Wallace might deliver them from the imagined perils of forced integration. In March 1972, Wallace won Florida's Democratic Party primary in a landslide, carrying every county except Dade (now Miami-Dade).[15]

When the Alabama governor ran for president as an independent in 1968, he had blamed the nation's problems on eastern elites, communists, Black radicals, and other assorted "anarchists," including hippies. At rallies Wallace frequently addressed long-haired men as "Sweetie" and told audiences that the only four-letter words hippies did not use were "w-o-r-k" and "s-o-a-p." Sometimes the governor baited protesters who showed up to heckle him, once telling a vocal young man, "Take off your sandals and I will autograph them for you." He had softened his rhetoric some by 1972, but his message was still clear: people like Stan Altland and his long-haired friends were responsible for much of what ailed America.[16]

Stan not only detested Wallace, but also decried the "copout of the Democratic and Republican parties." In the spring of 1972, Altland embraced the People's Party and its presidential candidate, Dr. Benjamin Spock, author of the famous childcare book. A vocal opponent of American involvement in Vietnam, Spock had urged others to resist the draft and had once been indicted for conspiracy against the United States government. He argued for an immediate end to the war, free medical care, legalization of marijuana, legal abortion, mandatory busing as a short-term remedy for segregation, and a national *maximum* wage to alleviate poverty. As Spock put it, "We've got to substitute brotherhood and the simple life for dog-eat-dog behavior." That was a near-perfect expression of Stan's political philosophy, and he quickly signed on as Central Florida Coordinator for the People's Party.[17]

Later that spring, with Spock's third-party presidential campaign going nowhere, lots of young people in Clearwater and elsewhere turned toward South Dakota senator George McGovern. He favored ending the war in Vietnam, amnesty for draft-resisters, and abortion as defined under 1972 law, when each state decided the issue. He spoke against harsh sentences for first-time drug offenders, criticized police brutality, and hinted that he might favor legalizing marijuana. Some party leaders thought he was out of step with mainstream America and warned of his imminent defeat in November. But the delegate count and convention rules worked in McGovern's favor. By early summer, his nomination seemed all but certain.

When it became clear that McGovern would be the Democrats' choice, Nixon's campaign painted the South Dakota senator as a "hippie candidate," who favored "amnesty, acid, and abortion for all." The upcoming election loomed as a referendum on American culture.[18] Would voters side with hippies or with the establishment? Freaks or cops? Peace or war? To paraphrase a lyric from Gil Scott-Heron, a radical Black poet and songwriter prominent at the time, the nation would decide whether it wanted to be Bob Dylan or Marshal Dillon.[19]

Stan Altland leaned heavily toward the former. Would he have gravitated to McGovern? We will never know. The shotgun blast that took his life deprived him of his first chance to vote for the political changes he deemed so important. I am contemplating all that when I hear Roger say, "Let's head over to the Bungalows." I jump back into Roger's truck, eager to see what most of the Clearwater crowd regarded as Party Central.

We roll through another maze of four-lane streets, traffic lights, and crosswalks, until Roger gestures toward a row of evergreens on the left, "Right there, right by those Australian pines, that's where you turned in to the Bungalows." Linda points to a small gully close to the trees. "Every weekend someone's car ended up in that ditch." We avoid the ditch, make the turn, and drive a short distance to an area about the size of a city block with sidewalks, neatly kept lawns, live oaks, and several two-level apartment buildings. "None of this was here in '72," Roger explains. "The entire place was nothing but pine trees and sand. And, of course, the Bungalows—I think there were six or eight buildings or something—looked nothing like these."

Fortunately, he has photographs to prove it, and I have those old images on my cell phone. Looking around, staring at the modern terrain and then at the fading color pictures from 1972, is like entering a time warp. In the photos, modern sidewalks, paved streets, and manicured yards disappear, replaced by a narrow sandy road, barely wide enough for a single vehicle. The grass is patchy and uncut, beaten down by cars parked at random just off the sand. A few pines dot the landscape, but you can see for hundreds of yards in every direction across the level terrain. Telephone and electrical lines dangle from old-style wooden poles. The Bungalows, low-slung structures with tiny, covered porches, shuttered windows, peeling paint, and no air-conditioning, sit clustered along the dirt drive. The small two-bedroom dwellings once housed migrant workers who harvested strawberries, vegetables, and citrus during the heyday of commercial agriculture. By the early seventies, they had been converted into cheap apartments. "Cracker shacks," Kevin Shea called them, "just the worst kind of low-rent places around."[20]

According to Sue Cello, the chief attractions were minimal cost, outdoor space, and isolation from Clearwater's suburban neighborhoods. "Most of us came from good families," Cello told me, "but we all had jobs and cars and liked living on our own." Her father, a produce buyer for the Florida-based grocery chain Kash n' Karry, helped Sue get a job at one of the larger stores. Ron Olson drove for Biff-Burger, a fast-food franchise, delivering supplies to restaurants across central Florida. Max Johnson worked for the local gas company. Phil Lokey labored as a carpenter and had a part-time job at his father's car dealership. Kevin Shea remembers working "off and on" at various jobs to pay for rent and frequent trips to the beach.[21]

Like Stan, Sue was "pretty political," but most other Bungalows residents were not, though they did "keep up with the news." According to Cello, "We were not radicals or anything, just weekend hippies" who shared a festering distrust of authority and a penchant for partying with their friends. Some retained at least a modicum of respect for their elders, but everyone had a friend who had been "turned in" (to police) or "kicked out" (of their house) when they defied parental authority.[22]

On weekends as many as fifty or more local kids found their way to the Bungalows to drink, smoke pot, and groove to rock and roll. Some of the largest gatherings took place on the last Sunday of every month. "It was nuts," Phil Lokey recalls. "An FM radio station at the University of South Florida had a show called *The Underground Railroad* where they played hard

Sunday afternoon at the Bungalows.
Courtesy of Roger Altland.

rock. The DJs would make announcements, 'Party at the Bungalows Sunday afternoon,' and people just came out of the woodwork."[23]

Roger shows me pictures of long-haired guys in cutoff jeans, shirtless or wearing tank tops, and barefoot girls in shorts and T-shirts, leaning on old Plymouths, Chevys, and VWs, cans of beer on car roofs—the essence of an early seventies happening. It was spontaneous, out-of-control, and by all accounts, "a helluva lot of fun."[24] Linda Mancini first partied at the Bungalows when she was sixteen. "It sounds crazy now," Linda tells me, "but as teenage girls in high school we felt perfectly safe there, even with all the drinking. The older guys like Phil, Ron, and Max were like our big brothers, and they looked out for us."

Poonie Porter could not be sure how he heard about the Bungalows, maybe on the radio or from someone at Pier 60. In 1972 he was back from Vietnam where, as he told it, he had been "wounded in the buttocks like Forrest Gump" and eventually ended up working with the military police. "I wasn't doing much of anything when I got home," he recalled. "Just growing my hair out, drinking, smoking a little pot, and trying to get over that shit." He "spent a lot of time at the beach." Some nights he and his friends slept under the pier.[25]

Poonie explained, "Me and a couple of others just kinda showed up at the Bungalows and got to know the kids there." He did not remember any serious problems at the weekend parties, only an occasional Camaro in the ditch or a stranger passed out on someone's porch.[26] But others recall that some of those in attendance got staggering drunk on vile concoctions like Purple

Jesus, a potent combination of Welch's grape juice and grain alcohol. Some partygoers experimented with quaaludes, and the heavy sedatives known as "reds." Various forms of acid and mescaline occasionally made the rounds. However blissful things might appear on a given Sunday afternoon, the alcohol-and-drug-saturated, potentially violent underside of youth culture lurked just below the surface. "My parents knew I went to the Bungalows," Linda says as we drive away, "but they definitely did not know everything that went on out here."

Given the crowds, underage drinking, and controlled substances, Bungalow parties might seem like the sort of gatherings that would interest local authorities. Residents often heard rumors of narcs trying to blend in with the weekend crowds, but the Bungalows lay outside the jurisdiction of the Clearwater police, and for some reason, the Pinellas County sheriff never raided the place. Isolation and open terrain helped. With few straitlaced suburbanites to complain about parties and loud music, law enforcement rarely got noise complaints. Occasionally a deputy might drive by, but as Kevin Shea noted, "you could see them coming from a mile away."[27]

In 1971 Florida passed a law that reduced possession of five grams or less of marijuana from a felony to a misdemeanor. By 1972 Clearwater authorities focused their efforts on those selling and using harder drugs. Anyone caught smuggling or moving large quantities of pot could still expect prison time, but casual users hardly seemed worth arresting. Several Bungalow regulars, including Stan Altland, got busted for possession, but no one went to jail, and police eventually dropped the charges against Stan. Linda remembers getting stopped by a local cop while smoking dope in a car, but she and the other passengers suffered no penalty other than surrender of the offending joint and a promise to drive carefully. Later, some partygoers who did not live at the Bungalows did time for dealing drugs, but most of the residents were more interested in smoking marijuana than selling it.[28]

By the time Roger and Linda drop me back at my hotel, the sun is setting, and the locals are bracing for a "cold front." Noticing that I am still in shorts and a T-shirt, the desk clerk offers me some advice: "Better dress warmer tomorrow; it's only going up to 65." Checking my phone, I learn that last night in Burnsville, temperatures dropped into the high teens. I am still chuckling about that as I take the elevator back to my room.

The much-ballyhooed Florida cold wave never materializes. The next afternoon, I turn my car air-conditioning on full blast as I battle the traffic in search of a restaurant/delicatessen called Lucky Dill. Even with help from Google Maps, I drive by the place twice and make a couple of U-turns before I find the parking lot. I sit in the car for a few minutes to settle my nerves. I am about to meet ten more of the Clearwater campers face to face.

Roger and his wife Debbie organized the gathering, reserving a room at the restaurant, sending out invitations, and providing nametags for everyone present. I grab a glass of ice water and start introducing myself to people that it seems like I already know: Kim Burns, Phil Lokey, Max Johnson, Ron Olson, Kevin Shea, and Sue Cello. Roger and Stan's younger brother, David, is here too. Although it defies logic, I half expect them to look like they did in 1972, but of course they do not. And neither do I. We are all on the back side of middle age now, with all the trappings, physical ailments, and problems of older adult life.

At first, it feels like a high school reunion: old friends hugging, smiling, snapping pictures with their phones, flipping through photo albums, laughing at images on ancient Polaroids. But this gathering has an undercurrent of seriousness and sadness. Ron Olson has a thick folder of newspaper articles, letters, and pictures from that ill-fated excursion to see the Rolling Stones. Others tear up as they remember Stan. I feel a twinge of guilt about intruding on their personal tragedy to write a book, but they are eager to talk with me.

Drinks arrive, followed by food, and I meet several other Briar Bottom campers whose names I have seen in the Florida papers. Sue Cello introduces me to Doreen Sofarelli and Diane Cracolici. I discover that Doreen and I both drove Plymouth Dusters in the early seventies. Diane tells me that she "spent a lot of time with David Satterwhite that night." She was sitting with him at the fire, but they somehow got separated before the gun went off. I also talk with Martha "Marty" Watkins, who was standing so close to Stan that his blood splattered onto her clothes. The afternoon slips by, and eventually people begin to drift away, out of the past, back to their lives. I do the same, driving back to the hotel with a half-eaten club sandwich. That will suffice for dinner. I head up to my room, open my laptop, and try to make sense of what I have learned over the last two days. Running on adrenaline and diet soda, I am still pounding the keyboard at 2:00 a.m.

———————————

Some of the contrasts between Clearwater and Yancey County are as stark as the variations in topography and weather. Though not nearly as overcrowded and developed as it is today, Pinellas County had forty-five times as many year-round residents as Yancey in 1972; Clearwater alone had four times as many. Daily newspapers and metropolitan television stations routinely brought the major issues of the day, including Vietnam and federally mandated integration, into every home. In 1968 and 1972, most white voters in Clearwater favored either George Wallace or Richard Nixon, just like white people in and around Burnsville. But given the much larger population, dissent and antiwar demonstrations were far more common in Pinellas.

Young people in Yancey County drank beer, smoked pot, and cruised favored spots on weekends like their counterparts in Pinellas. But the Clearwater kids grew up in a more cosmopolitan environment where much of the population, including the Altlands, had moved in from elsewhere. Everyone seemed to be from off. At Philippe Park, Clearwater Beach, and especially at the Bungalows, mingling and partying with strangers became routine. Pot and pills were as common as beer. Friend groups formed and occasionally spats developed, but as one Clearwater camper told me, "It was no big deal. Just bring your own dope and try not to be a pain in the ass." There, as among my friends in Raleigh, the ubiquitous descriptor "cool" evolved into a euphemism for those who drank and smoked pot, as in, "Is she cool?" If so, she was more than welcome.

Pop music reinforced those attitudes. According to Sue Cello and Phil Lokey, "Led Zeppelin, Cream, Grateful Dead, Creedence [Clearwater Revival], Stones. Those were the standards. No one listened to country." A few of the girls liked James Taylor and, according to Max Johnson, Linda and her friends tortured him by insisting that he play Carole King's *Tapestry* album constantly when they rode in his car. Otherwise, as the FM radio DJs liked to say, it was "hard rock, all day every day."[29]

I hang around Clearwater for another half-day before heading back to Boone, again by way of Brunswick, Georgia. Sitting in the same ale house, near the same hotel, tired after another day of fighting interstate traffic, I remember again just how far it is from central Florida to western North Carolina. Throw in the demographic and cultural disparities between Pinellas and Yancey Counties and it seems improbable that these freewheeling urban kids would ever encounter a high-handed mountain sheriff like Kermit Banks. And they might not have, had it not been for circumstances unfolding thousands of miles away. In Los Angeles, during the first months of 1972, the Rolling Stones began planning a thirty-two-city tour of North America.[30] By early summer, the swirl of events around rock's biggest band would put twenty-four kids from metropolitan Florida on a collision course with seven Yancey County lawmen and bring the national epidemic of intergenerational violence to an out-of-the-way place called Briar Bottom.

4

It's Only Rock and Roll

On April 14, 1972, radio stations across America began playing a new 45 rpm single from the Rolling Stones. A quirky, guitar-heavy tune, with a boozy juke joint feel, it featured slurred, sometimes indecipherable lyrics. Only on the chorus were the words reasonably clear as Mick Jagger wailed, "Gotta roll me; keep on rolling; call me the tumbling dice." It did not matter. "Tumbling Dice" and its B side, a tribute to Angela Davis called "Sweet Black Angel," started climbing the US charts, eventually making it to number seven.[1]

Out at the Bungalows, the dedicated hard rockers did not buy 45s, but they turned up the volume whenever "Tumbling Dice" came on the radio. Other than a greatest-hits set released the previous December, no one had heard much from the Stones in over a year. Their last album of original songs, *Sticky Fingers*, had appeared in April 1971. Even in the wake of bad publicity associated with Altamont, *Sticky Fingers* had served up the same bluesy decadence that made the band popular in the first place, including lyrics that celebrated interracial sex, drugs, and "juiced up and sloppy" drunkenness. As if to bolster their outlaw credentials, the band had refused to pay English taxes and fled to France just as *Sticky Fingers* landed in the United States.[2]

By the spring of 1972, with fans around the world desperate for fresh Stones material, rumors of a new two-disc, eighteen-song album had been circulating for months. April brought the teaser "Tumbling Dice." A month later, Stones aficionados, including those at the Bungalows, flocked to record stores to buy *Exile on Main St.*, two LPs' worth of wonderful, hard-rocking excess that made *Sticky Fingers* look tame. With songs like "Rocks Off," "Turd on the Run," "Rip This Joint," and "Sweet Virginia" (which spoke of drug-induced "waves behind your eyeballs"), the band again offered the establishment a giant middle finger. Like a lot of their fans, the Stones were cynical, disillusioned, and fist-in-the-air angry, though they offered few solutions to the turmoil of the times. Just turn up the volume and party hard.

Almost before the band's devotees could play all four sides of *Exile*, bigger news leaked out of California. The Stones were in Los Angeles rehearsing for a summer tour of the United States and Canada. Wherever rock fans gathered that spring, one question dominated the conversation: "Hey man, did you hear about the Stones?"[3] By late May, everyone at the Bungalows had heard. Living close to Tampa and St. Petersburg, the Clearwater crowd had ample opportunities to attend concerts and they kept an ear out for which bands might be coming to town. Sue Cello and her roommate papered the doors and walls of their Bungalow apartment with ticket stubs from various shows. But the Rolling Stones? Live? Nothing in their previous experience came close. A Stones concert was more than a rock show. Being there was a cultural and political statement, an opportunity to commune with fellow freaks, flaunt your contempt for traditional values, give in to rebellious impulses, and be the envy of every longhair who could not get a ticket. They had to go.[4]

The Stones had scheduled no concerts in Florida or Georgia, and because of riots during the 1969 tour, ticket sales for most venues were "mail order only" with a required dated postmark. Just a few sites planned to offer tickets to walk-up customers. Department stores like Sears and Montgomery Ward, which usually functioned as outlets for major arenas, had limited supplies. In California, some of the retailers had recently installed a new computer service called Ticketron that supposedly allowed for faster sales. Whether by mail, in person, or via computer, an individual could buy only four tickets and at some venues, only two. It was all for the fans, the Stones said, a way to thwart the scalpers.[5]

A ticket cost $6.50, a healthy sum for a rock show in 1972. But it seemed more than reasonable (*Exile* retailed for $9.98), and any serious Stones enthusiast could afford it. The biggest obstacle for prospective concertgoers was the sheer magnitude of the event. As Robert Greenfield, who covered the tour for *Rolling Stone* magazine and turned his experiences into a critically acclaimed book, explains, "The Stones had been together for *ten years* . . . the only great band of the sixties still around in original form playing original rock and roll." More than mere royalty, "they were kings. Undeniably. By acclamation. And it was to America they came to receive their crowns." The tour, Greenfield writes, "was bigger even than the youth of America." Or as celebrity DJ Wolfman Jack put it, "If Jesus Christ came to town, he couldn't sell more tickets. Do ya understan'?"[6]

At the LA Forum, thousands camped outside the box office for five days. The place sold out in two hours. In Long Beach, more than 5,000 customers were in line when sales started. The Hollywood Palladium received 15,000 orders for the 4,500 tickets available via mail order.[7] As Greenfield notes, "In L.A., a ticket to a Stones' concert was better than a negotiable bond." A single ticket could be exchanged for fifty dollars or, if one preferred the coin of the realm, "seven grams of hash and a twenty-dollar lid."[8] A San Francisco radio station held a contest for free tickets asking, "What would you do to see the Rolling Stones?" The man who won promised to "shave off all the hair on [his] body and smoke it."[9]

In Chicago, Detroit, and other major cities, shows sold out faster than arena staff could count requests. Tens of thousands of mail orders went unread and unfilled. At the Montgomery Ward in Waukegan, Illinois, inebriated fans waiting to buy tickets for the Chicago concerts broke windows and started looting the store as soon as it opened. Even in the hinterlands, ticket sales smashed all previous records. Nashville sold out in seven hours. Promoters there called Stones representatives and desperately tried to schedule a second show—to no avail.[10]

These days, when music fans follow rock stars on Instagram, get text and email updates with tour info, and download set lists weeks in advance of local shows, it is impossible to recapture the curious mixture of excitement and uncertainty that engulfed Rolling Stones fans that summer. News of the tour spread mainly via radio and word of mouth; occasionally you could pick up something in the paper or in *Life* or *Newsweek*. Among my friends, "Hey man, did you hear about the Stones?" turned into "Hey man, guess what I heard about the Stones!" Everyone knew something, often only half-true. They just played Chuck Berry records at their post-concert parties. They were not playing "Sympathy for the Devil." The stage had a dragon painted on it. (Actually, two sea serpents breathing fire.) They were never coming back to America; this would be the last chance to see them live. Hells Angels planned to kill

Mick because he had blamed them for Altamont. That last one had some basis in fact. In addition to the usual bodyguards and enhanced security, Jagger apparently carried two .38 caliber pistols with him when not on stage.[11]

Such rumors only compounded the mystery and hype, especially for fans like me who had no tickets. I listened fanatically to Stones albums and constantly combed newspapers and magazines for any scrap of relevant information. My fascination with the band is difficult to explain. Rebellion was part of it, but in 1972, while Alice Cooper performed with a pet boa constrictor, and a band called Wicked Lester prepared to don circus makeup and reemerge as Kiss, the Stones just played rock and roll. Jagger became famous for his antics and wild gyrations, especially on songs like "Midnight Rambler," and in a few years, the Stones would perform with their own props on stages the size of movie sets. But that summer, the shows were mostly about the music.[12] At least that is what the rock magazines said. I could only imagine it. *Gimme Shelter* came back to the Cardinal's late show, but I did not go. It now seemed like a poor substitute for the real thing.

A lot of those in Clearwater felt the same way. "I was absolutely obsessed," Linda Mancini remembers. "We all were. We couldn't stop thinking about what it would be like to see the Rolling Stones." Stan Altland read about the Charlotte concert sometime in May. The city was within driving distance of Clearwater, and the timing seemed perfect, right in the middle of a holiday week when it would be easier get up to North Carolina and back. All seats for the Charlotte show would be sold by mail; no one had to go to the arena ahead of time. Stan and his friends needed twenty-five tickets to accommodate everyone who wanted to go. Since an individual could request just four tickets, several people had to place orders by the required date. And they had to collect $6.50 from each prospective concertgoer, a total of $162.50.[13]

By the time those plans took shape, *Exile* was the number one album in America and trying to get twenty-five tickets by mail might seem like a fool's errand.[14] But Stan Altland had a rare combination of organizational skill, naivete, and faith in human nature that made him want to try. With help from Phil Lokey, Gary Graham, and a couple of others, efforts went forward. Money had to be fronted and deadlines imposed on stragglers, but on the appointed day, all the envelopes and checks went into the mail, addressed to the Charlotte Coliseum. Now they waited.[15]

While his older brother labored to get Rolling Stones tickets, Roger Altland prepared for another, much-anticipated summer trip. For several years, he had wanted to hitchhike across the United States on a "voyage of self-discovery, just me and my dog Sam." (Apparently Sam just showed up one

Left to right: **Stan Altland, Gary Graham, and Ron Olson, a few weeks before they left Clearwater for North Carolina.**
Courtesy of Roger Altland.

day at the Bungalows. Roger took him home after he "bit a couple of people.")
However risky and far-fetched it might seem, hitchhiking cross-country was
a common enough occurrence in 1972. Lots of young people, especially
men, felt perfectly safe accepting rides from strangers and leaving the rest to
chance. As the *New York Times* later put it, once school ended, vast numbers
of young people left behind "the spring anti-war protests to hitchhike and
panhandle their way across the nation." Roger Altland wanted to be one of

It's Only Rock and Roll   49

Roger Altland, leaning on his 1948 Dodge, just before
he left to hitchhike cross country in 1972.
Courtesy of Roger Altland.

them. He said goodbye to Stan on Memorial Day weekend and promised to
call from the road.[16] It was the last time he saw his brother alive.

On June 3, the Rolling Stones, with Stevie Wonder as the opening act, played
their first gig at Pacific Coliseum in Vancouver, British Columbia. With
memories of Altamont still fresh, promoters hoped that the '72 shows would
come off without incident. They were wrong. Violence followed the Stones
wherever they went. When officials in Vancouver turned away about 2,000
fans, some of whom had unknowingly bought counterfeit tickets, the mob
stormed the arena. Hurling rocks and bricks, they tried to crash the front
gate, instigating the worst riot the city had ever seen. It took the Royal Cana-
dian Mounted Police to restore order and by the time they did, thirty-one of
them needed medical attention.[17]

   In San Diego on June 13, the 16,000-seat arena had been sold out for a
month, and about 1,000 young people under the influence of various substances gathered in the streets around the venue. A few had crudely printed
bogus tickets; the rest planned to crash the gate. They threw rocks and tossed
firebombs, not only at police, but also at passing motorists. The cops fought

back with tear gas. One policeman even heaved a rock at a car with an open window, injuring a teenage girl inside. In the coliseum parking lot, rioters smashed car windows, torched several vehicles, and kindled a bonfire with wooden traffic barricades. Officers later described the three-hour riot as "real guerilla warfare." Fifteen people suffered injuries and law enforcement made sixty arrests, eleven for felonies.[18]

The next night, in Tucson, 400 ticketless fans tried to break down the gate, smashing windows and ripping a door off the Tucson Community Center.[19] The story was much the same in Minneapolis on June 19, where "a man in his early 20s—blond hair tied in a ponytail—and his girlfriend and his dog" started organizing a mob outside the arena just as Stevie Wonder went on. "Come on, you hippies!" the man shouted. "Let's crash the gate. They can't stop us." They could and did. Police sprayed mace and set off tear gas, driving the rioters back into the parking lot. Inside, it was stifling hot with spectators sitting or standing in the aisles. Tear gas drifting in from the disturbance outside "made it nearly impossible to breathe."[20]

The *Minneapolis Star* took notice of the melee but relegated the story to page 7. After all, no one died, and police beating up kids at rock concerts was old news. In the late sixties, local cops and sheriffs in southern states had sometimes gone after the artists themselves. In March 1969, Jim Morrison allegedly exposed himself to an audience in Miami. Dade County sheriffs swore out a warrant and, in 1970, a jury convicted the Doors' front man of "indecent exposure and open profanity." He died before he could pay the fine or serve his sentence. In Tampa, police asked Janis Joplin to calm down a rowdy audience. Instead, she cursed the cops, who took her to jail for using "vulgar and obscene language." After Altamont, police presence at the biggest shows became even more pronounced. By 1972, law enforcement did not think twice about pulling out billy clubs and tear gas, even for minor misbehavior.[21]

Stones management blamed the problems on crowds outside the arena, not the paying customers, but as always, the band did nothing to discourage the mayhem. Street violence and contempt for authority were central themes in many of their songs. While onstage, Jagger, Richards, and guitarist Mick Taylor (who had replaced Brian Jones) swigged bourbon straight from the bottle. Officially, promoters called the enterprise the "Stones Touring Party" (S.T.P). Unofficially, it became known as the "Cocaine and Tequila Sunrise Tour." In mid-June, as they played Chicago, the band stayed at Hugh Hefner's Playboy Mansion and rumors flew about all-night orgies. As always, the Stones exemplified the clichéd trifecta of sex, drugs, and rock and roll—what *Life* had once called the "sacraments" of youth culture.[22]

During the third week of June, Jagger and company left Chicago headed for Kansas City and Texas, where at a Fort Worth show they played "Sweet Black Angel" live for the first and only time.[23] Just as the Stones' jet touched down in the Lone Star state, the long-awaited envelopes from the Charlotte Coliseum arrived in Clearwater. The impossible had happened. Altland, Lokey, and their friends had somehow secured twenty-five tickets to the now-sold-out show in Charlotte. They were ecstatic. Some of the girls shrieked with delight when they got a phone call with the good news. "I couldn't believe it," Linda Mancini said. "It was absolutely fantastic, like winning the lottery." More than 2,500 miles away, Roger Altland (still hitchhiking around the country) picked up a phone in Berkeley, California, and heard Stan's excited voice on the other end. They were going to see the Rolling Stones, and Stan had a ticket for Roger. All he had to do was find his way to Charlotte by July 6 and meet them at their motel.[24]

A few days after the kids in Clearwater got the good news, the Stones flew into Alabama. Fearful of southern law enforcement and their reputation for beating up rock fans, promoters had been reluctant to bring the band to George Wallace's home state. But the Stones, who made no bones about their affinity for southern gospel and Delta Blues, insisted on it. Still traveling with the entourage, Robert Greenfield thought that his stereotypical views of southern lawmen might be exaggerated. But when he got to Mobile, there they were "with stomachs bulging over their ammo belts, .38 Magnums hanging obscenely off their hips . . . baby blue riot helmets covering their faces."

Hotels near the arenas drained their swimming pools so longhaired concertgoers would not "foul the filtering system." Greenfield heard a Mobile policeman say of the Stones, "I heah they been causin' hell everywheah they go. They bettah know we mean business here." At the next show in Tuscaloosa, the band's bus got stuck in post-concert traffic. When one of the managers asked for help so they could make their flight, a local officer drawled, "Ah doan give a fuck if you make yoah plane or not. You the same to me as anyone else."[25] So it went between cops, kids, and rock bands in the American South, a portent of things to come.

Back in Clearwater, Altland, Lokey, and several others began to talk about turning the trip to Charlotte into a week-long vacation. Maybe they could spend a couple of days in the North Carolina mountains on the way to the show.[26] It was the kind of outing that held tremendous appeal for seventies youth. Sleeping in tents or a van, away from TV and phones, on the road, freed from school and the daily routine: it all had a vagabond gypsy feel to it, a sense of community and trust in each other that seemed painfully absent from everyday life.

Phil Lokey and some of his friends were avid boaters and fishermen who thoroughly enjoyed being outdoors. Sometimes they ventured out to Sand Key, a relatively isolated spit of sand and sea oats near Clearwater Beach, where they stayed overnight, fished, drank beer, and listened to music. Those small-scale get-togethers reflected a national trend. Every summer, across the country, young people crowded into public campgrounds and recreation areas, where they inevitably clashed with authorities.[27]

One of the more famous confrontations took place in 1970 at Yosemite National Park. Hippies poured into Yosemite that summer. They took up residence at various campsites and picnic areas, drove their vans across open meadows, and panhandled around park stores and restaurants. For weeks, tourists complained "about loud music, marijuana smoke, loose dogs, public nudity, and theft," all of which threatened to ruin family vacations.[28]

Stoneman Meadow, in the middle of Yosemite Valley, had long been a favorite place for longhairs to congregate. Around Memorial Day 1970, rangers and park police tried to put a stop to the partying by ticketing and towing abandoned cars and vans out of the meadow. When some young people resisted and one pulled a knife, the officers withdrew and allowed the vehicles to stay.

In early July, with young people again flooding the meadow, Yosemite officials decided that quiet hours would begin at 7:00 p.m. instead of the usual 10:00 p.m. and ordered the crowd to disperse. The 300-plus kids refused to move. Park police (whom the hippies openly derided as "pine pigs") and other law enforcement personnel on horseback formed a line and drove most of the crowd into a nearby area. The next night, July 4, when young people again ignored an order to vacate, chaos ensued. Rioters set fires and turned over a police vehicle. Once more, park officials on horseback rode through the meadow, this time at full gallop, dispersing the crowd and running over anyone who got in their way. By the time things settled down in the early hours of July 5, officers had made 174 arrests, and at least five rioters needed medical attention. Some witnesses held law enforcement responsible; others blamed the nation's "hedonistic youth."[29]

No one in the Clearwater group remembers the Stoneman Meadow riot, but some do recall a similar well-publicized hippie gathering that took place in 1972, just as they prepared to leave for North Carolina. Inspired by Woodstock, a group calling themselves the Rainbow Family of Living Light, headquartered in Eugene, Oregon, met for the first time at Strawberry Lake,

Colorado. The group planned "to meditate in the forest, to chant prayers together, talk over things, and play flutes and guitars and drums under the spruce and aspen trees."[30]

The governor of Colorado used every means at his disposal to keep them out. Police and sheriffs closed every road into the site. The hippies came anyway, hiking miles over steep mountain trails. Authorities tried to ban food from the giant meadow in which the visitors camped, but that proved unwieldy. When officials raised the issue of poor sanitation and suggested that deadly epidemics might follow, volunteers dug long, deep trenches for garbage and human waste that could be quickly covered with dirt. The group secured its own doctors and a generous supply of penicillin. Finally, as some 3,000 young people marched out of Granby, Colorado, headed for the gathering, the outnumbered cops gave up and opened the roads. The American Civil Liberties Union (ACLU) went to court on behalf of the Family, pointing out that the visitors were on public land and constitutionally entitled to assemble in a peaceful manner. Despite the disquieting appearance of several motorcycle clubs during the festivities, the gathering remained mostly peaceful. Various estimates put the crowd at 10,000 to 20,000.[31]

Twenty-four kids from Florida camping out on their way to a Rolling Stones concert hardly compared to the Rainbow Family or the rioters in Stoneman Meadow, but thanks to those and similar events, even small groups of unchaperoned young people met with immediate suspicion in public parks and campgrounds. Longhairs arriving in vans or other hippie vehicles invariably set local rangers' teeth on edge. Accustomed to the carefree atmosphere at the Bungalows, the Clearwater group either did not know or did not care about how they might be perceived. Nor did they seem to understand that they would have to camp cheek by jowl with people who had vastly different ideas about appropriate outdoor behavior. Just keep cool and things would be fine. They could play music, drink beer, and smoke a little dope, just like at home. Yeah, cops were always a threat, but how bad could it be if you were way off in the woods on public land? Poonie Porter had seen the Rolling Stones in Tuscaloosa, but when offered a ticket for the Charlotte show at the last minute, he jumped at the chance to join his friends and camp out in North Carolina.[32]

The group took the same relaxed approach to planning details of the outing. Ron Olson would take his white Volvo; Max Johnson had a Chevy Impala large enough to accommodate four or five concertgoers; Phil Lokey would drive his Mazda. Along with Doreen Sofarelli in her gray Duster, they became part of a six-vehicle caravan that would leave Clearwater on Saturday, July 1. They planned to stop overnight in Atlanta. Lokey's mother lived just outside the city and could find the group a place to stay. Fred McNairy, one of Stan's partners in Alternative Vittles, and Fred's girlfriend, Cathy Siebenthaler, would meet them there. Fred had an orange Volkswagen bus that could also provide transport for several others. Stan made reservations at a Charlotte motel near the coliseum. He did not worry about camping accommodations. Everyone could just bring their own gear or borrow from friends. If it rained, those without tents could sleep in the vehicles.[33]

Someone, maybe Phil or Fred, thought it best to go somewhere near Asheville because "it looked like a place with plenty of mountains and campgrounds." Once there, they could get some advice about where to stay on public land. Apparently, no one thought about the logistics of finding space for twenty-four people during the busiest vacation week of the year. Nor did they consider the difficulties of driving and parking seven vehicles anywhere off the beaten path. Roger Altland made it all the way to California relying on rides from strangers, and he would get to Charlotte the same way. Sleeping on the ground for a night or two seemed tame by comparison. Besides, they had more pressing matters: Who had a portable tape player? Could they get beer on the road? And who had the pot and other pharmaceutical necessities? They might be roughing it for a couple of days, but going to see the Rolling Stones without being in an appropriately altered state of mind? That was unthinkable.[34]

As the departure date got closer and news of violence at Stones concerts spread, some of their parents got nervous. The older members of the group were not subject to adult oversight, but the younger ones were, even if they lived away from home. Sue Cello's father told her she could not go. She ignored him and kept her ticket, figuring that she would deal with the consequences when she got back to Florida. Two girls just lied about where they were going, telling parents that that they would be spending July Fourth together in South Carolina with another friend. Linda Mancini persuaded her folks that this was the perfect "high school trip," a graduation gift to reward twelve years of hard work. Others argued or sulked until the adults gave in.

Naive and caught up in the excitement of it all, most of the group thought their parents were overreacting. It was only rock and roll. A concert. They had been to similar shows before, dozens of times. But Linda's dad seemed to grasp something that the kids failed to understand. Whatever their intent, given the tenor of the times, going to see the Rolling Stones might be interpreted as an act of defiance, the equivalent of waving a red flag in the face of conservative, law-and-order America. A seven-vehicle caravan, filled with long-haired guys and girls in T-shirts and cutoff jeans, all of whom hailed from a Florida city, might look to some like a hippie invasion, a beachhead from which to set loose the evil troika of sex, drugs, and rock and roll. Just before Linda left the house, headed for western North Carolina, her father offered her a piece of advice. "Remember," he said, "those people up there aren't like us."[35]

5

Disorderly Conduct

It was overcast and cool when the group gathered at Phil Lokey's house on July 1. The mood was light and upbeat as they loaded luggage and gear into the six vehicles. "I was sooooo excited," Linda Mancini recalls. "I had never been camping before, but I didn't care. It was summer. School was out. We were going to see the Rolling Stones. Everyone had their tickets. We felt good, ready to rock 'n' roll."[1]

The first day's drive from Clearwater to Atlanta went smoothly. They talked incessantly, listened to music, and "probably smoked a joint or two" as the caravan cruised up Interstate 75. They got to Georgia about 8:00 p.m. and met up with Fred McNairy and Cathy Siebenthaler as planned. Lokey's mother treated them all to a buffet dinner at the Conyers Motor Inn and arranged for them to camp at a nearby lake. "She fed all of us and found us a place to stay," one of the campers remembers, "It was an incredibly nice thing to do." The next morning, Lokey's mother served them breakfast before they left.[2]

The first sign of trouble came on July 2, as they drove through South Carolina on Interstate 85. Somewhere near Greenville, they stopped at a restaurant where some local youth had gathered. As Max Johnson describes it, "They all looked pretty straight [seventies slang for non-hippies], but when we spoke to some of the girls, they looked like they might want to go with us to the mountains." That did not sit well with their boyfriends, who immediately began to harass the longhairs and make lewd comments to the Clearwater women. "They were just local rednecks who wanted to start some shit," Lokey explained. "We tried to ignore them and got out of there as fast as we could."[3]

Just out of Greenville they passed a roadside fireworks stand. With Independence Day close, the place was hopping. Some in the group bought a few firecrackers and sparklers.[4] From there, they took US Route 25 toward Asheville, arriving between 5:00 and 6:00 p.m. They still had no place to stay, but in keeping with the casual vibe of the trip, no one panicked. They asked a couple of people in Asheville where they might camp for the night. The locals told them to try the Mount Mitchell area. It took a while to sort out the directions and even longer to navigate a route that took them from 19E to NC Route 80 and the Blue Ridge Parkway.[5] They had to move fast if they wanted to get settled before nightfall.

Just before 9:00 p.m., they found their way to NC Route 128, which runs from the parkway to a small campground at Mount Mitchell State Park. Halfway up the curvy road, Lokey looked in his Mazda's rearview mirror and saw a "cop car" (it turned out to be a state park ranger) with lights flashing. The car came up behind the caravan and pulled out to pass, speeding into blind curves, looking like it might crash any second. Lokey wondered if it might be on the way to an accident or some other emergency. Not until they got almost to the top did he realize that the ranger had passed them so he could beat their entourage to the campground. He parked his car sideways across the entrance, intent on keeping the group out. "Oh shit," Lokey thought, as he and Fred McNairy got out to talk with the ranger. By then it was almost dark.[6]

"You can't camp here," the man told them, "We only allow families." Phil tried to banter with him. "But we *are* a family," he said. Without another word, the man walked to his car and took out a .30-.30 rifle, brandishing it in front of the caravan. Lokey remembers him saying something like, "I told you that you can't stay here. Get off my mountain." Poonie Porter remembered it as, "We don't have facilities to accommodate people of your character." Porter asked the ranger for the name of his supervisor. He handed Poonie a business card and told him to call anyone he "damn well pleased."[7]

From there, the group somehow found their way to Black Mountain Campground, a larger US Forest Service facility just off NC 80. They arrived well after dark and met Blaine Ray, a "recreation technician," who "pulled a log across the road" to stop them from entering that site. After fifty years, no one from Clearwater can recall exactly how they got from Mount Mitchell to Black Mountain, just that they were not welcome at either place. As Jay Barrett explained it, "There were just so many people camping. Everywhere. We weren't ready for that, and we didn't know where we were going anyway."[8]

Tired and frustrated, they drove a short distance down Forest Service Road 472 and pulled off less than a quarter mile from Black Mountain Campground, near a small dam and fish barrier designed to protect South Toe River trout from invasive species. A sign read "No Camping," but it was late, and they were exhausted. In the dark, they either did not immediately see the notice or at that point "really didn't give a damn." Happy to be off the road, Max Johnson rolled up his jeans and waded out into the river. He got out quickly because "the water was freezing."[9]

They built a fire, ate, "smoked some pot and drank a little liquor." A couple of the girls took a small dose of mescaline and ended up sitting awake in a car all night while one of them insisted that the other "looked just like Mary Tyler Moore." None of their friends slept much either. Late that night or early the next morning, someone chopped down the No Camping sign and threw the post into the fire, in part because they needed wood, but also as an act of defiance.[10]

About 7:45 a.m. on July 3, part-time ranger Jack Olinger left Black Mountain Campground headed for the Forest Service office in Burnsville. Olinger worked summers as a "compliance officer," taking fees from campers and enforcing regulations. Each day he drove to Burnsville with money collected the night before. On the morning of July 3, he saw the Clearwater group near the fish barrier and noticed that the No Camping sign had been chopped down. Some of the young people were still asleep on the ground or in cars, and Olinger did not stop. He went on to the Forest Service office and reported the illegal campers to ranger Johnny McLain and assistant ranger Harold Rivers.[11]

Around 8:30 a.m. Terry Shankle, a state game warden, drove past the fish barrier. Shankle kept a close eye on the South Toe because it had lure restrictions and creel limits different from nearby streams. Local fishermen frequently ignored those rules, and with the holiday, violators figured to be out in force. Shankle noticed several vehicles with Florida license plates parked in the restricted area. As a game warden, he had no authority to issue a citation (except for illegal fishing) or even ask the campers to move but decided to check out the group anyway. He saw trash strewn about and the signpost burning in the campfire, but he said nothing about illegal camping or their source of firewood.[12]

Later that morning, Phil Lokey and a couple of others left to gas up one of the vehicles. They pulled into that country store that I visited where, as Sue Cello remembers, the local people "looked at us like we had five heads." One person there looked a lot like them; he had long hair, well-worn clothes, and a large white dog. He introduced himself as David Satterwhite, said he was from Mebane (pronounced *Meh-bin*), North Carolina, and often came to the mountains to escape the summer heat. When he heard the group had no place to stay, Satterwhite told them that he knew "a great place to camp." He had already set up his stuff there and would be happy to show them the way. According to Lokey, Satterwhite was "just a cool hippie, extroverted, who had no problem talking to us and was basically like, 'Follow me, man.'" Phil and the others headed back to give the group the good news.[13]

Meanwhile, Warden Shankle drove up the river, turned around, and went back past the illegal campsite. About a mile or so farther down Road 472, he ran into Blaine Ray driving upriver and told him about the Clearwater group. Ray, who had refused them entry to Black Mountain Campground the night before, decided to call the Forest Service office in Burnsville. Jack Olinger was already there talking with Johnny McLain when Ray's call came in. McLain suggested that Shankle and Ray just tell the hippies to go somewhere else. Then McLain went off duty, leaving assistant ranger Harold Rivers in charge.

Shankle and Ray drove back to the campsite, where they spoke with a "white male in his twenties, wearing blue pants," who had "a ponytail a foot or a foot and half long." According to the game warden, this man (probably Poonie Porter) asked the two officials where the group could go so that they would not be bothered and would not bother anyone else. The warden drew them a map showing the way to Curtis Creek Campground in McDowell County, a less popular site about eight miles away. Blaine Ray gave the campers some plastic garbage bags, asked them to pick up the trash, and suggested they move on within the next couple of hours. Apparently neither he nor Shankle made an issue of the signpost still smoldering in the firepit. As one camper remembered, the two men were "not confrontational at all." By 3:00 that afternoon, when Shankle drove by again, the litter and the Florida cars were gone. But instead of going to Curtis Creek, the Clearwater group followed David Satterwhite to Briar Bottom. It proved a fateful decision.[14]

The modern sign pointing the way to Briar Bottom.
Photo by the author.

These days, getting to Briar Bottom is easy. You turn right off Forest Service Road 472, drive across a bridge over the South Toe River into Black Mountain Campground, and turn left. A well-maintained gravel road takes you up the river. Drivers must still cross a small tributary, but the Forest Service has thoughtfully placed large paving stones along the creek bottom to smooth the way. From there a one-way loop road winds past a site occupied by the campground host, a full-time supervisor who keeps an eye on things during the camping season. Briar Bottom is now a group campground with six large sites named for a variety of local flora: Laurel, Red Oak, Maple, Dogwood, Ash, and Poplar.

Each site can accommodate fifty campers and ten cars. All have running water, a shelter that covers multiple picnic tables, charcoal grills, and designated space for tents. Campers use well-lighted, tiled bathrooms with flush toilets and have access to hot-water showers at Black Mountain Campground.

Group camping costs one hundred dollars a night and reservations must be made online in advance. Just as in 1972, quiet hours begin at 10:00 p.m., when the host locks the gate. Even with all its new features, Briar Bottom remains breathtakingly beautiful. Fifty years of forest growth have filled in some of the once-open area with more poplars, oaks, maples, and yellow birch. Floods have altered the river's course over the years, but the stream remains remarkably pristine, with clear, cold water that supports a healthy trout population.

One autumn afternoon, I decide not to drive in the easy way. Accompanied by a professional surveyor and another friend, I hike up Road 472 in search of the route that David Satterwhite, Phil Lokey, and the others took on that July afternoon in 1972. Armed with geographic information systems (GIS) data, portable global positioning system (GPS) trackers, printouts from Google Earth, and some old topographic maps from the 1930s and 1960s, we locate a particular curve in the gravel road where it crosses a tiny tributary to the South Toe.

Finding what might be an old roadbed off to the right, we fight through a tangle of rhododendron and greenbriers until we cross the tributary a second time. From there we spot a break in the thick woods that opens into a shallow depression leading to the river. A vehicle would have no trouble making it through the streambed here (assuming the larger rocks were gone). On the other side are the group campsites at Briar Bottom, where you can still find a grassy area punctuated by large trees. Though we cannot be certain, our maps and data indicate that this is where the group from Clearwater forded the river.

Today the place is deserted and dead quiet. A hurricane, which ironically enough crossed Florida perilously close to Clearwater, is working its way up the Atlantic coast, and the Forest Service has decided to close Briar Bottom in anticipation of heavy rain and floods. We will be the last three campers to leave. I get an eerie feeling as I imagine six cars and a van fording the river on that July afternoon, one of them carrying a twenty-year-old passenger who would be dead by midnight.

Doreen Sofarelli worried that her new Plymouth Duster might be permanently damaged if she drove across the river. Only after several others successfully navigated the stream did she attempt it and was "nervous as a cat" as she put the car in gear. In 1972, Briar Bottom served as an overflow area for Black Mountain Campground and had few of its present amenities. Doreen

Approximate site of the old river ford into Briar Bottom.
Photo by the author.

and the others found only a few privies, a couple of metal trash cans with lids attached via chains, and a single pump that dispensed fresh water. They had to schlep their gear from the parking area and spread out as best they could to avoid others already staying there. No one remembers paying a fee to camp.[15]

A couple of the guys built crude lean-tos for shelter. Given the clear weather, others just opted for the ground. The group found some rocks for a fire ring and dragged up some wood to burn later. Sue Cello and several of the other women set up a large tent and dubbed it "the girls' dorm." Fred McNairy and Cathy Siebenthaler planned to stay in Fred's van. Gary Graham shared a tent with his girlfriend, Sandra Drucas.

Once the sleeping arrangements had been decided and the camp chores done, Satterwhite rode his motorcycle in the meadow, and some of the men organized an impromptu game of tackle football. Paul Brayly, an Elon College student camping nearby, got his van stuck crossing the river, and the kids from Clearwater helped him get it going again. Fred took six of the girls to a store to purchase food and do some laundry while Lokey and two others headed to Asheville for beer.[16] Finally, it seemed, things had started to go right.

Three campers from Greensboro—Frank Lasnick, Joel LeFebvre, and Margaret Kowalski—had been staying at Briar Bottom since July 1. About

5:00 or 5:30 p.m. on July 3, they returned from "a trip into town" and discovered that the Clearwater group had moved in beside them, about sixty-five yards away. According to Lasnick, the Florida kids were "having a good time" and listening to music. After the alcohol arrived, the group invited Lasnick, Lefebvre, and Kowalski to join the fun. The three stayed for about an hour, drank some beer, and talked with Poonie Porter and several others. When someone set off a few firecrackers, Lasnick advised Porter that fireworks were illegal in North Carolina. Poonie told him that the Clearwater crowd did not need more problems with the rangers, especially after one "had actually drawn a gun on them" the day before.[17]

Porter had other reasons to be concerned. Earlier that afternoon, he had encountered a camper from Burnsville who passed along a rumor that the local sheriff planned to "bust the campground" that night. The young man warned Poonie to be careful and suggested the group go elsewhere. David Satterwhite told everyone not to worry. He had camped at Briar Bottom for three years and nothing like that had ever happened.[18]

Maybe because of his training in the military police, Poonie still could not relax. He drank some beer but continued to fret about what might occur if the group again drew attention from local authorities. Poonie moved nervously about the campsite, telling each of his friends to put away any fireworks, turn down the music, and hide their drugs, just to be on the safe side. A few complied immediately, but many were having too much fun to care. By then Kevin Shea was well into his rattlesnake hunt. A couple of others had been drinking hard and had passed out or fallen asleep in one of the lean-tos. It took a while for Poonie's message to get across. Sometime between 9:30 and 10:30 p.m., as Lasnick and his companions left the Clearwater campsite, they noted that Poonie's friends had turned off the music and appeared to be settling down for the night.[19]

Well before then, Forest Service employees at a nearby work center got complaints from other campers about the hippies and noise at Briar Bottom. One of the workers phoned Terry Shankle, the game warden who had encouraged the group to move that morning. Around 9:00 p.m., Shankle decided to talk to assistant ranger Harold Rivers (now filling in for Johnny McLain). By then Rivers had returned to his home, located only a mile or so away from the campground. Shankle stopped by and told Rivers that some of the campers he had spoken with that morning were now in Briar Bottom, drinking, setting off firecrackers, and making a lot of noise. With his boss out of town,

Rivers thought he should go to Briar Bottom and have a look. He saw beer cans on the ground and later stated that he heard "loud music, shouting, and a few loud reports that sounded like fireworks."[20]

That must have been about the time that Poonie began his efforts to tone down the revelry. Rivers walked up to within seventy-five or one hundred feet of the Clearwater campsite, where he stood unnoticed in the gathering darkness and watched for a few minutes. He did not approach the group or ask them to be quiet. Instead, he went to the work center, told the others what he had seen, and called the sheriff's office in Burnsville. Rivers told the dispatcher that "27 hippies or hippie types" were "drinking and misbehaving" and "trying to take over the campground."[21]

Kermit Banks ate supper at home that evening and had just gone out on patrol when the message came crackling over his radio. According to the sheriff's statements to reporters, he immediately deputized his brother, Robert, and contacted deputies Erwin Higgins and Bill Arrowood, along with Horace Biggs, a Burnsville policeman. Two deputies from the sheriff's office in neighboring Mitchell County, Paul Wheeler and Larry Dean Cox, were also cruising the roads that evening, monitoring radio chatter. Wheeler asked Banks if he needed help, and the Yancey sheriff told the two Mitchell County officers to meet him near Micaville, a tiny hamlet on NC 80. The seven lawmen drove six cars and brought at least five shotguns. It seemed like a lot of manpower and weaponry just to quiet an outdoor party. But the sheriff later explained that Briar Bottom was twenty miles from Burnsville; if he needed help, it would take a while to arrive. "So," he said, "I decided to take reinforcements with me."[22]

While waiting for Banks, Harold Rivers spoke to several other campers in Briar Bottom. After hearing what they had to say about the Clearwater group, he grew more agitated. He went back to the work center and called Burnsville again. "Where's the sheriff? Those hippies are still causing trouble." Someone at Banks's office told Rivers that the sheriff had just left. As planned, Banks met up with the Mitchell County deputies, and they all drove to Briar Bottom. Knowing they had to ford the river, the lawmen left their six vehicles parked along the road and climbed into two pickup trucks driven by Rivers and Olinger. After crossing the stream, Banks and his men leapt from the truck beds, shotguns at the ready. The two rangers waited by the river.[23]

By then, the three Greensboro campers had returned to their site. Margaret Kowalski went into her tent; Frank Lasnick and Joel LeFebvre decided to sit by their fire a while longer. They noticed that the three men from Orlando, Florida, staying in a nearby van, had turned off their lights and gone to bed.

No sounds came from the Clearwater site either. About 11:30 Lasnick and LeFebvre saw flashlights coming through the woods. Two sheriff's deputies walked into their campsite, demanding to know where they were from and how long they had been there.

Just then, someone began pounding on the doors of the van occupied by the Orlando men and yelling for those inside "to open up." A few moments later, Lasnick saw all three men from Orlando handcuffed and led away while an officer stayed to search the area. As Lasnick walked back toward his campfire, he heard voices at the Clearwater site, but no shouting. Then he heard the shotgun go off, followed immediately by screams and what sounded like moaning. Stan Altland was dead.[24]

———————————

Ron Olson, who had gone to bed early, around 8:30 or 9:00, was sound asleep in his pup tent when the shotgun fired. He rolled over in his sleeping bag and briefly wondered who could be setting off fireworks at that hour. Then he heard screams from the direction of the campfire, and someone hit him across his feet. "Are you with this group?" a deputy demanded. When Olson said yes, the man pointed a gun at him and told him to go sit down with the other campers. Olson asked if he could get his shoes. "You won't need them," the officer said.

Barefoot and half-asleep, Olson staggered from his tent and tried to make sense of the chaos unfolding near the firepit. Girls were screaming and in tears, "sobbing and wailing, 'They wouldn't let us help Stan.'" Sue Cello was cursing at men with guns. At first, it made no sense to Olson. Then someone told him Stan had been shot and that a ranger had taken him away in a pickup truck. For an instant Ron hoped it might all be a bad dream, but he knew better.[25]

As Olson remembers it, Banks told no one they were under arrest. Nor did he say which laws had been violated. Instead, the sheriff rounded up everyone in sight, including Paul Brayly, the Elon College student, and the three men from Orlando. At gunpoint, the sheriff marched all of them toward the cars parked across the river. Olson and several others waded the rocky stream barefoot in the dark.

Poonie Porter, who had not been handcuffed, hung back for a moment. When no one seemed to notice, he took one or two cautious steps away from the others, slipped quietly into the woods, and broke into a dead run. Two officers chased him but gave up when Porter disappeared into a rhododendron thicket. From that hiding place, Poonie heard the sheriff's vehicles drive away.[26]

Across the river, Ron Olson got into a car with Kermit Banks. The sheriff said little and "showed no signs of stress." He was "as cool as a cucumber. Just told us we were going to jail." Kevin Shea also rode with Banks. As Shea's buzz slowly receded and the evening's events came into sharper focus, the snake hunter felt jittery and paranoid. He, too, could not understand how the sheriff remained so "cold and perfectly calm." According to Olson, Banks drove to Burnsville "at high speed."[27]

Linda Mancini rode with Deputy Bill Arrowood. Unlike Banks, the deputy made conversation and seemed almost friendly. Sitting in the back seat, thoughts racing wildly as she tried to process what she had just witnessed, Linda pondered the officer's last name. Arrowood. It seemed so odd. A few minutes later, she vowed to remember it forever, because just as they left Briar Bottom, Bill Arrowood began to cry. As he drove down the dirt road away from the campground, Linda saw more tears rolling down his right cheek.[28]

An hour later, in Burnsville, Banks crowded his detainees—many of them still wet from wading the river—into one room in the Yancey County Courthouse. He did not have enough jail cells to house them all. According to the Clearwater kids, the sheriff still told no one that they were under arrest or what they had done wrong. The room was cold, with a dirty floor, and Banks provided no blankets for the shivering campers. Several requested Breathalyzer tests to prove they were not drunk. The sheriff refused. Olson and others asked to use the phone; Banks said no. Various deputies took statements from every camper, a process that went on until about 9:00 or 9:30 a.m. on July 4. The officers released Paul Brayly and the three Orlando men early that morning, but not the group from Clearwater. "We were all in shock," Linda explained, "and we figured Stan was dead, but we didn't know for sure."[29]

Meanwhile at Briar Bottom, it was weirdly quiet, serene, as if nothing had happened. Alone in the woods, Poonie Porter tried to calm down and think about what to do. He decided to search the area for drugs or anything else the sheriff might use as evidence against his friends. As he moved about the camp, he saw the large bloodstain by the big tree and felt faint. When the queasiness passed, Porter cautiously made his way to the cars and the van. He knew the group had more pot and pills but had no idea exactly how much contraband remained. He grabbed whatever drugs and paraphernalia he could find. He threw some of the stuff in the river and scattered the rest randomly in the woods.[30]

Just before 2:00 a.m., Poonie again heard vehicles on the access road and ran back to his hiding place. Kermit Banks had returned, accompanied by an agent from the North Carolina State Bureau of Investigation (SBI). Banks probably knew the SBI man well. The sheriff had worked closely with the agency on previous cases. From the woods, Porter watched as the men unpacked lights and searched the area. They crawled into tents, looked in garbage cans, shook out sleeping bags, and picked up articles off the ground. Then they went through the vehicles. The sheriff and the agent finally left an hour or so later, carrying whatever they had found.[31]

Shivering in the predawn dampness, Poonie desperately needed sleep. He could have crawled into one of the abandoned tents or sleeping bags but feared the sheriff might return. Spotting the flicker of a campfire some distance away, he walked over and found a man awake outside his tent. Poonie told the camper that he had been "up on the mountain meditating" when he heard the shot. Now his friends were gone. He was scared and cold, and he needed a place to sleep, preferably by a fire. The man told him it would be okay, and Poonie spent the rest of the night there. Not until the next day did Porter tell the man the truth, explaining that he did not want to upset him at three o'clock in the morning. Right after that, Poonie found a pay phone and began calling people in Clearwater, as well as newspapers in Charlotte and Asheville, to report what had happened.[32]

About 1:00 a.m. on July 4, Danny McIntosh and three of his friends drove into Burnsville. Normally, they were not out at that hour, but the night before they had gone up to the Northwest Utilities Dam on the Cane River and fished until midnight. "I can't remember if we caught anything," Danny says, "but it was just a chance to stay up late, the kind of thing county kids did for fun." They figured things in town would be "pretty quiet" and they were right—until they passed the sheriff's office. To their surprise, the parking lot was jammed with vehicles. No one seemed to be around, though, and only the usual lights burned in the jail. "We knew something had happened, probably something bad," Danny remembers, "but we didn't know what."[33]

Yancey County Assistant Solicitor Tom Rusher was asleep at home when his telephone rang. Given the hour, he knew the news could not be good. The caller said little, just that Rusher needed to come to Burnsville and meet the sheriff. Rusher dressed quickly and headed into town. He, too, was surprised to see all the activity at that hour. Inside the courthouse, he found more than two dozen young people still crammed into a single room. Banks and the SBI agent got back to Burnsville just before daybreak. Once Rusher heard what they had to say, he knew he would not sleep much for the next several days.[34]

The county medical examiner, Dr. W. A. Y. Sargent, also got a late-night phone call. He dutifully reported to the county hospital where he declared Stan Altland dead at 12:50 a.m. on July 4. He listed the official cause of death as "accident." In the space on the death certificate that required an explanation, he wrote "shotgun accident." Sargent took some pellets from Altland's body, as well as blood and tissue samples that he sent to North Carolina's chief medical examiner in Chapel Hill. Later that morning, Sargent spoke to the *Native Stone*, a weekly newspaper in Asheville. Along with explaining the cause of death, he felt compelled to add that Altland and his friends "all had long hair" and that "the Sheriff confiscated five or six cases of whiskey after it was over."[35]

The Clearwater kids remained confined in the courthouse, but Banks knew he could not detain the group much longer; he had nowhere to put them. His mother, who still served as the jail's cook, dutifully made breakfast for everyone. Several campers recall that she "served us runny eggs." If the new inmates stayed past noon, she would need a lot more help in the kitchen, not to mention that the courthouse had only a few sinks and toilets.[36]

Sometime before 10:00 a.m., the sheriff officially charged the remaining twenty-three detainees with disorderly conduct. They each signed a $300 personal recognizance bond and promised to appear in district court in Burnsville on September 6. The campers put up no money; their signatures authorized the sheriff to collect $300 from anyone who did not show. Practically speaking, though, Banks lacked both the resources and jurisdiction to retrieve defendants from another state. If the kids stayed out of North Carolina, he could not touch them.

Someone finally asked about Stan. Either Banks or a deputy said flatly, "He's dead. Body's at the hospital." At that point, the sheriff allowed Fred McNairy to use a phone. McNairy was not sure who to call, but Cathy Siebenthaler suggested he talk to a lawyer. He knew only one attorney, Michael Plunkett, who had invested in Alternative Vittles and helped Stan with some legal work at the store. Plunkett told McNairy and the others to cooperate with the Yancey authorities. He would notify people in Clearwater and see what might be done when they got home.[37]

North Carolina's disorderly conduct law had long been a source of controversy. As in much of the South, the state legislature created the statute to replace the old Jim Crow ordinances against vagrancy and unlawful assembly used against African Americans. The original North Carolina statute defined the offense as "a public disturbance by any person who: (1) Engages in fighting or in violent, threatening, or tumultuous behavior; or (2) Makes any offensively coarse utterance, gesture, or display or uses abusive language, in such manner as to alarm or disturb any person present or as to provoke a breach of the peace; or (3) Willfully or wantonly creates a hazardous or physically offensive condition." It was a vague, catch-all law that might be interpreted any number of ways, especially when it came to "using abusive language," alarming or disturbing "any person present" or creating "a breach of the peace." Many legal experts believed that, as originally written, the law infringed on free speech.

In 1971, about a year before the incident at Briar Bottom, the legislature amended the wording to read "*abusive language which is intended and plainly likely to provoke violent retaliation* and thereby cause a breach of the peace." Whether Sheriff Banks knew about the change is unclear. He might well have thought the old law was still in effect and that he could arrest the campers simply for milling around and cursing in public. The offense was a misdemeanor, punishable by no more than a $500 fine or six months in jail.[38]

The accused found the charge frivolous and insulting. In their view, Banks and his deputies had created the disturbance that got Stan Altland killed. The peace might have been breached earlier that evening, but it had been restored before the sheriff got there. Phil Lokey got the sense that Banks's deputies felt the same way. "That's why they did the bonds the way they did," Lokey explained. More than one deputy told him that "nothing would happen if we did not return. They just wanted to be rid of us and forget the whole thing." Ron Olson echoed those sentiments, noting that once the group signed the bonds, "They put us all in an old bus or something, took us back up to the campground, and told us we could go. Poonie came back and we tried to decide what to do."[39]

6

Somebody Has to Be Lying

Most of the Clearwater kids wanted "to get the hell out of Yancey County as fast as possible."[1] But Stan's younger brother Roger was hitchhiking across the country, planning to meet them for the concert, and they had no way to contact him. They also needed food and showers. Kim Burns, Sue Cello, and Marty Watkins still wore clothes stained with Stan's blood. After talking it over, the group resolved to drive to Charlotte, where they had motel reservations. Their campsite had been ransacked, "tossed" as the police might say, by Banks and the SBI agent. Some of the tents were still standing, but sleeping bags, blankets, and cookware lay strewn across the ground. They packed up what they could find, throwing it quickly into the cars and van. They were all short of sleep, and some nursed bruises and abrasions from the night before.[2]

Dazed and despondent, they settled in for a depressing two-and-half-hour drive and checked into a motel "almost across the street" from where the Stones would perform two nights later. No one remembers what David Satterwhite did. Apparently, he and his dog went home, though one of Satterwhite's Mebane friends thought he saw David two days later at the concert. The Clearwater group still had their tickets for the Stones, but for the moment, no one said much about that. They ate, showered, and made some more phone calls.[3]

Roger Altland arrived later that day right on schedule. He had come from Chicago, by way of Knoxville, bone tired and miffed that he had gotten a ticket for hitchhiking on an interstate. He had to pay a sixty-dollar fine in Tennessee but immediately got right back on the highway and stuck out his thumb. His last ride let him off not far from where his friends were staying. According to Roger, he and his dog had traveled more than 7,000 miles around the country. They ran into Poonie Porter in the motel parking lot. Roger did not know Poonie well but recognized him from the Bungalow parties and immediately asked, "Where's Stan?" Apparently unaware that he was speaking to the dead man's brother, Poonie came right out with it. "Stanley got killed last night," he said. "We had some trouble with the cops, and they shot him."

Stunned, Roger thought it was some kind of bad joke. Then he saw Fred McNairy and Gary Graham walking toward him. Phil Lokey was right behind them. Phil remembers that talking to Roger that evening was "the hardest thing I've ever had to do." They consoled him as best they could, and then went inside where Roger sat shell-shocked as others recounted the grim details of Stan's death. "Somehow I just didn't really comprehend it," Roger told me. "The girls were crying. Everyone was telling me how sorry they were about Stan, but it just didn't sink in."[4]

Tipped off by Poonie, reporters from the *Charlotte Observer* showed up that evening. They described the group as "jittery and excited, displaying anger and suspicion as they room-hopped at the motel rehashing the incident with each other." "I don't think anybody really realizes that Stan is dead," Linda Mancini told the reporters. "He was the one who was trying to calm everybody down . . . telling us that everything would be all right." Several Florida newspapers called, seeking details. It was another long night with little sleep.[5]

Some in the group decided to return to Clearwater the next morning, July 5. A few of them called parents and friends to arrange transportation. Sue Cello, there without her father's permission, hated the thought of calling home, but did not want to stay. Doreen Sofarelli phoned her dad, who flew up from Florida and drove them back in Doreen's Duster. Both Cello and Sofarelli remember that it was "one helluva long ride home." After all that had happened, Phil Lokey decided "there was no friggin' way" he was going to the concert. "I love the Stones, man," he told me, "but I just couldn't do it." Kevin Shea and several others felt the same way. They, along with Cello and

Sofarelli, got back to Clearwater on Wednesday, July 6, the day the Rolling Stones arrived in Charlotte.[6]

The rest of the group, including Roger Altland, stayed for the show, joined by a few other friends who had driven up from Clearwater to meet them at the motel. Roger felt that he somehow "owed it to Stanley who had worked so hard to organize the whole thing and get me a ticket. I decided to go and sit in his seat. Besides, I still could not wrap my head around what had happened."[7] Several others expressed similar sentiments, noting that after all they had been through, Stan would have wanted them to go. They eventually joined other Stones fans, long-haired and in hippie garb, who gathered around the coliseum early that afternoon.

As they lined up to enter the arena, it seemed for a moment like any other rock concert. Cops searched anyone who looked suspicious, confiscating quart bottles of Budweiser and Boone's Farm. In 1972 the Charlotte Coliseum allowed smoking indoors, and once the lights went out it could be difficult to tell the difference between a joint and a conventional cigarette. That provided more than enough cover for those who preferred pot to tobacco. Long before Stevie Wonder finished his set, "the heavy odor of marijuana floated through the air." By the time Mick Jagger (whom the *Charlotte Observer* described as "a modern symbol of rebellion to many of the young people") took the stage, "non-smokers said they were feeling the effects of pot, just by breathing."[8]

As at their previous gigs, the Stones opened with "Brown Sugar" and "Bitch," two songs from *Sticky Fingers*. When 500 ticketless fans outside the coliseum heard the familiar riffs, they began beating on windows, throwing bottles, and demanding entry. But compared to some of the other concerts, the one in Charlotte proved tame. Officers quickly dispersed the bottle-throwers, and no one got hurt. All told, police arrested thirty-one people, mostly for trespassing and drugs. (They also charged a sixteen-year-old from Charleston with larceny when he swiped a policeman's hat and ran across the coliseum floor.) By all accounts the Stones put on one of the best shows of the tour. According to Robert Greenfield, the band's fifteen-song set seemed "to fly from beginning to end, the musicians completely locked into one another . . . like a championship team in its finest, most fluid moments."[9]

For the remaining kids from Clearwater, it quickly became a concert like no other, but not because the Stones were in peak form. The group had good seats, but as events of the previous days began to sink in, fear and paranoia took over. Ron Olson thought plainclothes officers had watched them leave their motel and enter the coliseum. He believed they might be from the SBI or the Yancey County Sheriff's Department. Or maybe they were from the FBI, sent to protect them from Banks and his minions. Even as the air filled with acrid marijuana smoke, some in the group felt uneasy about getting high (a little pot and mescaline had somehow eluded both Poonie and the sheriff). Their story had been in the papers. Maybe Kermit Banks had alerted the local narcs about what happened in Briar Bottom.[10]

All around them Stones fans screamed, drank smuggled booze, smoked joints, and danced in the aisles as they relished the concert of a lifetime. "What I remember," Linda Mancini says, "is that the show was really, really good, but no one felt like dancing." Jay Barrett was "paranoid and restless the whole time." As the band worked into the slower, bluesy part of the set with "Love in Vain" and "Sweet Virginia," he wandered off into the far reaches of the arena where he tried to calm down and watch the rest of the show. Finally seeing the Stones, but knowing Stan was dead, made for "a very weird experience."[11]

When the last chords of "Street Fighting Man," the showstopper finale, echoed through the coliseum, Barrett and the others could hardly wait to get back to Florida. They left the next morning, hoping somehow to put the awful reality of the last two days behind them. The Rolling Stones departed Charlotte bound for Knoxville and nine more venues before wrapping up the tour in New York City on July 26, with a celebration of Mick Jagger's twenty-ninth birthday. Along the way, police clashed with ticketless fans, a bomb exploded under one of the band's trucks near Montreal, and Mick and Keith got arrested in Rhode Island. The shows went on. Nothing stopped the Stones.[12]

In Burnsville on the morning of July 4, Danny McIntosh and his friends asked some townspeople about all the commotion the night before. Kermit Banks had a reputation for remaining tight-lipped about anything involving his office, but in a small community like Burnsville, word got out anyway. A few residents owned the new electronic devices known as police scanners; others had citizens band radios. The equipment was expensive and by modern standards unsophisticated, but it allowed private citizens to hear and discuss police and fire calls. Before the days of satellite television and personal computers, scanners and CBs were staples of home entertainment in rural areas. Someone listening the night before had heard some news from the sheriff's office, the gist of which was: "Some hippie got shot last night up at the campground." No one seemed to know anything else.[13]

Early that morning, while the Clearwater group sat in the courthouse, Banks, Tom Rusher, and district solicitor Clyde Roberts drafted a press release. According to the statement, at about 10:30 p.m. on July 3 the sheriff and several deputies responded to "an urgent plea for help" from the United States Forest Service. A large group of young people at Briar Bottom Campground were drinking, exploding fireworks, and disturbing other campers. The sheriff and his deputies made the twenty-mile trip from Burnsville, surrounded the campsite, and immediately placed everyone there under arrest for disorderly conduct. As reported in the *St. Petersburg Times* on July 5, Banks's statement went on to say, "Several of the group actively resisted and advanced upon me, striking me and grabbing my weapon. In the ensuing scuffle, my shotgun was accidentally discharged, fatally wounding Altland."[14]

A day later, the *Yancey Record* carried a brief, 250-word article based solely on the press release. Buried on the bottom left corner of the front page, the small headline read "Vandalism, Plea for Help Result in Fatal Shooting." It told the same abbreviated story, adding that "numerous acts of vandalism [presumably perpetrated by the Clearwater campers] had been reported" and that the SBI would conduct a thorough investigation. Regarding the shooting itself, the *Record* stated that "*a shotgun*," not Banks's shotgun as reported in the *St. Petersburg Times*, discharged accidentally and killed a twenty-year-old white man.[15] Banks's strategy seemed clear: Say as little as possible, let the SBI investigate, and hope the whole mess would quickly blow over.

It did not. A bevy of reporters from Tampa, St. Petersburg, Clearwater, Orlando, Miami, Asheville, Charlotte, and Raleigh clamored for more information. A few of them descended on Burnsville, asking pointed questions: Were the campers disturbing the peace when the sheriff arrived? Why did the men bring loaded shotguns and enter the camp with the safeties off? Did they point the weapons at the campers? Who held the gun that fired the fatal shot? Did Altland bleed to death because the sheriff offered no aid? Were the group's civil rights violated during the arrest?[16]

Kermit Banks had little experience with urban reporters and did not like talking to the press anyway, but given all the publicity and speculation, he decided to grant interviews. Insisting that his office had nothing to hide, he spoke to newsmen from Florida and North Carolina on July 5. According to the *St. Petersburg Times*, the sheriff seemed "upset" during the interview, continually picking at his nails and refusing to make eye contact with reporters. Banks did not say why the lawmen brought shotguns or whether the guns had been cocked with their safeties off. He acknowledged that some of the youth were asleep when he arrived, but denied kicking, hitting, or pointing weapons at them.

Then, according to Banks, the campers turned on the officers. "I was attacked by more than one person and all my deputies were attacked. I don't believe there wasn't [*sic*] a police officer there that wasn't assaulted." At one point, the sheriff claimed, at least six of the youths tried to take his weapon and tore his clothes. When Chief Deputy Erwin Higgins rushed over to help the sheriff, the deputy's shotgun somehow discharged and killed Altland. Did Stan Altland attack him or Higgins? Banks could not be sure because "everything was so confused." The sheriff said nothing about why he and the deputies did not immediately help the dying man. Banks concluded with, "It's just unfortunate that this happened. The death could not be prevented and I'm sure any level-headed citizen understands that."[17]

When the Clearwater kids heard the sheriff's story, they were livid. To this day, they insist that "it's ridiculous. Absolutely pure bullshit." They agreed that the shotgun had discharged accidentally but insisted that Banks held the weapon. It fired when the sheriff hit David Satterwhite on the arm with the gun butt. Max Johnson avowed (and continues to avow) that he saw smoke rising from the sheriff's shotgun and watched him reload. Everyone in the group fervently denied (and still deny) attacking the lawmen. Poonie Porter swore, "As Jesus Christ is my witness, there was no young person in that camp that assaulted one of those men with weapons." Why, he asked, would unarmed kids go after officers holding loaded shotguns? "Why weren't assault charges placed against us," Phil Lokey wondered. "I've never known police to be hit by people and not charge them with assault."[18]

Sheriff Banks had a simple answer right out of the national headlines: drugs. "Quite a few drugs, pills, grass, and other narcotics were confiscated from the campers after the shooting," he told reporters. No one had been charged with possession, but the substances had been sent to a Raleigh crime lab for analysis. Asked if any of the campers had been tested for drugs or alcohol, the sheriff said no, but the medical examiner planned to run a thorough analysis of Stan Altland's blood. "We advised them over and over that they were under arrest and what the charges were," Banks said, "but they just didn't seem to understand. They wouldn't cooperate. They said they wouldn't go to jail, refused to put their hands in the air, and kept milling around. From their actions, I would definitely say they had been using drugs." Drug-crazed hippies might be capable of anything, including an unprovoked attack on seven heavily armed officers, five of whom carried sawed-off shotguns.[19]

When local reporters asked the campers about Banks's allegations, the group admitted to drinking beer and liquor, but denied using drugs. That, too, was bullshit. But Poonie had jettisoned a lot of contraband before Banks and the SBI returned to the campsite. Since no charges had been filed, the cops must not have found anything too incriminating. Besides, the sheriff's account was sheer fantasy. Marijuana slowed things down; it made you mellow, not violent or homicidal. Kevin Shea might have twirled his stick and howled at some point, but he was waiting to be searched when the gun went off. Sue Cello admitted screaming and cursing after the shotgun blast, but as another camper later said in her defense, "When they blew Stanley away, I think all of us were freaked out. I mean, I have never seen nothing like that."[20]

While Banks and the campers argued in the newspapers, the Clearwater community grappled with emotional fallout from the killing. Some of the kids had to deal with angry parents. Linda Mancini said, "[My folks] found out about it on the news. My mom and dad were losing it." Sue Cello's father, who had ordered her not to go, "temporarily disowned" her and used his influence to get her fired from her job at Kash n' Karry. Phil Lokey remembers that his father "basically thought it was all our fault." Jay Barrett found it impossible to concentrate after he got home: "I had PTSD. For days all I did was walk the streets. I couldn't focus on anything." He soon had "trouble with the law" over an allegedly stolen car.[21]

Meanwhile, those who knew Stan Altland mourned a promising life cut short. Attorney Mike Plunkett remembered him as "an emerging leader." A supervisor at a store where Stan once worked poignantly told a reporter, "A lot of people didn't think we should hire a long-haired boy, but we hired him because he was a real nice person and a real good person. His friends were a little on the hippie side, but they were never out of line." John Conyers, one of Altland's partners at Alternative Vittles, described those friends—including the group from the Bungalows—as "20 or more youths who treated each other like brothers and sisters."[22] One editorial noted that Altland "was troubled by what he saw around him—moved by the plight of the poor, outraged by his nation's role in Vietnam, fearful that the environment was being carelessly and needlessly destroyed." He was also "one of the few" who cared enough to get involved in politics and try to change the things he could not accept.[23]

Some were also quick to point out that Stan smoked marijuana and drank beer. He occasionally hosted loud parties at the house on Tioga Avenue. But those who knew him were sure that he "could not have been a leader" of events that "preceded the violence" at Briar Bottom. That made his death even sadder and more ironic.[24]

On Saturday, July 8, one week after the group left Phil Lokey's house to see the Rolling Stones, 250 people gathered at a small chapel for Stan Altland's funeral. The family agreed to an open casket, and Stan's mother wove a strand of purple flowers through her son's long hair. A wreath shaped like a peace symbol stood to one side of the coffin as an organist played the Beatles' song "Yesterday." A Lutheran minister offered a few remarks about the fragility of life and the inability to change the past. Then, with the casket still open, friends and family filed past. As one newspaper described it, "With few exceptions, the mourners appeared to be members of the local 'alternative culture.' They dressed casually—many in blue denims and jerseys or shirts." Several remained "in front of the coffin, crying and embracing each other." The family had Stan's remains cremated and, in a private ceremony, scattered his ashes along the Florida beaches he loved.[25]

Talking with others after the service, Stan's friends again insisted that "their campsite wouldn't have been raided if they weren't young with long hair and grubby clothes." If they wore crewcuts and neat outfits, "they wouldn't have had any trouble."[26] Lots of people in and around Clearwater agreed. Another employee at Alternative Vittles said Altland's death proved that "a radical is anyone who tries to use his mind in this society."[27]

In the ensuing weeks, as more details about the killing emerged, the collective grief over Stan's death hardened into deep-seated suspicion and anger. Mike Plunkett, still the attorney of record for the group, said he "received a call from a 64-year-old Yancey County man" who had heard Kermit Banks say, "I'm not going to let any long-haired hippy ruin my life." Plunkett noted that the sheriff's comment came after Stan's death and that the man who heard it "would testify in court if necessary." Editorials in the Tampa and St. Petersburg newspapers called for the Florida attorney general to get involved "to guard against a biased investigation." Reviewing the conflicting stories told by Banks and the campers, the *Clearwater Sun* put it more bluntly: "Somebody has to be lying. . . . Justice demands a full and complete report and that it be made public."[28]

Three days after Stan's funeral, Poonie Porter, Jay Barrett, and Fred McNairy appeared before the Clearwater City Commission to ask for assistance. Given the close ties between Kermit Banks, the SBI, and Yancey County solicitors, Porter believed he and his friends would need help from "the politically powerful people" in Clearwater. He told the commission that Banks held the gun that killed Altland and again swore that he "had never seen a greater example of police brutality and harassment than occurred at the Black Mountain Campground." Porter then asked the commission to pass a resolution condemning the sheriff's actions. After discussion, the commissioners adopted a measure supporting an investigation, but included no allegations against Banks or the deputies.[29]

Fred McNairy and a group called the Clearwater Neighbors met with the city's mayor and petitioned Florida governor Reuben Askew, asking him to "use the power of [his] office to assure that Floridians of every age and race can travel peaceably into other states without fear of physical abuse or harassment." Until then, the group called for a moratorium on travel to North Carolina. McNairy also collected affidavits from witnesses, including Frank Lasnick, the camper from Greensboro. The Greater St. Petersburg Chapter of the ACLU demanded a thorough inquiry and agreed to work closely with North Carolina chapters on the matter. In addition, the ACLU promised to assist the campers with their defense against the disorderly conduct charges.[30]

Results from the tests on Stan Altland's blood and tissue came back from the state medical examiner in mid-July. The samples showed "only a very faint trace of alcohol" in Altland's system, roughly "the equivalent of one or two beers at the most." In 1972, neither marijuana nor LSD could be detected by testing blood and tissue. All the state lab could say for sure was that Stan Altland was not drunk the night he died. In Yancey County, Dr. Sargent quickly filed a supplemental report changing the cause of Stan Altland's death to "homicide." This time the description read, "Apparently accidental homicide."[31]

Such supplemental reports are not unusual, but medical examiners routinely list the cause of death as "pending" or "undetermined" while awaiting an autopsy, lab results, or further investigation. Deadly shootings were rare in Yancey County, and Sargent had been called out in the wee hours of July 4 to conduct his examination. Perhaps he acted hastily or from a lack of experience, especially when he talked to the press about long hair and falsely stated that the sheriff had confiscated numerous cases of whiskey. But the shift in cause of death now reads like an attempt by Sargent to protect himself as more information emerged and the case moved forward. He would not be the last to change his story.[32]

Chapter 6

7

Local Boys and Feds

In the days immediately after Stan Altland's death, lots of questions swirled around who should investigate the incident. Banks had immediately called in the SBI, but Briar Bottom was part of Pisgah National Forest, land owned by the federal government. The FBI could easily claim jurisdiction. Besides, the campers insisted that their civil rights had been violated, clearly a federal matter. Initially, when the Charlotte FBI office asked about getting involved, the Yancey officers and the SBI falsely stated that the killing occurred on state-owned land. When challenged on that point, the SBI admitted that they misspoke but insisted that they still had jurisdiction because a Forest Service ranger had called the local sheriff. Apparently, no one questioned that rationale. The SBI produced a one-hundred-page report a mere two weeks after Altland's death.[1]

Fifty years later, I desperately wanted to see that document. Naive in the ways of state agencies, I fired off an email to the SBI office in Raleigh and politely asked for a copy of the report. The agency's response was swift and unequivocal. All SBI reports are strictly confidential. No one in North Carolina or anywhere else can see them. Not now, not ever.

Fortunately for me, that policy did not stop regional SBI director J. N. Minter from talking about the case in 1972. Two days after the inquiry wrapped up, he told Florida reporters that "all the evidence and what the witnesses say" indicated that Chief Deputy Erwin Higgins's gun had fired the fatal blast. The director went on to explain that Kermit Banks's 12-gauge had been loaded with a type of shot different from that in Higgins's weapon. Asked about those disparities, Minter said he could not elaborate, because he personally had not investigated and could not remember which weapon had been loaded with what or which kind of shot had killed Stan Altland.[2]

Solicitor Clyde Roberts received the SBI report on July 24, stating again that it would remain confidential. But in mid-August he spoke to the *St. Petersburg Times* and dropped a bombshell. In sharp contrast to what Kermit Banks had said a month earlier, Roberts dismissed the notion that drugs played a major role in the killing. "There was not that much [*sic*] drugs involved to be of consequence," he told the *Times*. "And just because it was in the camp doesn't mean that much." Asked about analysis of the substances confiscated from the site, the solicitor said that lab results were not included in the SBI report.[3]

Roberts did not know that Poonie had disposed of everything he could find the night of the raid. Exactly what the SBI recovered remains a mystery, but the solicitor's comments gave the lie to Banks's statement about drug-addled hippies attacking armed lawmen. Asked about discrepancies between Banks's account and that of the campers, Roberts replied, "The tales they tell in public are distinctly different than the tales in the report." As the *Times* dryly noted, the solicitor "did not elaborate."[4]

He did not have to. No one outside law enforcement would ever know what the SBI had found unless they revealed it, or it somehow surfaced as evidence in a trial. And Roberts quickly made it clear that he had no immediate plans to investigate or file charges against Banks, Higgins, or anyone else involved in the shooting. "It's plainly a little indeterminate when I will make a decision," he explained, adding that he needed more information from the SBI. It would be at least three months before he could convene a grand jury. When a Charlotte reporter suggested that Roberts might be dragging his feet to protect the sheriff, the solicitor's only response was to say that he had "spent hours and hours" going over the one-hundred-page SBI report.[5]

Back in Clearwater, some of the parents shared the press's skepticism about "the local boys."[6] Fred McNairy's mother Emma decided to call an attorney she knew in Washington, DC. After hearing the story, the lawyer agreed to contact the Justice Department and insist that the FBI investigate.

On July 13, the FBI dispatched agents to interview witnesses in Florida and North Carolina. Asked why the bureau had waited so long to get involved, a spokesman told reporters, "Let's just say that publicity helped bring it to our attention."[7]

Still living in Raleigh, I had been following the case as best I could. When I learned of the FBI investigation, I felt a little better. So did the kids from Clearwater. Like a lot of Americans at the time, we thought of the FBI as an agency dedicated to solving crimes. In fact, it had long since evolved into something far different. For decades, the bureau's main mission had been gathering information about potential spies and terrorists, foreign and domestic. Nixon had frequently exhorted the bureau to pay particular attention to the "thousands of Americans under thirty" who were plotting "to destroy our society."[8] That might not bode well for FBI objectivity on the Altland case, but at least the bureau had no obvious ties to Kermit Banks, his family, the SBI, or the Yancey solicitors.

As a federal agency, the FBI is also subject to the Freedom of Information Act (FOIA), meaning that any citizen has a right to see their findings after the documents have been vetted to remove sensitive information. Or so I thought. The moment I learned that the FBI had investigated Altland's death, I filed an online FOIA request for their report. Three weeks later, I received a form letter from FBI headquarters, explaining that because I was neither a subject of the investigation, nor a relative of Stanley Altland, the bureau could neither confirm nor deny that they had such a document. Stan's brothers, Roger and David, who were by any definition relatives, made a request and got essentially the same letter. Thoroughly frustrated, with my latent suspicions of the FBI awakened, I filed an appeal that included a white-hot narrative about the bureau's obstinance, my right as a citizen and professional historian to see the file, and the blatant unfairness of it all.

It took eighteen months, with several more back-and-forth exchanges, before I finally learned that the FBI report had been moved into storage with the National Archives and Records Administration (NARA) in Maryland. If I wanted to see the entire 400-page file, I would have to wait another *three years and three months* until the archivists vetted and processed it. It took a call to my congresswoman's office and some diligent work by her staff before NARA offered to let me see part of the report, specifically ten of the bureau's interviews with those involved. The archives agreed to process that request within sixty days. In exchange I had to rescind my application to see the entire file.

As much as I wanted to see all 400 pages, I had a book deadline looming and could not wait thirty-nine months for whatever NARA might deign to release. I swallowed my frustration, thought carefully about what might be most useful, and requested FBI interviews with three of the lawmen (Kermit Banks, Erwin Higgins, and Horace Biggs), five of the campers (Linda Mancini, Sue Cello, Max Johnson, Ron Olson, and David Satterwhite), and two of the three witnesses from Greensboro (Frank Lasnick and Margaret Kowalski).

The other officers were on record elsewhere, either in court documents or direct trial testimony. I could check what the Clearwater witnesses told me versus what they said to the FBI immediately after the incident, and the two Greensboro campers could provide something approaching objective accounts. I also wanted to see if Satterwhite's interview matched what he had told the press about the incident. The day the pdf files from NARA landed in my inbox—roughly two years after my initial FOIA request—I sat down to read. A lot of it sounded familiar, especially the conflicting accounts between lawmen and campers about what happened that night. But the more I read, the more I realized that the interview transcripts contained crucial new details.

Questioned at his home on July 13, David Satterwhite told agents that during the afternoon of July 3, he "heard from someone from the Clearwater group that the rangers and police were going to raid the camp site that night." Having camped there before without incident, he figured they had nothing to worry about. Satterwhite also described the man holding the lethal shotgun as six feet tall, with a "slender build," wearing "a pair of dark pants, possibly brown, a pale yellow or white shirt, with a brown tie with yellow checks." The youth was certain he "did not see a uniform or a badge on this man."[9]

To my surprise, Satterwhite did not immediately identify the man as Kermit Banks. Instead, in a careful, measured statement, he noted that he encountered him later at the Burnsville courthouse and would recognize him if he saw him again. The young man also told the FBI that he had a bruise and burn on his arm after being struck with the shotgun. The agents inspected his arm but at that point, ten days after the shooting, saw nothing.[10]

A day later, special agents Austin A. Andersen and John M. Quigley interviewed Banks in Burnsville. When the FBI men asked Banks why he took so many cars to Briar Bottom that night—six by my count—the sheriff said that Harold Rivers had requested that "several vehicles be sent, as a single vehicle would not be sufficient to handle this number of campers."[11] Banks did not say what he meant by "handle," and the FBI did not ask.

The FBI did want to know why Banks brought loaded shotguns to the campsite. The sheriff alluded to an incident two weeks earlier in Durham, where "several young motorcyclists" (in fact, a motorcycle club/gang called the Outlaws) had been involved in a shootout with North Carolina officers and "several individuals were killed." The sheriff told the FBI that "because he did not know what to expect" from young people "camping in an extremely remote rural area, he decided the shotguns were necessary."[12]

Even on paper, fifty years after the fact, the sheriff's antipathy for the campers is palpable. He remembered a girl (probably Sue Cello) saying "Fuck you, you bastards!" Banks said it happened immediately upon his arrival, not after the shooting. Satterwhite, the sheriff noted, "kept telling everyone else not to cooperate and that the group did not have to leave the campground." Banks also said that Satterwhite whispered to the other campers and then pointed at the sheriff, as if organizing an attack. According to Banks, the Mebane youth yelled, "You god-damned son of a bitch, I'm going to kick your ass."[13]

The sheriff was "not sure, but he may have hit Satterwhite on the elbow with the barrel" of his shotgun, but the weapon did not fire. At that point, at least six other campers came at him "scuffling with him, tearing his shirt and scratching the left side of his neck." When Erwin Higgins came to help, the sheriff said he could not see what the chief deputy was doing, but "heard Higgins's shotgun discharge approximately six feet to his right." Altland fell and "all resistance ceased." The sheriff added that when he grabbed two blankets "in order to carry and wrap [Altland's] body," one of the Clearwater campers said, "Don't use my blanket on that bloody son-of-a-bitch." Asked about whether those detained had been allowed to make phone calls, Banks told the agents that he allowed the group to make calls, even without reversing charges, but "Satterwhite monopolized the telephone during much of the evening," making it difficult for the others to call anyone.[14]

The sheriff seemed especially concerned with refuting stories published in the Asheville papers accusing him of "slashing" at Satterwhite by bringing the butt of the shotgun down across the Mebane youth's upper arm. Poonie Porter had described it that way to the *Asheville Citizen* and the *Native Stone*. (National Guard training manuals list this action, called a "butt-stroke," as an effective means of riot control.) According to Porter, who was familiar with the maneuver from his military training, the slashing motion had caused the gun to fire. Banks assured the FBI that he had never "chopped anyone with

Blaine Ray (*left*), Sheriff Kermit Banks (*center*), and FBI agents re-creating the scene of the shooting, July 1972.
FBI photo, courtesy of the National Archives and Records Administration, College Park, MD.

his rifle [*sic*] and that he did not witness any other officer strike or mistreat any camper." He also said that his weapon, a 12-gauge pump shotgun with a sawed-off single barrel, had been loaded with double-aught buckshot, while Higgins carried a double-barrel shotgun with "number 5 shells, or duck shot." Banks then drew a diagram of the campsite at the time of the shooting. It showed at least three people standing between the sheriff and Higgins.[15]

After his formal interview, Banks and Agent Andersen, along with another FBI man named John Willis, drove to Briar Bottom, where they met Blaine Ray. Banks, Willis, and Ray took up positions to illustrate where the sheriff, Higgins, and Stan Altland stood on the night of the shooting. Andersen snapped several thirty-five-millimeter photographs of the scene. Andersen noted that Banks, representing himself, was the man in the photo "wearing a light sport coat." I stared at those color images a long time before I noticed that, beneath that sport coat, the sheriff appeared to be dressed almost exactly as David Satterwhite had described him on the night of the shooting—in brown pants, a light-colored shirt, and a dark tie. Asked to sign the report that summarized his remarks to the FBI, Banks refused. He did not want to commit to any statement because he feared that "he may be charged with a wrongful death action or other civil suit to collect monetary damages."[16]

Chief Deputy Erwin Higgins backed up Banks's account, explaining that the dispatcher told the deputies that they would encounter "27 individuals who were drunk, using fireworks, and who had damaged a sign at the campground." Then, almost casually, the deputy added that he got the call to go to Briar Bottom "about 10:30 or 10:45 p.m., *while on duty and in uniform* [emphasis mine] as a deputy for the Yancey County Sheriff's Office." He made no mention of changing clothes before he left or while enroute.[17]

At the campsite, he "moved in to assist Kermit" in fending off an attack by "a tall individual." Holding his weapon "pointing straight up," in his right hand, the chief deputy placed his left hand on the tall individual's shoulder and "attempted to pull him away." At that moment his gun discharged and killed Stanley Altland. Higgins said he had "not released the safety before moving to assist the sheriff" and could not explain how the weapon fired. He also drew a crude diagram of the campsite that showed Banks standing between Higgins and the sheriff's attacker. Concerned that Higgins, who had not graduated from high school, might not understand everything in a written statement, the FBI agent went over it "sentence by sentence" with the deputy, who, unlike Banks, had no problem signing the document.[18]

Horace Biggs, the Burnsville policeman, told the FBI that he "heard loud noise and a radio playing" when he got to Briar Bottom. From the first, the Burnsville policeman said, "members of the group indiscriminately began cursing the officers," calling them, among other things, "you sons of bitches." He and another deputy encountered Kevin Shea in the woods with his snake stick. As the officers confronted Shea, he repeatedly reached for his pocket, so Biggs "tapped him" on the right side of his head with the barrel of a shotgun. The other deputy then "shoved Shea lightly" before he and Biggs placed him under arrest. The officers searched him but found only a flashlight and a small knife in his pocket.[19] The two deputies then went to arrest the three men from Orlando. Like Banks, Biggs refused to sign his statement.

I approached the FBI interviews with the four Clearwater kids with some trepidation, wondering if those accounts would square with what the campers told me fifty years later. Sue Cello told the FBI she had three beers that night. Ron Olson noted that he had only two and went to bed before nine.

Linda Mancini told the agents that she had nothing to drink. They did not admit to using drugs.[20] Max Johnson carefully stated that he "did not see anyone using any type of drugs." Cello said that, "to the best of her knowledge," no one had used "drugs or narcotics of any nature." They told the agents that the music had been turned off and that many people had gone to bed before the officers arrived, though they disagreed about exactly what time the tape player went silent. Around 8:45 p.m., Cello said, someone set off two firecrackers and some in the group played with sparklers.[21]

Linda Mancini saw Banks stick the shotgun in David Satterwhite's stomach and, a short time later, heard the weapon go off. Max Johnson was standing by the fire and turned around to see an officer, later identified as Sheriff Banks, "holding a gun that was still smoking." Max noted that someone asked about constitutional rights "and they said, 'Animals do not have rights.'"[22] They all recounted wading the river, and riding to Burnsville where, as Cello said, they were "put in one big room with one bathroom where we sat for 5½ hours, wet, hungry, and cold, before given our rights and then sat for another 4½ hours before our warrants were issued to us." All of them signed their statements.[23] Except for the comments about drugs, their accounts were identical to what they related to me fifty years after the fact.

I knew little about Frank Lasnick and Margaret Kowalski before I read their interviews, just that they were from Greensboro and had socialized briefly with the Clearwater group. Kowalski, a junior at UNC Greensboro, told the FBI that the Florida kids were "playing rock music, eating, talking, and drinking beer" that afternoon. But she said that "in general, the group was orderly and was not causing any disturbance and at no time interfered with their camp site or bothered them." In fact, "a group that had camped in that site the previous night consisting of a large family were much louder and rowdy." That group "kept the music going until late in the night and did disturb their sleep."[24]

She, LeFebvre, and Lasnick left the Clearwater site "between 9 and 9:30" and went to sit by the river, "talking and striking stones causing sparks." At that point, Kowalski explained, "it was so quiet" in the campground "that the sound of the rocks striking echoed throughout the area."[25] After returning to their campsite, she went into her tent. She said that "it was at least an hour and 15 minutes" before she heard "some voices talking to Joel and Frank." Then she heard "a large amount of banging" on the side of the van belonging to the three Orlando men. A short time later, the gun went off and she "heard people crying and moaning and wailing."[26]

The next morning, when the Clearwater group returned to their site, Kowalski walked over to speak with them. One girl showed her a badly bruised leg and said "she had been kicked by a deputy sheriff while she was in her sleeping bag." Kowalski also saw male campers with "abrasions about the face and bruises on their arms." David Satterwhite showed her his left arm "and above his elbow was a large welt and black and blue marks."[27]

Frank Lasnick was thirty-two and worked full-time for a Greensboro printer. He corroborated much of what Kowalski said, adding that during the afternoon, some in the Clearwater group were riding motorcycles in the "meadow section" of the campsite and "most were observed to be drinking beer." The music was loud, but not disturbing; in fact, "they enjoyed listening to it." Lasnick also referenced the "large family" that had occupied the space the night before. They had "played music late into the night and were singing and yelling country folk songs."[28] Lasnick said he, Kowalski, and Lefebvre left the Clearwater site sometime between 10:00 and 10:30. By then, the Florida kids "had stopped playing their tapes and radios and settled down for the night." After going down to the river where "everything was absolutely quiet," he and his companions returned to their site.[29]

About an hour after they got back, Lasnick and LeFebvre were sitting around their fire, when they "saw flashlights coming through the woods." Three men walked up and said they were from the sheriff's department. Lasnick asked for identification, but the men refused to provide it. They asked Lasnick his name, where he was from, and how long he had been there. He "told them that he would not identify himself as he did not know who they were and what their authority was." The men instructed Lasnick and his friends to stay put "for their own protection."[30]

A few moments later, Lasnick heard someone "beating on the van" occupied by the three Orlando men and telling them to "open up." Lasnick told the officers that the group in the van were not with the people from Clearwater and "had been absolutely quiet and had apparently gone to bed as all their lights were off." One of the lawmen said that the van "had Florida license plates and had been observed down by the dam [fish barrier] earlier" that day with the Clearwater group.[31]

Shortly after that, Lasnick heard the shotgun blast, followed by "continuous moaning and what sounded like wailing coming from the Clearwater campsite." The next morning, Satterwhite showed Lasnick a bruise inflicted by the shotgun just before it fired. Several others "had bruises on the face and one girl in particular had an extremely bad bruise on her leg." Later that day, Lasnick met the "older ranger" (probably Jack Olinger) and "asked him what had happened the night before that caused all this difficulty." The ranger told him that the people from Clearwater "had all been arrested because they were drinking beer in a dry county." When Lasnick said that he "could not believe that a young man was killed" for that, "the ranger walked away and had no further conversation with him." Neither Lasnick nor Kowalski signed a statement.[32] Lasnick noted that he had already signed a statement for an attorney in Florida (probably Mike Plunkett). Kowalski did not give a reason for withholding her signature.

Lying to the FBI is a federal crime, punishable by five years in prison, but that is no deterrent to witnesses who face worse consequences if they tell the truth. Two of the Clearwater kids had claimed that they had no knowledge of drugs at the campsite, something I knew to be false, even if I understood why they might not admit that to FBI agents. Otherwise, I found their statements consistent and credible. They had all been eager to tell their stories—to the newspapers, the FBI, and me.

Neither Banks nor anyone else in law enforcement spoke with me about that night, so I could not make a similar comparison with their interviews. But I found reason to question some of what the lawmen told the FBI. Banks said he feared violence akin to what one might encounter from a motorcycle gang. That lent credence to the notion that the raid had been contemplated in advance of Harold Rivers's allegedly urgent phone calls, something also supported by Satterwhite's statement about hearing rumors of an impending bust. Banks brought plenty of cars and shotguns, an indication that he went to the site fully intending to remove the Clearwater group from Briar Bottom, or as he put it, to "handle" them. That suggested that he did not go only to investigate a noise complaint.

Horace Biggs claimed to have heard loud music and shouting, but every other witness who acknowledged hearing noise earlier that evening told the agents that things had been quiet when the sheriff arrived. According to Kowalski and Lasnick, another group had been drinking and playing loud music the night before. Evidently that had not bothered the rangers or anyone else. The officers refused to show Frank Lasnick any identification, corroborating what the Clearwater kids had said about Banks and the other deputies.

Biggs's statement that he "tapped" Shea with a shotgun and that another deputy had "lightly" shoved him sounded like a partial admission of roughing up the campers, as did Banks's note that he "might" have hit Satterwhite on the arm with a shotgun. By the time the FBI talked with Satterwhite, he had no visible injuries, but the sheriff could not know that. Telling agents that he accidentally struck Satterwhite with the shotgun but denying that he "chopped" him with the weapon could explain away any marks the FBI might find on the Mebane youth's arm.

The tone of the sheriff's interview and his memories of the dialogue that night also seem suspect. Amid all the confusion and conflict, did Satterwhite have time to organize an attack, whisper the plan to other campers, and then yell, "You goddamned son of a bitch, I'm going to kick your ass," before going after the sheriff? And, given what I knew about the group from Clearwater and their high regard for Stan Altland, I could not imagine any of them refusing their mortally wounded friend a blanket or referring to him as "that bloody son-of-a-bitch."

The diagrams drawn by Banks and Higgins both showed one or more persons between the chief deputy and David Satterwhite. Banks depicted himself standing between the two men. I wondered how the deputy could reach across the sheriff or several other individuals to grab Satterwhite by the shoulder. Most important, Erwin Higgins told the FBI that he had been in uniform that night. Satterwhite swore that the man who hit him with the shotgun before it fired wore civilian clothes. The young man's description of those garments resembled an outfit Kermit Banks wore in photographs taken by the FBI ten days later.

Any shotgun can go off accidentally, and a 12-gauge loaded with duck shot can easily kill someone eighteen feet away. But I did not understand how a weapon "pointing straight up" could do it. It seems more likely that a shotgun held parallel to the ground, maybe one that had just struck someone on the arm, fired the fatal shot. Eyewitness accounts of Altland getting hit and flying backward as well as Poonie Porter's description of the extensive wounds to Stan's chest and neck are more consistent with a load of double-aught buck than with duck shot.

The FBI investigation went on for another six months. Concerned that the agency might not be objective, Stan Altland's mother wrote to Lawton Chiles, a US senator from Florida, asking him to make sure the bureau did its job.

Chiles responded quickly, saying that he had spoken directly with FBI director L. Patrick Gray and John McGuire, chief of the US Forest Service, about the incident. Would the FBI or the Department of Justice press charges if warranted? Not until Clyde Roberts decided what to do, the bureau said. "We normally defer to local authorities if they are handling an investigation."[33] In other words, despite Chiles's best efforts, it might not matter that the FBI had turned up evidence to refute statements by Banks and his deputies. "The local boys" could still delay any action against the Yancey lawmen for weeks, months, or years—maybe forever.

The Clearwater campers and David Satterwhite did not have that luxury. They were due in Burnsville on September 6 to answer charges of disorderly conduct. Most of them were eager to go back. They hoped the court proceedings would not only exonerate them, but also pin the killing on Kermit Banks and provide a measure of justice for Stan Altland. For that, they needed good lawyers.

Emma McNairy again took the lead. Senator Chiles put her in touch with more attorneys in Washington, who suggested she contact Levonne Chambers, an African American civil rights lawyer practicing in Charlotte. The ACLU also agreed to speak with him. After hearing details of Stan's death and the raid at Briar Bottom, two attorneys from the Charlotte firm agreed to take the case. Neither Emma McNairy nor the Clearwater kids knew it, but they had just hired Julius Chambers and Adam Stein, two of the most celebrated civil rights lawyers in North Carolina.[34]

8

All Hippies Look Alike

Levonne Chambers, who later changed his name to Julius, grew up during the Great Depression in Mount Gilead, a tiny Piedmont town in Montgomery County, North Carolina. There, as in similar small communities across rural North Carolina, white sheriffs and small-town cops, aided by an active Ku Klux Klan, enforced a rigidly segregated social system. In the 1930s, Black people did not vote or participate in local politics. The Black high school graduated barely a third of its students; only a tiny fraction of those went to college.[1]

Julius Chambers defied the odds. After finishing high school and graduating from North Carolina College (now North Carolina Central University), he completed a master's degree in history at the University of Michigan and entered law school at the University of North Carolina. At UNC, he became editor-in-chief of the *North Carolina Law Review*, the first African American to hold that prestigious post. Upon graduation, when white law firms refused to employ or even interview him, Chambers worked as an intern with the NAACP's Legal Defense Fund (LDF). He continued to represent the organization after he opened his own practice in Charlotte and began a lifelong fight to make life better for Black North Carolinians.[2]

It was dangerous work. In 1965, as Chambers spoke on behalf of the LDF in New Bern, the Klan blew up his car in a church parking lot. Later that year, Chambers set out to integrate the Shrine Bowl, an all-white high school football game that showcased talented players from the Carolinas. He succeeded, but not before persons unknown hurled a bomb made from five sticks of dynamite at his Charlotte home. He and his wife escaped unscathed.[3]

In 1967 Chambers took on two new partners: an African American attorney named James Ferguson and Adam Stein, a white lawyer with a keen interest in civil rights litigation. When they signed on, Chambers, Stein, and Ferguson became Charlotte's first biracial law firm and the *only* one in the state where white attorneys worked under supervision of a Black man.[4] By then, the firm had begun litigating one of the biggest civil rights cases in North Carolina history, *Swann v. Charlotte-Mecklenburg Board of Education.*

It took six long years and an eloquent argument by Chambers before the United States Supreme Court, but in 1971 the Swann case established mandatory busing of white students to predominantly Black schools as a legal and viable remedy for segregation. The same lawyer who would defend the Clearwater campers also won the landmark case that created so much consternation about school integration and busing in their home state. Chambers's victory proved equally unpopular in North Carolina. In the dark of an icy February morning in 1972, a still-unidentified arsonist sloshed gasoline on the steps of the Chambers law office and struck a match. With help from firefighters, the lawyers and staff salvaged what records they could, but the building was a total loss.[5]

I heard those stories and more when I met Adam Stein on a late summer afternoon in Carrboro, North Carolina. As we sipped beer at a table outside Weaver Street Market, I asked how he and Chambers ever got involved with two dozen white hippies from Clearwater. Stein mentioned the ACLU, but also noted that, by the early seventies, the Chambers firm had a reputation for defending anyone, Black or white, who had been harassed or abused by law enforcement. "There was violence everywhere," he explained. "Cops were beatin' the hell out of people. Somebody firebombed our offices. If you were up against authority in North Carolina, we were the people to call. We took cases other lawyers would not touch." As Richard Rosen, one of Chambers's biographers and a former law clerk in his firm, later told me, "That's what Julius had in common with those campers. As a Black man, he knew what it was like to seek justice in a system stacked against you. When Julius and

Adam took a case—any case—they were all business. They didn't care what anyone thought, or really, how much they got paid."[6]

According to Phil Lokey, the Clearwater campers had never heard of Chambers and Stein. "We just knew they were supposed to be good lawyers."[7] That quickly proved an understatement. Chambers, Stein, and Robert Young (now the campers' Clearwater attorney) immediately got the Burnsville proceedings postponed until October 30. Then Chambers, appearing with seven of his clients, managed to get the trial rescheduled again, this time for the end of November.[8] The attorneys needed that extra time to prepare. They had been hired to defend the campers against the disorderly conduct charges, but their clients wanted more. Stan Altland was dead, and not one of the officers had been placed on leave or had their motives publicly questioned, even as state and federal agencies investigated the matter.

Unlike police, who are hired by municipalities and must abide by the city's employee regulations, county sheriffs are elected public officials who serve at the pleasure of the voters. Even now, in the age of cell phones and body cameras, when questionable officer-involved shootings make national news, the choice of whether to investigate a North Carolina sheriff rests mostly with local people. Recent legislation allows the governor or a district attorney to call in the SBI "to investigate and prepare evidence," but does not require that a sheriff be removed from duty during the investigation.[9] Likewise, the North Carolina Sheriff's Association currently has guidelines for investigating officer-involved shootings, but plainly states, "There is no legal mandate that an officer must be placed on leave following a use of force incident."[10]

Solicitor Clyde Roberts and his assistant, Tom Rusher, took full advantage of the protections afforded North Carolina sheriffs in 1972. Both prosecutors read the full SBI report and received additional information from the FBI but saw no reason to convene a grand jury to hear evidence against Banks or anyone else. At the October 30 hearing, Chambers requested that the state provide the defense with the full SBI report and the names of any witnesses whose accounts might aid the defendants. He and Stein eventually got some names, including those of the Greensboro campers, but the two defense attorneys never saw the SBI report or anything that the FBI had uncovered.[11]

Chambers and Stein also faced other obstacles, mostly owing to the incestuous nature of Yancey County justice. In his position as sheriff, Banks also served as the court bailiff, meaning that he would be present throughout the trial and could hear all the witnesses, even though he (or his brother and other deputies) might later be called to testify. Worse, William Atkins, an attorney who would assist Rusher with the prosecution, had also agreed to represent Banks pro bono should he be charged with anything in connection with Altland's death. That was business as usual. North Carolina allowed solicitors, especially those in rural areas, to take on other clients to supplement their income. Apparently, no one in Yancey County cared about the potential conflict of interest. As a deputy told Frank Lasnick on the night of July 3, "Justice is funny up here. All the sheriffs and deputies are all brothers and cousins, and the judge is the daddy of them all."[12]

Fortunately for the defense, an out-of-town judge, Robert T. Gash from Brevard, North Carolina, got the assignment. Because the case would be heard in district court, the judge—not a jury—would decide the campers' fate. Robert Young, the Clearwater attorney, preferred it that way, because, as he put it, "I'm not sure we could get an impartial jury up there."[13] As far as anyone could tell, Gash had no family ties to Kermit Banks or the prosecution. The campers would also be tried as a group, something else the defense thought might work to their advantage.[14]

Neither side had much physical evidence. DNA testing, of the sort that might have shed light on who held the gun or whether the defendants had attacked the deputies, would not be available for another forty-five years. Unless one has access to the spent shells or pellets, ballistic evidence can also be hard to come by in a shotgun killing. Apparently, the ammo that killed Stan Altland had been turned over to the SBI, but no one seemed to know for sure. On the night of the shooting, a simple paraffin-based test for gunshot residue might have determined who fired the gun, and the SBI had access to that technology. Why the agency did not administer the test to Banks or Higgins remains an open question. At the October hearing, assistant solicitor Tom Rusher mentioned a torn shirt, allegedly worn by Sheriff Banks on July 3, that might be introduced into evidence.[15]

From the first, Chambers and Stein saw the Burnsville trial as a prelude to the federal civil rights lawsuit that Emma McNairy and others had requested. If the Yancey prosecutors failed to convict the Clearwater group of disorderly conduct, that would provide solid evidence that Kermit Banks and his men had acted maliciously and without provocation on July 3. A blanket acquittal could go a long way toward establishing law enforcement's liability in a civil suit.[16] Jay Barrett put it more starkly: "We want to find out why Stan was killed that night for no reason. We want to let the people who have that kind of power know they can't shoot people without answering for it."[17]

Tom Rusher was new to the solicitor's office, and this was his first high-profile case. Aware that a federal lawsuit would likely follow, he did not intend to be cowed by Chambers's reputation as a litigator. Kermit Banks also seemed ready for a fight. The Florida newspapers had not treated him kindly, constantly questioning his account of the killing and deriding him as a "small-town sheriff." As the trial got closer, Rusher noted that he intended to call as many as twenty witnesses, including Banks.[18] Unfazed, Chambers and Stein calmly responded that they planned "to demonstrate that the parties are not guilty of any offense that night."[19]

On Saturday, November 25, some five months after the caravan left Phil Lokey's house to see the Rolling Stones, a group of young people again departed Clearwater bound for Yancey County. They had held a couple of carwashes and raised about sixty dollars; the rest of the travel expenses came out of their pockets. Not everyone went back. One camper had more serious legal problems, stemming from a conviction for selling marijuana. Marty Watkins and another woman elected not to return, knowing that Kermit Banks could not arrest them if they stayed out of North Carolina. One defendant came down with the flu a week before the trial. That left nineteen kids from Clearwater, including the Bungalows residents and their close friends. Thanks to his midnight escape, Poonie Porter had never been charged. David Satterwhite, also defended by Chambers and Stein, drove to Burnsville from Mebane, accompanied by his father.

This time the Clearwater contingent did not travel together. Phil Lokey and Gary Graham left early, hoping to reach Atlanta in time to watch a college football game on television. Fred McNairy drove up with Cathy Siebenthaler; Sue Cello and Doreen Sofarelli rode together. Linda Mancini and Kim Burns flew to Asheville (Linda's first time on a plane). Jay Barrett rode with attorney Robert Young and Allen Cowan, the reporter from the St. Petersburg Times, who had covered the story from the beginning. Fred McNairy's parents, Roger and David Altland, and several other supporters and family members also made the trip. A few of them met for dinner in Atlanta, but as Cowan wrote, "It was almost as though the shot that killed Altland had splintered the once-close group."[20]

Chambers picked up Stein in Chapel Hill and drove to Asheville. It was windy and spitting snow on Sunday when the attorneys and their clients checked into a Ramada Inn. The lawyers immediately went to work. "Julius Chambers was great," Phil Lokey remembers. "He had each of us write down what happened. He was amazed at how consistent our stories were." Chambers, Stein, and Young then went to Chambers's room and worked

The Clearwater campers, with family and supporters, filing into
the Yancey County Courthouse for their disorderly conduct trial.
Courtesy of Roger Altland.

until about 2:00 a.m. Monday morning. They left the motel in plenty of time
to get to Burnsville by 9:00 a.m., but as Stein remembers, "Julius got lost
somewhere on those mountain roads and we were running late."[21] After a
preliminary conference with the judge, court convened at 10:15 instead of the
scheduled time of 9:30.

Dressed in "jeans, bellbottoms, minis, and maxis," the Clearwater friends
paused to take photographs outside the courthouse. As they filed in, some
local people (who evidently had their own problems with Kermit Banks)
shouted encouragement. Others just stared. The courtroom furnishings
were spare, consisting of a US flag and a North Carolina state flag, a nonde-
script clock like the ones in public school classrooms, and a paper calendar
directly behind the judge's chair that advertised a Burnsville funeral home.
In his capacity as bailiff, Kermit Banks took a seat at the prosecution table
alongside his personal attorney, prosecutor William Atkins.[22] The sheriff
wore "a brown pinstriped suit" and carried "a large blackjack in his right rear
pocket." Chambers, Stein, and Young were at the defense table, with their
twenty clients seated behind them, along with fifty other curious spectators.
Judge Gash called the proceedings to order, and the legal wrangling began.

Knowing that the prosecution witnesses had spent only a few hours with the campers in July and could not identify most of them by name, Tom Rusher asked that each defendant come forward and stand with their lawyers so that the state could be sure they were in court. Chambers objected, emphatically stating that it was up to the prosecutors to identify those charged with disorderly conduct, and that his clients had no intention of doing that for them. Trying to keep things from quickly going off the rails, Judge Gash had the names read from the court calendar. Adam Stein responded for each defendant present.

That still did not satisfy Rusher, who argued that the prosecution needed to hear from the defendants themselves, in effect suggesting that Stein could not be trusted. Chambers called that "an insult to the defense" and moved that all the state's witnesses be immediately sequestered so as not to taint future testimony. Judge Gash calmly denied that motion and allowed another roll call. Each defendant answered when they heard their name but did not come forward or stand beside their lawyers. Perhaps hoping to turn down the temperature a bit, Gash called a short recess. When court reconvened, the defendants had all "switched their seats." Some "had adjusted their clothing to appear different," and Sue Cello wore different glasses.[23]

The first prosecution witness, assistant ranger Harold Rivers, recounted what he had observed when he walked up to the campsite on the night of July 3. William Burt, a man from Charlotte staying at the adjacent Black Mountain Campground, testified that he heard a lot of noise on Sunday night when the Clearwater group camped near the fish barrier, and again on July 3, but on cross-examination admitted that he did not know who made "the racket."[24]

Blaine Ray and Terry Shankle attested to their encounter with the Clearwater campers at the fish barrier and destruction of the No Camping sign. Chambers objected to all that testimony as irrelevant to events at Briar Bottom. Judge Gash let it stand. During cross examination, Ray could not identify any of the defendants as being present that day, nor could he say for certain that the post smoldering in the firepit came from the damaged sign. Neither could Shankle.[25]

Ronny Hoyle, a nearby camper who had complained to the rangers about noise, testified that the hippies "had more or less taken over the campground." He saw "a long-haired boy" riding a motorcycle but could not identify him. He thought he recognized another defendant whom he had seen drinking beer but could not be sure. Hoyle then testified that one of the Clearwater kids came into his campsite about 2:00 a.m. and asked to sleep by the campfire. That had to be Poonie Porter, who was not among the accused. Asked if he saw the person who came into his camp in court, Hoyle confidently and erroneously pointed at another camper named Jimmie Seifert who had been in custody in Burnsville at 2:00 a.m. on July 4.[26]

The leader of a Boy Scout troop driving in Briar Bottom said that he saw young people playing football. Questioned by Rusher and Atkins, the witness said he could not tell if they were men or women because "they were all long haired, had on denim and stuff like that." He claimed to have seen a girl emerge bare-breasted from a tent but could not identify her or anyone else as being present in the courtroom. Apparently, once they switched seats, all the hippies looked alike.[27]

Kermit Banks took the stand right after lunch, stating again that David Satterwhite incited the drunken campers, cursed him, and threatened to kick his ass. The group then attacked him and tried to take his shotgun, ripping his shirt in the process. For the first time, Banks noted that officers took a large hunting knife from Satterwhite. The sheriff added that he smelled burning marijuana "in the air" when he and his men arrived at the campsite. Chambers objected, pointing out that no one had been charged with smoking marijuana and no drugs were in evidence. Gash agreed but did not strike the sheriff's testimony.[28]

When Rusher asked if the sheriff remembered who he arrested that night, Banks replied yes, but said nothing more until the solicitor handed him a list of names to read aloud. That again brought Chambers out of his seat to object. When Gash allowed Chambers to inquire about the list, Banks said he had made it the night of July 3 and referred to it only to refresh his memory. Chambers glanced quickly at the papers and then asked, "Where is the description of the incident involving Stan Altland?" Rusher shouted an objection. Gash sustained it, saying, "I don't believe we need to get into that now, sir."[29]

Things got tense as Chambers began his cross-examination. Convinced that Banks had gone to Briar Bottom intent on removing the campers at gunpoint, Chambers methodically poked holes in the sheriff's sworn testimony. He inquired about Banks's brother, Robert, and how often he worked as a deputy. "Just when I need him," the sheriff replied. Chambers then wanted to know how all those officers, including a Burnsville policeman, just happened to be near the courthouse when the sheriff got the call from Rivers. Banks responded, "I don't know."[30]

Asked how he had determined that the "eight or ten campers around the fire" were drunk, Banks replied that he "gave them the walking test." Pressed to elaborate, the sheriff explained that the "test" consisted of "observing them walking." Did he know how to issue a Breathalyzer or conduct a roadside drunk-driving test? "Yes." Did he do so on the night in question? "No."[31]

On redirect, Rusher and Atkins had Banks identify the shirt supposedly torn during an attack on the sheriff. During recross, Chambers simply ignored the garment and again went after Banks. Every time the defense attorney asked about the fatal shot, the prosecution objected, stating that the sheriff was not on trial and the shooting had nothing to do with the disorderly conduct charges. But Chambers persisted. If the sheriff had done nothing wrong, why did he need a lawyer? Banks had no good answer. Chambers noted that Atkins had accompanied Banks to court that day and was assisting with the prosecution. Then Chambers asked, "Following the death of Stanley Altland, you found it necessary to have some legal protection?" Banks replied no, but Chambers ignored him. "And your interest in this case has been in trying to protect yourself, has it not?" "No, sir."[32]

Sensing an opening, Chambers said, "I just want to get one thing straight. After you crossed the river, you heard noise, but that was not what you used to place anyone under arrest, is that right?" Banks agreed, saying he only arrested them after they cursed him. Did he arrest them because they cursed him? "No sir," Banks responded, "not because someone cursed me, after they cursed me." Chambers wanted to make sure. "After they cursed you, you then placed them under arrest?" When Banks answered yes, Chambers pounced. "How much time expired between that time and the time you shot Stanley Altland?" At the prosecution table, Atkins was apoplectic. "Objection!" "Sustained." Chambers calmly said, "I have no further questions," and took his seat.[33]

In one final attempt to prove claims that the campers were drunk, Rusher called a campground worker to the stand to testify that he had emptied the trash before the Clearwater group arrived. That proved, the solicitor contended, that the beer cans Banks saw at the site had been left by the defendants, something the Clearwater kids did not dispute. Chambers quickly established on cross-examination that the worker had no knowledge of any of the events at Briar Bottom that night. After calling Paul Wheeler and Larry Dean Cox, neither of whom added anything new, the prosecution rested.[34] Chambers immediately moved to dismiss charges against all twenty defendants due to lack of evidence. Gash did not go that far, but he released eleven of them on the spot, including Linda Mancini, Jay Barrett, Ron Olson, Max Johnson, Diane Cracolici, and Doreen Sofarelli.[35]

Day two immediately brought more victories for the defense. After arguments from both sides, the judge dismissed charges against three more defendants, including Kim Burns. That left only six of the original twenty who still faced possible conviction: David Satterwhite, Phil Lokey, Sue Cello, Kevin Shea, Gary Graham, and Fred McNairy.[36]

Tensions ratcheted up again as Satterwhite took the stand. Questioned by Adam Stein, the young man said that he and several others "from the main campground" rode motorcycles early on the afternoon of July 3 and admitted that the group drank beer and a little liquor that evening. Before Banks and his men arrived, the tape player had been turned off, because it had severely drained the battery in Ron Olson's Volvo. Most of the campers had gone to bed.[37]

Satterwhite then told the court what he had told the newspapers and the FBI: that he had been sitting by the fire when the sheriff kicked him and stuck a loaded shotgun in his belly. Banks got mad when Satterwhite asked about his rights, struck him with the weapon, and it fired. Stein did not ask if the shot killed Altland, but the implication was clear.[38]

Questioned as to whether he had attacked Banks, Satterwhite vehemently denied it, stating that he was too afraid to do anything except follow the lawman's orders. He added that he used no profanity before the gun went off. After the blast, things got confused, and he might have said something unseemly. Asked about the knife, Satterwhite described it as a family heirloom and said he voluntarily gave it to Paul Wheeler as the officers marched them across the river to the cars. Wheeler took it and never gave it back.[39]

Throughout his testimony, Satterwhite stared straight at Banks while the sheriff either put his head down or looked away. Satterwhite kept his gaze riveted on the sheriff as Rusher began his cross-examination.[40] Asked about how much he drank that night, Satterwhite testified that he "had around four beers" and "a drink of tequila." He heard no fireworks. When Satterwhite again noted that he had been too frightened to assault the sheriff, Rusher asked, "You weren't too scared to ask about your rights, were you?" Glowering at Banks, Satterwhite shot back, "I never lost my fear." Then, gesturing toward the sheriff (who still did not look up), Satterwhite said, "I'm scared to death of that man right now. I wouldn't walk down this street at night for nothing."[41]

Paul Brayly, the Elon College student who had been taken into custody with the campers, followed Satterwhite to the stand. Brayly explained that he had loaned the Clearwater campers a lantern early that evening. He heard some noise from the Clearwater site, but it did not bother him "in the least." A few fireworks went off well before dark, but he could not say where they came from. He went over to the site to retrieve the lantern just before the sheriff showed up. Brayly saw no scuffle involving Banks and Satterwhite. "The scuffling," Brayly testified, "was made by the officers that were prodding and pushing and there wasn't any reaction from the campers other than to try to get out of the way." Asked how he was treated, Brayly said that he was pushed, shoved, and "verbally taunted by the police officers for having long hair and just being there."[42]

Joel LeFebvre, the Greensboro man who camped with Frank Lasnick and Margaret Kowalski, was next. He heard some fireworks before dark, but nothing from the Clearwater campers between 9:30 and 11:00. Sometime after 11:15, he heard officers banging on the van belonging to the Orlando campers saying, "Come out, you son of a bitch." On cross, Atkins asked LeFebvre how many beers he had. "Two." Atkins then tried to shake the direct testimony about noise. "From about ten until eleven o'clock you hadn't heard much noise?" The Greensboro camper did not hesitate. "You could hear a pin drop."[43]

On redirect, Stein asked LeFebvre if he had heard any noise the night before, on July 2. "Yes," the witness replied. "There were about three pickup trucks with campers on the back, people drinking beer, drinking liquor, and playing a tape player, very loud, very late." Stein sarcastically inquired, "Did Sheriff Banks come out that night?" LeFebvre responded, "If he did, I did not see them [sic]."[44]

Chambers and Stein then called each of the remaining defendants: Sue Cello, Gary Graham, Phil Lokey, Kevin Shea, and Fred McNairy, along with Sandra Drucas (Graham's girlfriend) and Cathy Siebenthaler (McNairy's girlfriend). All five defendants acknowledged drinking on the night of July 3. They denied exploding any fireworks, riding motorcycles, or directing any profanity at the officers before the shot. All seven witnesses described being searched and pushed around by the officers and the difficulties they encountered in trying to use the phone at the courthouse.[45]

Julius Chambers had one more question for Fred McNairy: "Do you know Jimmie Seifert?" When McNairy answered yes, Chambers brought up Ronny

Hoyle's earlier testimony about Seifert being in his camp at two in the morning. McNairy made it clear that Seifert had been with the group detained in Burnsville at that time. Chambers took his seat, confident that Hoyle, like most of the other prosecution witnesses, had been discredited.[46]

Jay Barrett, who told me that he "saw Banks's gun go off and Stanley just go flying," desperately wanted to testify, but the attorneys feared the prosecution might bring up his recent trouble over the stolen car in Clearwater. They were right to be concerned. On cross-examination, Rusher and Atkins tried to rattle every defendant by repeatedly asking about previous arrests, especially drug offenses. Fred McNairy had to admit that he had been convicted of marijuana possession and was on probation. The prosecutors also focused heavily on the amount of alcohol consumed, especially by Kevin Shea. Rusher suggested that had Shea been sober, he would have stayed at the campsite with the girls and not gone off in search of rattlesnakes. The solicitor also implied, without admissible evidence, that Shea had used barbiturates that night. Shea denied it.[47]

Atkins then questioned Gary Graham and Fred McNairy about sleeping with their girlfriends. He caustically asked Graham, "Sandra Drucas, is that a girl or a boy?" Chambers objected that it was an insult and uncalled for. Gash let it stand. When McNairy testified that he had gone to his van because he wanted to be by himself, Atkins sneered, "If you wanted to be alone, why was Cathy Siebenthaler there?" McNairy did not flinch. "Well, I wanted to be alone with her."[48]

When Siebenthaler took the stand, Atkins asked, "Were you sleeping in a van?" "Yes." "Was anybody else sleeping in that van?" "Fred McNairy." "Who?" "Fred McNairy." "Fred McNairy?" "Yes, sir." "Did you have any of the beer that was flowing around or the whiskey?" "No." "You were in the van when the officers came?" "That is correct." Atkins still would not let it go. "About how long had you been in bed do you think before you went to sleep?" Without a hint of embarrassment, Siebenthaler replied nonchalantly, "I don't know, maybe fifteen minutes. We were pretty tired." Atkins sat down.[49]

Sandra Drucas testified that she had been in a tent with Gary Graham when the officers arrived. On cross, Rusher immediately asked Drucas how old she was on July 3. "Sixteen." That was and is the age of consent in Florida and North Carolina. The solicitor then asked how much she had to drink. "Nothing." "You were about the only one not drinking anything, is that correct?" Drucas responded, "No, sir," and quickly named several others all under eighteen, who she said were not drinking.[50]

Gary Graham and Sandra Drucas outside the Yancey County Courthouse. Prosecutors questioned them extensively about the sleeping arrangements at the campsite.
Courtesy of Roger Altland.

The defense called one final female camper (who asked that I not use her name) to testify that she saw the gun in Satterwhite's stomach. She heard a few firecrackers early in the evening, but no profanity directed toward the officers. In a barely audible voice, she also told the court that during the search, while she was against a tree, someone "went like this [the court reporter did not describe the gesture] down here," a statement that suggested sexual assault. The solicitor asked if she knew "who did that to [her]." "No." After her testimony, Chambers said, "That is the evidence for the defendants."[51]

At about 5:20 p.m., Judge Gash called a recess while he reviewed the evidence. Afterward, he held a closed-door meeting with attorneys for both sides while the defendants and the spectators waited anxiously in the courtroom or wandered around nervously outside the building. It was after dark when Gash reconvened the court and announced his verdicts. He found Phil Lokey, Gary Graham, Sue Cello, and Fred McNairy not guilty; he convicted Kevin Shea and David Satterwhite—the only two defendants the state's witnesses could identify as being present on July 3—of disorderly conduct.[52]

After another meeting with the attorneys and Satterwhite's father, the judge fined Shea twenty-five dollars and Satterwhite one hundred dollars, assessments that included court costs. Gash issued warrants for the three campers who did not show but elected not to prosecute the one who stayed home with the flu. The defendants passed the hat and paid the fines on the spot. Smiling and hugging each other, they left the courtroom and headed back to Asheville, where they gathered at Lum's, a chain restaurant that specialized in gourmet hot dogs, burgers, and beer. They stayed well into the night before returning to the Ramada Inn to sleep off the celebration and prepare for their return to Florida.[53]

9

A Perverse Twist of Irony

As they left Yancey County that November, the nineteen Clearwater campers had ample reason to be pleased with the verdicts. All but one of them had been found not guilty or had their charges dismissed. Kevin Shea had been fined a paltry twenty-five dollars. Given the statute governing disorderly conduct, which allowed for a $500 fine or six months in jail, even David Satterwhite's one-hundred-dollar assessment seemed lenient.

Considering the solicitors' home-court advantage, a lot of reporters present saw it as a stunning victory for the Clearwater kids. Allen Cowan called the whole proceeding a "quixotic prosecution." According to another observer, the two-day trial "provided little evidence to support the raid on the camp or the arrests" and "the first round of a continuing mountain drama has ended with the defendants on top." Even Assistant Solicitor Rusher admitted, "There are a certain number of people who we don't have anything on except general identification to them being there." Julius Chambers told reporters that he "was happy with the results," but "would've been happier if all the kids were acquitted. There was really no evidence to convict anyone."[1]

As more time passed, the Clearwater friends recognized that despite the favorable outcome, the trial had provided little in the way of justice for Stan

Altland. Chambers had accused Banks of killing Stan in open court, and the sheriff had not denied it, though his attorney had objected to Chambers's assertion. Banks had told the newspapers (and the FBI) that Chief Deputy Erwin Higgins accidentally fired the fatal shot, but Higgins had not taken the stand in Burnsville to say so under oath. Shortly after the trial, the *Charlotte Observer* reported that "sources close to the case" said Higgins "privately denie[d] he was holding the gun." When the chief deputy spoke with the *St. Petersburg Times* after the verdicts, he seemed evasive. "I won't make no comment about nothing. I want to be nice to you, but that's my privilege." Asked if he "was willing to stand by while the sheriff accused him of the fatal shooting and not defend himself," Higgins shrugged and said, "I've told the SBI everything I could about that night. If and when the authorities clear the air about this, I'll be willing to make a statement." Higgins also said that Rusher had advised both him and Banks not to talk about the case.[2]

Allen Cowan attempted to interview the sheriff anyway. By then, the Florida reporter knew what to expect as Banks again "picked at his nails and refused to look at" the interviewer. The sheriff did say one thing that surprised the reporter. Asked about the argument over which gun fired the fatal blast, Banks told Cowan, "I never made a statement on whose gun shot the young man. You can put whatever you want in your story." Was the sheriff now saying that Higgins did not shoot Altland? Cowan never found out, because Banks refused to answer any more questions or explain why he needed a lawyer.[3]

For his part, Rusher noted that he did not ask about Altland's death, because "it was not relative [*sic*] to what happened before the shooting occurred and that's what they [were] charged with." Choosing their words carefully as always, Chambers and Stein did not say that the killing was irrelevant, just that "[they] didn't care to go into any details" about it. They cleverly left that to the press.[4]

The lone voice in defense of the sheriff came from the *Yancey Record*. The local paper had not mentioned the killing since July, but now led with a front-page story that focused on the prosecution witnesses and the campers' alleged transgressions. On the prosecution's failure to identify the defendants, the *Record* took a potshot at the outsiders' appearance, saying that "the state's witnesses . . . had difficulty identifying the longhaired youth as boys or girls," adding, as if in surprise, that "eleven of those arrested were females." The account ran on Thursday, November 30, after the case had been decided, but the *Record* did not report the verdicts or punishments, only that Gash dismissed charges against eleven defendants on Monday and three more on Tuesday. Anyone reading the article might conclude that the other six had been convicted.[5]

If the cultural crosscurrents underlying the case were not already clear enough, another editorial in the *St. Petersburg Times*, published a week after the trial, threw the conflict into sharp relief. Pointing to the acquittals, dismissals, and the officers' shifting stories, the author argued that simply because the campers' "appearance and lifestyle did not blend in with the way of life around the mountain town," the sheriff and his men had no right to "rush in and touch off a scuffle" that left Stan Altland dead. The writer again demanded that both the SBI and FBI reports "be made public to clear the air" and urged the Justice Department to weigh in on "whether the civil rights of these young people, including Altland, have been violated."[6]

As usual, Chambers remained guarded. "We're waiting on our clients," he told the press. "We have to see what they want to do about this thing." The campers soon made it clear that they would do whatever it took to get justice for Stan, including filing a federal lawsuit and returning to North Carolina to testify. As one of them put it, "We're not going to forget about this—ever."[7]

They did not forget, but the newspapers did, at least for a while. George McGovern had lost the presidential election in a landslide. Nixon's appeal for law and order triumphed over youthful concerns about peace, tolerance, and justice. In January 1973, the United States signed the Paris Peace Accords and agreed to pull its troops out of Vietnam. By then, Selective Service took only nineteen-year-olds, and with America's involvement winding down, most undrafted young men felt safe. Meanwhile, a jury convicted G. Gordon Liddy and James W. McCord of burglary, illegal wiretapping, and conspiracy in connection with a 1972 break-in at the Watergate Hotel in Washington.

Now living in Burlington, I still read an early edition of the *News and Observer* but saw nothing about the Burnsville trial or what might follow. Bootleg live albums from the Stones tour appeared in record stores under the title *Goin' Back to the Roots*. I bought one, despite the terrible sound quality. Listening to the record, I wondered what became of those kids from Clearwater.

Emma McNairy, Stan Altland's family, and several others hoped that when the FBI finished its report, the Justice Department would bring federal charges against Kermit Banks and his deputies. In mid-December 1972, a Justice Department spokesman advised Senator Chiles that the FBI report "is still pending." In Yancey County, Clyde Roberts continued to sit on the SBI document, saying that he had no intention of releasing it to anyone, and bragging that he had turned down a request from "the federal folks" to see it.[8]

Eager to help his constituents, Chiles constantly sought updates from the FBI; finally in early March 1973, he got an answer from J. Stanley Pottinger, assistant attorney general of the Justice Department's Civil Rights Division. According to Pottinger, a careful review of the finished report indicated "that the facts of this matter will not support federal prosecution under criminal statutes which this Division is responsible for enforcing." Murder or involuntary manslaughter charges had to be filed by the state. The FBI could only determine "whether there is a conspiracy to deprive civil rights; whether civil rights are denied intentionally without conspiracy; or whether local law enforcement had interfered with certain federally protected activities." The investigation found no evidence of a conspiracy or interference. Pottinger said nothing about whose gun killed Altland, only that the "element of willfulness" could not be established, because the shotgun "discharged accidentally during a scuffle." Pottinger added that "numerous witnesses, including law enforcement officers and companions of the victim, Stanley Altland," had provided evidence to that effect.[9]

The Clearwater campers had indeed told agents that Banks's gun fired accidentally, but they insisted that David Satterwhite had done nothing more than ask about his constitutional rights and push Banks's shotgun aside. Everything that followed, they felt, should be blamed on the sheriff. The FBI had apparently accepted at face value Banks's story that the youths brazenly attacked him and six other heavily armed men. Never mind that eighteen of twenty defendants had either been found not guilty of disorderly conduct or had those charges dismissed for lack of evidence. Or that the Greensboro campers had repeatedly told FBI agents that the Clearwater campsite had been quiet before Banks arrived. The bureau closed its file on the Altland killing and refused to release the report to Senator Chiles or anyone else, citing the likelihood of future litigation. With Clyde Roberts zealously safeguarding the SBI findings, Chiles could only offer condolences. "Stan's death is a great tragedy," he wrote to Ron Olson's mother, "and I know this incident is something that will bother all of us for a long time."[10]

Meanwhile, David Satterwhite went home to Mebane, a small town that had more in common with Burnsville than with Clearwater. Founded in 1831 on the eastern edge of the North Carolina Piedmont, Mebane had remained a sleepy agricultural crossroads until the 1850s, when the state railroad connected it to some of North Carolina's larger towns. Rail transport eventually brought furniture, textiles, and other industries to the area. Following World War II, local scion June Crumpler established the Mebane Lumber Company and equipped it with a large sawmill, perfectly situated to take advantage of the Piedmont's vast hardwood forests and the railroad. By the early 1970s, Mebane Lumber had emerged as one of the largest suppliers of building materials in the Southeast and one of the region's major employers.[11]

Most of Mebane lies in Alamance County, but in two places the town spills over into Orange County, home to Chapel Hill and the University of North Carolina. That geographic quirk made for interesting politics in and around Mebane. Because of antiwar demonstrations at the university, Orange County developed a reputation as a hippie enclave and haven for draft resisters, while Alamance remained much more conservative. In the 1972 presidential election, George McGovern carried only two counties in North Carolina. Orange was one of them; Alamance went solidly for Nixon.[12]

Marshall Stephenson, who grew up in Mebane and went to Eastern Alamance High with David Satterwhite, recalls that in 1972, a lot of guys there still had short hair. Playing football or basketball provided the surest path to local glory. "We were," Stephenson notes, "mostly in the mode of keeping our noses clean." He and his friends sometimes drank at parties, but "usually went to church on Sunday." Most of them were "pretty conservative, GQ types who dressed neatly. We weren't hippies."[13]

None of that mattered to David Satterwhite. Because his father's job often required the family to move, Eastern Alamance was David's second high school in as many years. He showed up in the fall of 1972 with shoulder-length dark hair, faded jeans, and ragged flannel shirts. He cared little about high school sports and made no apologies for his liberal politics. In a current-events class, he routinely bashed Nixon and US involvement in Vietnam, something that frequently prompted arguments with other students and occasionally the teacher. He also projected an air of self-confidence and independence. Some classmates found him arrogant; others thought of him as an odd hippie kid who marched to his own drummer.

Stephenson remembers the first time he met Satterwhite: "I was driving my Volkswagen Beetle and I saw David hitchhiking home from school. I had seen him in class, so I picked him up. At that time, for some reason, he didn't have a car. I started giving him rides, and we started hanging around together a little bit." Mebane still had a traditional downtown drugstore, complete with a soda fountain, where Stephenson worked part-time serving up ice cream

**David Satterwhite, from the 1973 Eastern
Alamance High School Yearbook.**

and Cokes. Before long Satterwhite showed up there with his white dog in
tow, and the boys became friends.[14]

Stephenson's father, a prominent local banker who later served for more
than thirty years as Mebane's mayor, initially seemed leery of his son's new acquaintance. In fact, Marshall told me, "A lot of parents didn't want their kids
hanging around with David." They feared that his hippie style and carefree
attitude might be corrupting influences in the small town. When Satterwhite
finally came home with Stephenson, Marshall worried about how his father

might react. But when he left the room for a moment, he returned to find his dad and David laughing together and engaged in friendly conversation. From that point on, Satterwhite was welcome in the Stephenson home.[15]

David seemed to have a similar effect on anyone who got to know him. In time, some fellow students came to respect his intelligence and willingness to speak out against anything he found unfair. As Stephenson put it, "He was smart, opinionated, and didn't mind calling bullshit when he thought something was wrong." Women found Satterwhite attractive, and he liked "being with them" at parties or in some other group setting. But apparently, he never had a steady girlfriend, perhaps because he had so little time for the high school social scene.[16]

He preferred being outdoors, especially hiking and camping in the North Carolina mountains. He and Stephenson ventured out together a few times, and once backpacked into Linville Gorge on an overnight trip. Marshall, who made do with an inexpensive tent and sleeping bag, marveled at David's pricey "North Face gear" and state-of-the-art equipment. "He was a serious camper and had all that stuff a long time before anyone else did," Stephenson recalls. In keeping with his independent streak, Satterwhite sometimes camped solo, with only his dog for company, just as he did in July 1972.[17]

Satterwhite also enjoyed marijuana, something else that set him apart from many of his peers at Eastern Alamance. He was open about it with people he trusted, even those who did not partake. His attitude seemed to be, "Yeah, I get high, so what?" He usually had pot or knew where to get it, either locally or via out-of-town connections. He liked beer and occasionally liquor, though he seldom got falling-down drunk. As Stephenson described it, "David gave off a Jim Morrison–type vibe." He liked to party, but "you just got the feeling that there was a lot going on in his head." He could be "mouthy and argumentative," but also "very deep and philosophical."[18]

Shortly after the Burnsville trial, Satterwhite got a part-time job at Mebane Lumber, where he worked as a "stacker," arranging freshly milled boards and helping keep the yard organized. There he met Marty Krumnacher, who was a couple of years older and employed full-time in June Crumpler's business. Krumnacher shared Satterwhite's affinity for the outdoors and pot. The two also became friends with Ned James, age seventeen, another part-time stacker at Mebane Lumber.[19] During the early months of 1973, Satterwhite seemed content with his job, new friends, and life in Mebane. Like the Clearwater kids, he went to school, worked, and waited for the lawsuit against Kermit Banks to go forward.

Spring came early to the Carolina Piedmont that year. On Sunday, February 25, afternoon temperatures climbed into the mid-sixties under sunny skies. Satterwhite, Krumnacher, and James took advantage of the good weather to work on an old sailboat they planned to restore. It was a small craft, best suited for use on nearby lakes, and they intended to try it out a month or two later. It was just the sort of project Satterwhite loved. He always seemed to be repairing or tinkering with his outdoor gear. While they worked, Satterwhite had a beer; Krumnacher and James had two each, enough to provide a slight buzz, but not impede the task at hand. The boat's rusty mast posed the biggest problem because it did not rotate properly. That had to be set right if they ever hoped to get it on the water.[20]

The boys decided that some penetrating oil might break through the rust and free up the mast to swivel in the wind as it should. Unfortunately, no one had any oil at home, and the hardware stores were closed. Someone suggested that they might find what they needed at Mebane Lumber. It, too, was closed on Sunday, but as employees they knew a way to get in. Perhaps still a little buzzed from the beer, the three headed over to the lumber yard to see what they could find. It would not take long, and no one would miss something as common as penetrating oil, especially if they returned it the next day.

They got into the yard as planned at about 4:00 p.m. and went into a shed where they found an oil can. To their dismay, it was almost empty. No way they would get enough out of it to fix the mast. Figuring that they were not going to accomplish anything else that afternoon, one of them rolled a joint. They smoked it and half of another right there in the shed, all the while laughing and talking in loud voices. No one seemed to be around, and now they had nothing else to do on a sunny Sunday afternoon.

Clifton Ernest Whitley, age seventy-one, worked security that day at Mebane Lumber. He periodically made rounds to check various entry points but spent most of his time near the main gate. Sometime between 4:00 and 5:00 p.m., a man in a light-blue pickup truck rolled up to the entrance. The driver said that he had heard voices near one of the sheds and thought somebody might be "taking lumber out over the back fence." Whitley decided to have a look. He saw no one stealing lumber, but as he later explained, he heard Satterwhite, Krumnacher, and James "talking and cussing and swearing in the shed."[21]

Exactly what happened next is unclear, but at some point, Whitley unholstered his .38 caliber revolver and confronted the boys. According to Krumnacher, Whitley told them "not to go anywhere or he would shoot [them]," a threat the guard repeated at least three times. Krumnacher knew Whitley, but the guard apparently did not recognize him or Satterwhite and James as employees. The boys asked Whitley to put the gun away, saying, "You know us. We work here." But the guard kept pointing the .38 in their direction and said, "Never mind, just keep moving along." He seemed to be taking them back toward the main gate to call the cops.

For the second time in seven months David Satterwhite faced an angry man with a gun, and for the second time, the youth did not back down. Staring right at Whitley, he said something like, "You're not going to shoot; you can't shoot us; you know us." As Whitley continued to wave the .38 and walk them toward the gate, the two had another exchange about whether Whitley would use the weapon. When Whitley again said, "Keep moving," Satterwhite crouched low, and blurted, "Well why don't you shoot, then? Go ahead and shoot." Without another word, Whitley pointed the gun at Satterwhite and pulled the trigger.

The guard later said that he aimed at the young man's legs, but the bullet struck Satterwhite almost squarely between the eyes, killing him instantly. He made no sound as he collapsed in the sand and sawdust of the lumber yard, blood seeping into his long hair from the round hole in his forehead. Horrorstruck, Krumnacher and James looked on in absolute shock, unable to speak or make sense of what had just happened. Whitley left them there, staring at their dead friend and fighting back tears of panic, while he headed off to call the authorities.[22]

Mebane Lumber was in Orange County, and within a few minutes an ambulance showed up and took Satterwhite's body to a nearby hospital. A little while later, still barely able to talk, Krumnacher and James told Orange County sheriff's deputy Arthur Hamlet that they had gone into the shed in search of penetrating oil for the sailboat. They showed him the empty can and admitted that they had been drinking beer earlier and had smoked marijuana just before Whitley found them. When Hamlet asked Whitley what happened, the security guard refused to say anything. Orange County sheriff C. D. "Buck" Knight thought he had had no choice but to arrest Whitley for murder. As Knight later told reporters, "They claimed they couldn't find any [oil] and as to what happened after that your guess is as good as mine." He took Whitley to jail in Hillsborough, the county seat, to await a preliminary hearing.[23]

Marshall Stephenson was at home that Sunday evening when the telephone rang. His dad answered. After a short conversation, he turned to Marshall and said, "I have bad news. David Satterwhite got killed this afternoon." Marshall "could not believe it; there was just no way he could be dead." But he was. The principal at Eastern Alamance announced it over the intercom the next morning and asked students for a moment of silence. Once again, friends of a Briar Bottom camper prepared for a funeral, this time at Mebane United Methodist Church. Stephenson, James, and Krumnacher served as pallbearers. They laid David Satterwhite to rest late in the afternoon, on the last day of February 1973. He was nineteen years old.[24]

Clifton Whitley still said nothing, but the court released him on his own recognizance pending the preliminary hearing. It took place on March 13 in front of Judge Coleman C. Cates.[25] Judge Cates had long been something of a legend in Alamance and Orange Counties. When he was three years old, he tried to cut some threads off an old rag rug with a pocketknife. A thread snapped and the knife blade went straight into his right eye, damaging it beyond repair and leaving doctors no choice but to remove it. Shortly after that, an infection set in and spread to his left eye; within days, he was blind. Refusing to let that stand in his way, Cates earned undergraduate and law degrees from UNC. By 1973, he had a reputation as a "humane and compassionate" jurist. Prosecutors who locked horns with Cates often found him "much too lenient." He went especially easy on youthful offenders, preferring to lecture them from the bench rather than send them to jail.[26]

When the preliminary hearing began, district solicitor Bill Graham questioned Deputy Hamlet about his initial investigation at the lumber yard. Summarizing statements from Krumnacher and James, the deputy reported that both admitted to drinking beer and smoking pot. He noted that he found an empty oil can and "part of a marijuana cigarette" on site the day of the shooting. Krumnacher had also said that David Satterwhite had been "cussing" Whitley and "giving him a hard time." Both Krumnacher and James explained that Whitley repeatedly threatened to shoot them and that Satterwhite told him to "go ahead and shoot" just before he fired.

Hamlet then read a formal statement from Whitley, the first time the security guard had gone on record about the killing. According to Whitley, when he got to the shed, he heard the three boys "cussing and swearing" and "didn't know what to do." He took out his gun and told them to come with him. Then, he said, David Satterwhite threatened him, stating "We're going to kill you. We're going to grind you up [in a woodchipper]." He also noted that the youth crouched down as if to jump at him. Asked why he shot Satterwhite, Whitley responded, "I was scared of him. They were all acting like crazy men." Whitley concluded by saying that he had only intended to wound Satterwhite by shooting him in the leg.

The security guard's attorneys asked Hamlet a few questions and then requested that Judge Cates remember three things: the defendant's advanced age, that he had acted as a law enforcement officer, and that the boys had used foul language. In response, Solicitor Graham told Cates, "It seems to me that this would be the utilization of excessive force and that therefore the man should be bound over" for a grand jury. Both sides conferred with Cates before he left the room to deliberate. When he returned, the judge noted the discrepancies between the statements by Satterwhite's friends and Clifton Whitley but explained, "It really is not up to this court to determine who is telling the truth." He found probable cause for the case to go to a grand jury and ordered Whitley held without bond.[27]

It took a week for news of Satterwhite's death to reach Clearwater. On March 7, Allen Cowan broke the story in the *St. Petersburg Times*, noting that somehow "fate has brought violent death to a companion of Stanley Altland." After learning what he could about the circumstances surrounding the Mebane killing, Cowan phoned Adam Stein. Whether Stein had already heard the news is not clear, but he seemed shocked when he described Satterwhite as "a very impressive kid, a very nice, attractive kid." In Mebane and in Clearwater, those who knew Satterwhite hoped that his killer—unlike Altland's—might soon stand trial in criminal court. They should have known better.[28]

The grand jury is an anomaly in American jurisprudence. Originally intended to prevent politically motivated prosecutions, grand juries are supposed to allow unbiased ordinary citizens to hear evidence and decide whether a suspect should be indicted. In practice, grand juries strongly favor the prosecution, putting them at odds with a system supposedly skewed toward protecting rights of the accused. In North Carolina, a grand jury consists of eighteen citizens. It sits for a year, with half its members replaced every six months. Its proceedings are secret, with no press, no public, and no judge. Only the prosecutor, jurors, and court reporter attend; only the prosecutor calls witnesses and presents evidence.[29]

The suspect has no right to be there or have an attorney present. Hearsay is admissible, as is physical evidence procured without warrants. Nothing compels a solicitor or district attorney to acknowledge anything that might exonerate the accused. The standard of proof is low. North Carolina requires that only twelve grand jurors find enough evidence for a case to go forward. After hearing the prosecutor and witnesses, a grand jury either issues a true bill of indictment and sends the matter to trial, or the jurors declare the evidence inadequate, offer "no true bill," and the charges are dismissed. Though we lack reliable statistics for state grand juries now or in 1972, a 2010 study of federal grand juries found that out of 162,000 cases presented that year, only 11 resulted in no true bill.[30]

The man who killed David Satterwhite beat those incredible odds. On March 23, 1973, an Orange County grand jury found that "the charge of murder in connection with the slaying of David Satterwhite 'is not a true bill.'" Solicitors dropped all charges against Clifton Whitley, and he walked away a free man.[31] When that news reached Florida, some of the Clearwater campers thought that Satterwhite's death and Whitley's release had to be more than coincidence. "When I heard David got killed," Jay Barrett recalls, "I figured Kermit Banks had something to do with it, that it was a conspiracy." Roger Altland expressed similar sentiments: "I thought it was just too convenient. I mean, what are the odds that two kids on the same camping trip would both be shot by cops, and no one would go to jail?" Sue Cello remembers that "it all sounded way too familiar to all of us."[32]

Suspicions aside, I found nothing to suggest that Clifton Whitley knew Kermit Banks or any of the Yancey deputies in 1973. Whitley worked for a private security firm and apparently lived in and around Mebane most of his life.[33] The connections between the two killings were real, but more subtle. David Satterwhite did not suffer fools or cops gladly, and he liked to challenge authority. In much the same way that he pushed Kermit Banks's shotgun aside and asked about his rights, Satterwhite dismissed Whitley's threats as the rantings of an overzealous elderly security guard. Both men took offense at Satterwhite's attitude, especially when he questioned their power and tactics. At Mebane Lumber, his bluster cost him his life.

Within the confines of the grand jury, "prosecutors can decide to let an officer's version of events go unchallenged or try to discredit it with cross-examination. They can do the same with other witnesses." That permits solicitors and district attorneys to use grand juries as political cover, especially when police or sheriffs are involved. Because prosecutors work closely with law enforcement, they can be reluctant to indict officers in questionable killings of civilians or suspects, even in the face of public pressure to do so. If grand jurors, guided and advised by a prosecutor, return no true bill, they take the heat for the unpopular decision. Because the proceedings and names of the jurors are secret, the public has no one to blame.[34]

When he shot David Satterwhite, Clifton Whitley was not a police officer. He worked for the Security Patrol and Detective Agency, a private firm that provided guards for enterprises like Mebane Lumber. Many security guards, especially of Whitley's age, had previous experience in law enforcement, but with so little information about his past, it is difficult to know whether he had ever been employed as a police officer or sheriff's deputy. At the preliminary hearing, his status as a private citizen did not prevent Whitley's attorneys from urging Judge Cates to remember that the security guard had "acted as a law enforcement officer."

Solicitor Graham made the case for prosecution at the hearing, but assistant solicitor Herb Pierce took the evidence to the grand jury. By then, rumor had it that June Crumpler, owner of Mebane Lumber and one of the town's most influential citizens, did not want Whitley indicted. Apparently, lots of townspeople felt the same way. They blamed Satterwhite and his friends for entering the lumber yard illegally on a Sunday.[35]

Whatever his reasons, Pierce never intended to indict Clifton Whitley. We know because he said so. After the grand jury proceedings, Pierce told the *St. Petersburg Times* that Satterwhite and his friends had been drinking and smoking marijuana when Whitley found them in the shed and that Satterwhite had lunged at the security guard. Given those circumstances, the assistant solicitor found it astonishing that the case ever got to a grand jury. As he told the Florida papers, "It sounded to me like an old fellow trying to do his job." Pierce explained that he could take no further action unless presented with additional evidence, something he described as "not likely." Even in one of the most liberal counties in North Carolina, an unarmed hippie's death at the hands of a private citizen went unprosecuted. Few around Mebane seemed to care. As Marshall Stephenson recalls, "the whole thing just sort of went away."[36]

Justifiable or not, Clifton Whitley's decision to fire his .38 had enormous repercussions for the planned federal lawsuit against Kermit Banks and his deputies. Given his pugnacious personality, Satterwhite would have liked nothing better than to stay in the fight against the Yancey County officers. He had been convicted of disorderly conduct in Burnsville and might not have made the best witness at a civil trial, but he could have provided critical details about the night in question, especially his encounter with Banks. As

Adam Stein noted, Satterwhite's death was "a perverse twist of irony." It was also a serious setback for those who sought justice in another tragic and complicated case.[37]

On July 3, 1973, the anniversary of Stan Altland's death, John York of the *Charlotte Observer* revisited the Briar Bottom killing in a lengthy article. Noting that Clifton Whitley had at least gone before a grand jury after shooting Satterwhite, York found it odd that "no one had a chance to make a similar finding in the campground killing of Altland." When he contacted Clyde Roberts, the solicitor remained as noncommittal as ever. "I thought of going to the grand jury," he told the reporter, but "the kids disagreed about whose gun it was. Some of them didn't even know what was going on." Asked if the SBI report named the shooter, Roberts pled ignorance: "I'm not positive if the report made any statement or not." Then, perhaps unintentionally revealing his strategy, he added, "I haven't looked at that file for a good long time." As usual, Kermit Banks kept mum. "I'd rather not talk about it," he told York. "It's sort of quiet and that suits me fine."[38]

When York contacted Ron Olson, he stated again that Banks had held the shotgun and that all the campers agreed on that point, as they still do fifty years later. Olson also recounted his harsh treatment by Banks and the deputies. And to what end? To find out in court that Kevin Shea had a stick and that David Satterwhite had asked about his rights. Now Satterwhite was dead, too.[39] And the district solicitor did not even know what was in the SBI report? That was rich. The legal maxim that "justice delayed is justice denied" appeared to be alive and well in Yancey County.

Given the peculiarities of mountain justice and Clyde Roberts's self-serving inertia, the Clearwater group had only one recourse: a civil rights lawsuit in federal court. As the anniversary of Stan Altland's death passed, plans for that action seemed to be in limbo. A few of the parents thought it best for the group to let the whole thing go. As Roger Altland put it, "We are waiting right now for all the kids to get together to let [Adam] Stein know which ones are still willing to file a civil suit." Roger implored them not to give up. "That's wrong," he said. "They saw it happen. They ought to be there."[40]

10

Our Least Favorite Judge

Roger Altland need not have worried. Stan's friends kept fighting, with or without parental support. In the early months of 1974, seventeen of the original campers filed the long-anticipated federal civil rights lawsuit.[1] By then, as my freshman year of college wound down, I had lost touch with the case. Two stories dominated the national headlines. In February, radical anarchists in the Symbionese Liberation Army kidnapped newspaper heiress Patty Hearst. Two months later, a camera caught her wielding a gun as she assisted her captors in a bank robbery. The FBI launched a nationwide search to find her.

Elsewhere, a federal grand jury indicted seven of Nixon's top aides and named the president as an unindicted coconspirator in the Watergate coverup. In July 1974, when the Supreme Court ordered Nixon to surrender dozens of the original White House tapes, I hoped that my cynicism about government and the justice system might be unfounded. While I waited for the FBI to catch Patty Hearst and rooted for Nixon to get his comeuppance, the Chambers law firm went back to work on behalf of the Clearwater campers.

Adam Stein made many of the initial contacts through letters and long-distance phone calls. The task of drafting the complaint fell to Karl

Adkins, one of the firm's younger attorneys, just three years out of the University of Michigan Law School. Born in Germany in 1946, the son of a Black US soldier and a white German woman, Adkins had been adopted by an American family who brought him first to Savannah and later to Fayetteville. When he arrived in the States, he spoke no English and, as a "brown child," inevitably faced discrimination in the Jim Crow South. But by the time Adkins got to E. E. Smith Senior High School, he had become a serious student and a standout on the football and track teams. He graduated from UNC and, after completing his law degree at Michigan, came back to North Carolina to work with Julius Chambers.[2]

Adkins planned the Clearwater group's litigation carefully. Every camper who signed on had either been found not guilty of disorderly conduct or had their case dismissed during the Burnsville trial—powerful evidence, Adkins thought, that the campers had done nothing wrong on that July night. The list of plaintiffs included some of Stan Altland's closest friends: Phil Lokey, Linda Mancini, Kim Burns, Ron Olson, Max Johnson, Fred McNairy, Gary Graham, Jay Barrett, Sue Cello, Doreen Sofarelli, and Diane Cracolici.

To represent the Altland estate as administrator, Adkins called on Reuben Jasper Dailey, an African American attorney from Asheville who had campaigned vigorously for Black rights in western North Carolina. In the late 1950s, he played a key role in the successful efforts to integrate Yancey County schools. Like the lawyers in the Chambers firm, Dailey knew how to take on the white establishment and win.[3]

As with most civil actions, the lawsuit named as defendants anyone and everyone connected to Stan Altland's death: Kermit Banks, Robert Banks, Erwin Higgins, Bill Arrowood, Horace Biggs, Paul Wheeler, and Larry Dean Cox, along with Forest Service employees Jack Olinger, Harold Rivers, Johnny McLain, and Blaine Ray. Terry Shankle, the state game warden who had encountered the group near the fish barrier, also made the list.[4]

The complaint described the campers as "young white persons of somewhat unconventional appearance," looking to spend a few days outdoors on their way to Charlotte. On the morning of July 3, when told by Shankle and Ray that they had camped illegally, the group obeyed orders to leave that site and moved to Briar Bottom. Some of them were sitting or standing around the campfire and others were in tents or sleeping bags that night when Banks and his men showed up.

In the unflinching language common to civil litigation, the plaintiffs charged that Banks and the others engaged in "unlawful, unprovoked, wrongful, and malicious conduct" and breached the campers' rights under the United States Constitution. The search at the campground had been warrantless and without cause, a violation of the Fourth Amendment. The sheriff and his deputies had pushed the defendants around, beaten them with billy clubs, and held them in Burnsville without formal arrest, actions that infringed on Eighth Amendment protections against corporal punishment and excessive bail. The campers invoked the Fourteenth Amendment, arguing that they had been denied due process and equal protection under the law, and pointed to the Ninth Amendment, which provides for protection of rights not specifically named in the Constitution.

Then came the charge that the group had waited almost two years to put before a court. During one of "these wrongful assaults upon one David Satterwhite, Sheriff Banks discharged his shotgun into the body . . . of Stanley W. Altland thereby inflicting great pain and suffering upon [him] . . . and causing his death." The lawmen "made no effort to provide immediate medical attention" for Altland and denied the other campers "an opportunity to render emergency aid." Instead, the officers "recklessly and callously" placed Altland's body in the bed of a pickup truck. Based on those actions, the suit also held Banks and the others responsible for the wrongful death of Stan Altland.

Adkins asked that Altland's estate be awarded $1.5 million in compensatory and punitive damages. Each of the other plaintiffs should receive $50,000 ($25,000 compensatory, $25,000 punitive), bringing the total to $2.35 million. Adkins filed the action on May 6, 1974, in the US District Court for the Western District of North Carolina, Asheville Division. The court assigned the case to Chief Judge Woodrow Wilson Jones.[5]

Jones had been a fixture in North Carolina jurisprudence and politics since the early 1950s. Born in Rutherfordton, he went to Mars Hill College and Wake Forest Law School. After a short stint in private practice, he worked as the Rutherfordton city attorney and later as Rutherford County prosecutor. In 1949, running as a Democrat, Jones won a special election to replace a recently deceased US congressman. He held that congressional seat until 1958, when he voluntarily stepped down. Afterward, he chaired the state Democratic Party and in 1967, President Lyndon Johnson appointed him to the federal court's Western District.[6]

Ordinarily, civil rights lawsuits move through federal courts at a glacial pace. Once the plaintiffs file the complaint, the court issues a summons to every defendant, who must respond within a set time frame. In their answers, or pleadings, the defendants explain why the suit should not go forward and usually make motions to dismiss the action. The judge then rules on the motions and, if the complaint stands, establishes deadlines for submission of all documents and a tentative trial date. From there, "discovery," or gathering relevant information about the case, begins. Only after those procedures are complete and all relevant documents submitted for review does the trial take place.[7]

At almost any stage, litigants can ask for amendments to the complaint, seek extensions, argue motions, and request rulings, all of which delay the proceedings. Given the time required to type and mail documents, serve summonses, and make official notifications in the 1970s, a typical civil suit might take years to resolve—that is, unless the presiding judge happened to be Woodrow Wilson Jones. As he told more than one defendant, "you are entitled to a speedy trial, and I intend to give it to you." Jones thought no civil action should take more than a year and no trial should last longer than two days. In court, he often pushed attorneys to shorten opening statements and summations. Lawyers working in the Western District nicknamed him "Move Along Jones."[8]

Two weeks after Adkins filed the complaint, Kermit Banks and the other six lawmen, represented by Burnsville attorneys Garrett Bailey and Robert Long, made the usual motions to dismiss the case. They claimed that the statute of limitations for filing suit had expired and that the federal court had no jurisdiction. They also made clear their intention to put the blame for what happened on a dead man. David Satterwhite, they insisted, had been engaged in "unlawful activities and first assaulted and struck the defendants," who then had to act. In the process a shotgun somehow just went off.[9]

Because Olinger, Rivers, Ray, and McLain had been employed by the Forest Service in 1972, they had their own lawyers. By the end of July 1974, they had submitted affidavits saying that none of them had been present at the campsite when the gun went off (though Rivers and Olinger had driven the lawmen across the river and waited near the vehicles). State game warden Terry Shankle, defended by a North Carolina assistant attorney general, noted that he had no contact with the campers after they went to Briar Bottom. Like Banks and the deputies, all the federal employees insisted that the applicable statute of limitations had expired.[10]

With his penchant for speed, Judge Jones heard the various motions in early August 1974. Two months later, he found the lawmen's claims about jurisdiction frivolous and threw out their statute-of-limitations argument, explaining that the applicable law allowed three years to file suit. Unless Bailey and Long could come up with something better, the Banks brothers, Bill Arrowood, Erwin Higgins, Horace Biggs, Larry Dean Cox, and Paul Wheeler would go to court. Jones calendared the case for February 1975.

When it came to the Forest Service rangers, the judge found that because they were federal employees, a different statute of limitations—one year—applied to them. Moreover, Jones explained, the plaintiffs had presented no evidence that any of the Forest Service personnel had engaged in a conspiracy to deprive the campers of their constitutional rights. Nor had Adkins offered any proof that Warden Shankle had been part of any such plot. Earlier, when questioned by the judge about the issue during oral arguments, Adkins had said that he hoped to develop conspiracy charges as the proceedings progressed. According to Jones, that had not occurred, and the judge summarily dismissed the complaint against Rivers, Olinger, Ray, McLain, and Shankle. They were off the hook.[11]

North Carolina newspapers took scant notice of those preliminary proceedings. Nixon's resignation and Gerald Ford's path to the presidency overshadowed almost everything else. In Yancey County, Kermit Banks ran for reelection, touting his recent "law enforcement training" at "numerous institutions" and reminding voters that "there is no substitute for experience and training in law enforcement." Although named as a key defendant in the pending civil rights lawsuit, Banks won the 1974 election by 700 votes, more than twice his margin of victory in 1970.[12]

While Ford settled in at the White House and Banks geared up for a second term, Karl Adkins worked at breakneck speed to comply with Jones's ambitious schedule. In consultation with his clients, Adkins came up with 113 interrogatories to be answered in writing under oath by the sheriff and his deputies. In addition to standard questions about occupation, income, and the like (used to assess punitive damages), the interrogatories asked all the defendants to recount what happened that night in Briar Bottom. Question 101 asked if they had discharged or knew who had discharged a "firearm . . . into the body of Stanley Altland."[13]

Written interrogatories are not the best way to get at the truth. Defendants compose their answers with assistance from their attorneys, and no one from the other side is present to judge body language, time of response, facial expressions, or anything else that might determine an answer's veracity. Depositions, taken in person, are far more effective. Depositions are also expensive, primarily due to the time involved and the need to pay a court reporter. With the ACLU and a few parents footing the bill, perhaps Adkins lacked the funds or the time to question the defendants in person. If he took depositions, they do not survive as part of the official court records.

As might be expected, the written responses added little new information. Sheriff Banks stuck to his story of Satterwhite threatening to kick his ass and attacking him. In the ensuing struggle, "Deputy Higgins' shotgun discharged" and after that the campers gave him no more trouble "except that they kept [the officers] from immediately getting to Stanley Altland." In response to question 101, Kermit Banks replied no, indicating that he did not shoot Altland and did not know who did.[14]

The deputies again closed ranks around the sheriff and tacked on a few embellishments of their own. They could smell marijuana. The campers had brandished hunting knives. Satterwhite had a "large and vicious dog." They saw a couple "embraced," a statement intended to suggest lewd behavior. Someone yelled "Fuck you!" the moment they arrived. A stereo sat on top of a car, playing "at high volume," something none of the neighboring campers saw or heard after 10:00 p.m.

Strangely enough, no deputy except Higgins said in writing, under oath, that he saw the struggle during which Satterwhite allegedly tried to take the sheriff's gun. Robert Banks only observed Satterwhite step toward his brother. Bill Arrowood said, "My vision was blocked." Larry Dean Cox noticed Sheriff Banks standing "in a group of five or six persons," but had trouble seeing anything else in the dark. Shortly thereafter, he saw only a muzzle flash. Paul Wheeler and Horace Biggs had gone to arrest the three men from Orlando and were not at the Clearwater site when the shotgun fired.

For his part, Higgins did not identify Satterwhite by name, but again noted that he heard "a tall individual" threaten the sheriff. Higgins grabbed the tall man with his left hand while holding the 12-gauge in his right with the gun "pointed toward the sky with the safety on." The weapon discharged during the struggle. In response to the question asking if they knew who shot Stan Altland, all six deputies, including Higgins who had just written that his shotgun went off, answered no.[15]

Karl Adkins knew that his clients and other witnesses could refute tales of loud music and noise when the officers arrived. Almost anyone out camping carried a knife and by all accounts, no one had tried to use one against Banks or the others. Sue Cello admitted that she had cursed the sheriff and screamed "Fuck you!" but only after the gun went off. And if Higgins, as he insisted both here and to the FBI, had been holding the shotgun pointed skyward, then how did a blast from his weapon hit Altland, who was standing upright eighteen feet away?

Adkins also used the interrogatories to probe the officers' qualifications and training. When Higgins and Bill Arrowood went to work as Yancey County deputies in 1969, neither of them had a high school diploma. The job did not require it. The Burnsville Police Department had the same policy. Kermit Banks graduated from high school but had "no formal training" in law enforcement when he became sheriff. Between 1969 and 1972, he took courses on police and civil procedure, Breathalyzer use, jail detainment, and other related topics; he completed a formal course on firearms in 1973, after the incident at Briar Bottom. By the time they responded to the interrogatories in 1974, Horace Biggs, Larry Dean Cox, and Paul Wheeler had all found new employment, further evidence, Karl Adkins thought, of the lack of professionalism in Yancey County law enforcement.[16]

Interrogatory 26 asked, "Were there in existence, prior to July 3, internal administrative procedures designed to prevent and correct instances of abuse of the authority of law enforcement officers of your respective department?" All seven respondents answered no.[17] As Adkins saw it, the deputies not only lacked education and experience, but also operated with impunity, subject only to the whims of Kermit Banks. Adkins thought he might successfully argue that to a jury, even in Asheville. If Move Along Jones had his way, the trial would begin February 11, 1975, a mere nine months from the day Adkins filed suit.[18]

A few days before the trial, Adkins got some much-needed assistance when Charles Becton, another African American attorney from the Chambers firm, joined the plaintiffs' legal team. Becton had grown up in eastern North Carolina and had never known his biological father. When his mother went to New York City for a better-paying job, Becton moved in with his aunt in Ayden, a small town in Pitt County. As a youth, he spent a lot of time around his grandparents and extended family near Morehead City, where he picked cotton and "headed shrimp" (pulled the heads off before the catch went to market) for commercial fishermen. He was no stranger to hard work.

Encouraged by his mother, aunt, and grandparents, Becton went to Howard University and then to Duke Law School, where he was the only Black student in his class. Active in civil rights demonstrations at Duke and around Durham, Becton met his wife while picketing an all-white country club that had excluded a Black Duke football player from the team's annual banquet. After a brief stint with the NAACP Legal Defense Fund in New York, Becton joined the Chambers firm in 1970. Though he came late to the Clearwater lawsuit, he had been well-briefed on the case by Adam Stein.[19]

Adkins and Becton met their seventeen clients in Asheville on Sunday, February 9, 1975. The two attorneys immediately began prepping the group for the trial scheduled to begin the following Tuesday. The Clearwater kids were older and more cynical now, hardened by their experience in criminal court, David Satterwhite's death, and the hurry-up-and-wait civil proceedings. They knew that no amount of money could bring Stan back. But as Phil Lokey put it, "We still owed it to him to do what we could and see this thing through to the end."[20]

The campers' stories remained strikingly consistent with what they had said to Julius Chambers in 1972. They had been doing only what might be expected on the Fourth of July: camping out, picnicking, drinking beer, and maybe setting off a few fireworks. The group had quieted down shortly after ten o'clock and "some of them were asleep." As Becton told me with more than a hint of sarcasm, "You know, if you're a sheriff going to quell a disturbance, you would expect to hear some noise." Then he added, "But this is how law enforcement dealt with kids like that." In a federal civil case, the standard of proof is 51 percent (in legal terms, "a preponderance") of the evidence. Put another way, is it more likely than not "that the defendant is responsible for the harm the plaintiff has suffered?" After hearing what the Clearwater kids had to say, Becton believed that, given a fair chance in court, his clients had "a good chance to prevail."[21]

Neither of the two Black attorneys knew it, but they would have to argue their case before a judge who had once been a hardline opponent of integration and African American rights. In 1956, during an otherwise unremarkable congressional career, Woodrow Wilson Jones had signed *The Declaration of Constitutional Principles*, a document written by Senators Strom Thurmond of South Carolina and Richard Russell of Georgia in opposition to federally mandated school integration. Popularly known as the "Southern Manifesto," it had denounced the Supreme Court's ruling in *Brown v. Board of Education* as an egregious abuse of federal power and called for employing "all lawful means to bring about a reversal of the decision."[22]

The original draft of the manifesto also included a fiery defense of segregation and a blistering condemnation of the justices, accusing them of making southern race relations worse by inciting Blacks to violence against whites. Tempered by constitutional lawyers like North Carolina senator Sam Ervin, who also signed the document, the final version made a more conventional case against the Court based on states' rights, arguing that the US Constitution did not mention education and therefore could not regulate it.[23]

Perhaps the future Judge Jones sincerely believed the constitutional arguments, but his congressional correspondence suggests that he opposed Black rights for other reasons. In June 1955, about a year after the *Brown* decision, Jones learned of a speech delivered by the Reverend James E. Dees, rector of Trinity Episcopal Church in Statesville. Speaking to the local chapter of the Lions Club, Reverend Dees had insisted that integration would inevitably lead to miscegenation and "blood fusion" of the races, something Dees deemed detrimental to Black and white people alike.

The rector also blasted the NAACP for being in league with known Communists and stirring up "race hatred [of whites] among the Negroes." Characterizing the Supreme Court as "incompetent men," Dees added that *"integration should never come"* and that African Americans who supported it would commit "racial suicide." When Congressman Jones learned of the speech, he immediately wrote Dees a congratulatory note and asked for a complete copy of the rector's remarks, adding, "It is a like a breath of fresh air to read of a minister who sees the fight to abolish segregation in its true light."[24]

Dees's speech reflected the views of many white North Carolinians at the time. Maybe Jones saw opposition to the *Brown* decision as a political necessity. He received and kept correspondence from the NAACP and other organizations urging him not to sign the manifesto. But if Jones ever responded favorably to any of those pleas, the letters never made it into his "Civil Rights" file. A year later, the congressman also spoke and voted against the Civil Rights Act of 1957, a bill that established the Civil Rights Division of the Justice Department—the branch responsible for investigating charges like those filed against Banks and the deputies. Perhaps Jones's views had mellowed some by 1975, as integration became a fact of southern life, but as Adam Stein succinctly put it, "He was our least favorite judge."[25]

All of that boded well for Banks and the deputies, but their lawyers still feared they might lose. Attorneys Bailey and Long launched one more eleventh-hour effort to get the suit thrown out. Whether by happenstance or by design, they targeted Reuben Dailey, the Black attorney from Asheville who served as the administrator for Stan Altland's estate. The defense lawyers argued that because Stan lived in Florida and died in Yancey County, the clerk in Buncombe County, where Dailey resided, had no authority to name him as an administrator.

On Monday, February 10, barely twenty-four hours before opening arguments, Robert Long went to the Buncombe County clerk's office and somehow secured an order vacating Dailey's appointment.[26] How he got that compelling order on such short notice remains a mystery. Did someone owe Long or the defendants a favor? Did law enforcement get preferential treatment at the clerk's office? Did someone not like Dailey's role as an activist African American attorney? Or did Long just have the good fortune and legal acumen to get the work done quickly?

Jones allowed the defense to tack on the new motion to dismiss on the grounds that Altland's estate had no legal administrator, but the judge's immediate reaction to the rescinding order is not clear. No formal ruling survives. Newspaper accounts noted that just before the trial began, "Judge Jones denied a defense motion to set aside the suit."[27] Perhaps that referred to the flap over Dailey. Or maybe given the time required to get the documents properly filed, Jones just delayed his decision and waited to see what the jury would do. The trial opened as scheduled on February 11.

11

We Know We're Right

On Tuesday morning Adkins, Becton, and their unconventional clients from a city 700 miles away trooped into a drab chamber on the third floor of Asheville's federal building. Seated across the aisle were seven clean-cut, white lawmen and their attorneys, all from nearby mountain counties. The small courtroom embodied the cultural conflicts that had torn America apart for a decade: urban versus rural, counterculture versus establishment, Black versus white, individual rights versus law and order. The *Asheville Citizen* saw it as "an almost classic confrontation between generations, between young people on vacation and intent on having a good time and older, more conservative law enforcement officers intent on upholding the law."[1] Woodrow Wilson Jones took his seat, banged his gavel, and jury selection began.

Every attorney at the Chambers firm knew how difficult it could be to seat a jury of their clients' peers. Becton recalled, "It was almost impossible to find jurors who were not white and middle-aged. We had trouble getting Black jurors, even for Black defendants." "[And] when we did," he joked, "we always seemed to get the same two Black people, a maid and a janitor in their sixties." Nor was it easy to find young white jurors who might be sympathetic to the plaintiffs in the Briar Bottom case. Many of Asheville's younger people were either in school, working, or had found other ways to avoid jury duty. As Becton explained, "Asheville, you must remember, was a much more conservative town in 1975 than it is now."[2]

Judge Jones's obsession with moving quickly did not help either. "A lot of our challenges [to potential jurors]," Becton recalls, "simply were not allowed."[3] Eventually the attorneys had to settle for eight men and six women (twelve jurors and two alternates), all white, all over thirty. One of the male jurors had longish hair and a mustache, but another was "the son of a Western North Carolina sheriff."[4]

In their opening statements, Adkins and Becton made essentially the same arguments Chambers and Stein had made in Burnsville: that their "young somewhat naive" clients were as quiet as anyone else staying at Briar Bottom on July 3, 1972. Primarily because of their appearance, the Clearwater kids had been unduly rousted by overly aggressive, uneducated, poorly trained country cops. But now, in civil court, the attorneys could question all the witnesses, including Kermit Banks, about the shotgun blast that killed Stan Altland.[5]

Kim Burns, by this time a junior in college, took the stand and identified each of the defendants by name. She said that Robert Banks had thrown her "against a tree and frisked her." She saw Larry Dean Cox "hit several campers with a billy club" and watched as Banks stuck his shotgun in David Satterwhite's stomach. She also testified that Banks told them, "You don't have any rights. You're animals." "[We] pleaded with them to put their guns up," Burns told the jury. "We were all very scared and upset." While Robert Banks searched her, Burns heard a shot. She turned around and saw smoke coming from Kermit Banks's weapon.[6]

In testimony that again mirrored what he told me fifty years later, Max Johnson said that after the shooting, he saw the sheriff reload a shotgun with smoke curling from the barrel. Phil Lokey witnessed Banks poke Satterwhite with the shotgun and heard Satterwhite ask the sheriff to put the weapon away just before it went off. Others confirmed Lokey's account and noted that Banks told no one why they were under arrest. Nor had the sheriff advised anyone of their rights until much later at the Yancey County Courthouse.[7] All the plaintiffs' witnesses insisted that none of the lawmen came to Stan's aid after the shooting. The deputies seemed more interested in holding the campers at gunpoint until Sheriff Banks decided what to do.[8]

During their aggressive cross-examination, Bailey and Long asked Kim Burns to describe the sheriff's shotgun. She could not say if it had one barrel or two. She also admitted that she did not see the weapon go off because her back had been turned while Robert Banks searched her. Max Johnson acknowledged that none of the officers struck him but insisted that, like Burns, he saw Larry Dean Cox beating another camper with a billy club. Asked about drinking at the campsite, Lokey said that he drank five beers during the afternoon and evening. Just as at the Burnsville trial, several others testified that they had nothing alcoholic to drink that night.[9]

By 1975, some of the male plaintiffs had more conventional haircuts, but Bailey and Long repeatedly asked if they had long hair and beards at the time of the raid. Like the prosecutors in Burnsville, the defense attorneys honed in on the sleeping arrangements at the campsite, again soliciting testimony that "some of the males and females were sleeping near each other . . . or in the same tent." All the while, Jones kept urging lawyers from both sides to "move along."[10]

Judges have every right to expedite proceedings, but Charles Becton believes that kind of statement "can bear heavily on jurors because it suggests that we're wasting time here, that the issues are already clear. Of course, we didn't think the issues were clear; that's what we were trying to do with our witnesses, bring some clarity." When court recessed late Tuesday afternoon, Jones issued the standard warning to jurors not to talk about the case and to avoid news coverage of the trial. He then added the obligatory "Now don't make up your minds about this until you've heard all the evidence."[11]

Shortly after court reconvened on Wednesday morning, Adkins and Becton rested their case. As expected, the defense moved for an immediate dismissal due to lack of evidence. Jones denied their request but did rule that the plaintiffs had presented no evidence to show that Doreen Sofarelli, Fred McNairy, or Diane Cracolici had their rights violated. The judge dropped their names from the lawsuit. The defense still had to answer charges made by the other fourteen campers.[12]

In their opening statement, Bailey and Long depicted the Clearwater kids as wild, loud, profane, and a threat to others staying in the campground. Kermit Banks testified that the dispatcher who took Rivers's call said that the young people were all drunk, and that the sheriff "would need all the help he could get" to deal with them. The officers went to Briar Bottom "in good faith," Banks claimed. They only intended to investigate a reported disturbance.

In his responses to the written interrogatories, the sheriff had said nothing about noise at the campsite, but now he testified that he heard "unusually loud hard rock music" along with "hootin' and hollerin'." The campers were "staggering around drinking beer" and some were "passed out on the ground." As expected, Banks put the blame for what followed squarely on David Satterwhite. The sheriff now said that when he bent down to inspect a knife lying on the ground, Satterwhite jumped him from behind and struck him hard in the face with his fist. At that point, Chief Deputy Higgins came to his aid.[13]

On cross, Becton and Adkins went after Banks hard, questioning his account of loud music and drunken campers, and noting that previous witnesses had testified that they were asleep when the posse arrived. More than once the attorneys accused Banks of hitting Satterwhite with the shotgun before it fired. The cross-examination got so heated, and Banks seemed so overwhelmed, Linda Mancini told me, that she almost felt sorry for him.[14] Under the withering barrage of questions, Banks admitted that he had to wake up some of the campers before arresting them, but insisted that they, too, were drunk. Some of them had already testified that they drank nothing and had requested Breathalyzer tests (which Banks refused to administer) to prove it. Stan Altland's toxicology report, showing that he had consumed at most two beers, also came into evidence.[15]

Chief Deputy Higgins, who did not testify at the Burnsville trial, had always been evasive about his role in the shooting, though he had told the FBI that his gun fired the killing shot. Now Higgins took the stand and under oath came up with yet another story to explain how his gun killed Altland. Fearful that David Satterwhite (who Higgins now identified by name) "was gonna get the sheriff's gun away from him," the chief deputy said he rushed up and seized Satterwhite's shoulder "with my left hand." The deputy held his shotgun in his right hand, with the barrel pointed up. Then, adding a potentially crucial new detail, Higgins said the two wrestled briefly and "then [he] and Satterwhite and all went down. . . . Then's when the gun discharged." And that is how, Higgins swore, that the shot from his weapon, which had initially been pointed skyward, struck Stan Altland standing upright eighteen feet away.[16]

Higgins stated again that the 12-gauge was "on safety" and that he had no idea how or why it fired. The deputy further testified that he did not realize anyone had been hit until he saw Altland on the ground. To back up Higgins's account, the defense called a ballistics technician from the SBI who said his tests indicated the shot came from the deputy's gun. Apparently, he did not produce the telltale pellets that might have proven it.[17]

On cross-examination, Adkins and Becton made it clear that they thought Higgins had concocted the story as a last-minute ploy to aid all the defendants.

Becton told me, "Once Higgins confessed to the killing in open court, the jury could not just ignore that testimony." Becton also explained that he had seen "similar false confessions" used "more than once" to exonerate white defendants accused of killing Black men. With David Satterwhite conveniently dead and no access to the FBI report, the plaintiffs could not rebut Higgins's account with testimony about the different clothes worn by Banks and his chief deputy.[18] That critical evidence never came into court. And having filed the wrongful death suit naming Banks as the shooter, the plaintiffs could not now change course and accuse Higgins of pulling the trigger. All the lawmen knew that Clyde Roberts would never indict any of them on criminal charges. Higgins could effectively take the rap for the sheriff and everyone else, and Becton believes that is precisely what the chief deputy did.

At the 1972 trial, Judge Gash had sustained objections to testimony about drug use at the campsite. Only Banks's statement that he smelled burning marijuana had been allowed. In Asheville, over strenuous objections from Adkins and Becton, Jones permitted defense witnesses to testify that drugs had been found at Briar Bottom "after the raid."[19] No one identified the substances, brought them into court, or linked them to any camper, but the judge's ruling again raised the specter of drug-crazed hippies throwing caution to the wind and attacking seven heavily armed men.

As part of the ongoing effort to blame David Satterwhite, Bailey and Long tracked down Clifton Whitley, the security guard who had killed the Mebane youth two years earlier. (This only fueled speculation among the plaintiffs that Banks and the deputies had a hand in Satterwhite's death.) The defense brought the elderly man to Asheville on Thursday and Jones had him testify "outside the jury's presence." Whitley recounted his experience with Satterwhite, noting that the young man had made "threatening moves" and had forced him to shoot, a questionable claim, but something the defense saw as evidence of Satterwhite's allegedly volatile nature. Perhaps Jones found the testimony too prejudicial, or maybe irrelevant since it had happened seven months after the campground shooting. Letting it come into evidence might have provided grounds for appeal. Whatever the reason, the jurors apparently never heard from Whitley. Later that day, Bailey and Long rested their case and followed with another pro forma request that the judge dismiss the suit due to a lack of evidence.[20]

At that point, Jones dropped Bill Arrowood and Paul Wheeler from the complaint. According to the judge, neither of them had done anything to deprive the plaintiffs of their rights and were not involved in Altland's death.[21] With that ruling, Jones had whittled the original list of twelve defendants, including the rangers and the game warden, down to five: Kermit Banks, whom witnesses saw holding the proverbial smoking gun; Erwin Higgins, who now claimed to have been on the ground wrestling with Satterwhite when the 12-gauge went off; Robert Banks, whom Kim Burns had accused of rough treatment and an unconstitutional search; Horace Biggs, who had been involved in detaining Phil Lokey; and Larry Dean Cox, whom several witnesses had seen beating campers with his billy club. The jury would decide their fate.

In civil cases, plaintiffs make the first closing argument. Then, once the defense responds, the plaintiffs, who have the burden of proof, offer a final rebuttal. Aware that Jones would not abide lengthy statements, Karl Adkins got right to the point. He dismissed Higgins's story as a recently fabricated lie, and again made the case for Sheriff Banks firing the shot. Stan Altland's father, Glenn, had been present throughout the trial, and the plaintiffs made sure he sat where the jury could see him. As Adkins wrapped up his closing, he pointed at Glenn Altland and said, "This man's son was wrongfully killed." Nothing could make up for that, Adkins continued, but the jury should think about and calculate "how much money his son's remaining 50 years of life would have been worth" and act accordingly.[22]

Equally mindful of Jones's impatience, the defense lawyers countered with a quick rehash of evidence they found exculpatory. Banks and the deputies had gone to the campsite only in response to Harold Rivers's desperate calls, something called into question at both trials and in the FBI interviews. They had properly identified themselves as officers of the law and acted in accordance with their sworn duties, a statement several witnesses, including the Greensboro campers, had refuted under oath and in statements to the FBI. David Satterwhite had attacked the sheriff and caused Higgins's gun to fire accidentally, actions also disputed by plenty of witnesses, including Satterwhite himself before his death. The defense pointed to the large amount of alcohol purchased in Asheville, the alleged prevalence of drugs, the youths' disheveled appearance, lack of respect for authority, use of profanity, and loose morals. The jury, Garrett Bailey said, had to decide whether to believe these Florida hippies or five trusted local officers. All peace-loving citizens had a clear obligation to support law enforcement.[23]

Charles Becton gave the plaintiffs' rebuttal and urged the jury to put aside everything else, including his clients' appearance, and just consider the facts.

When asked to leave their illegal campsite by the fish barrier, the Clearwater kids had complied. During the afternoon and evening, they were doing what most Americans did on the Fourth of July: listening to music, drinking beer, and perhaps setting off a few fireworks. By the time the sheriff got to Briar Bottom, things were quiet. Indeed, Banks and the other officers had admitted pulling several campers from tents and sleeping bags.[24]

In short, Becton argued, the sheriff and his men had no reason to barge into the camp with loaded shotguns, push the young people around, beat them with billy clubs, and create the chaos that left Stanley Altland lying in a pool of blood with a third of his chest and neck blown away. Whether accidental or not, the shot came from Banks's gun. He and the rest of deputies were responsible for the young man's death because of their reckless behavior. To cover up their responsibility for the killing, they had violated the group's constitutional rights by searching the campers and holding them in Burnsville without informing them of their rights or placing them under arrest.[25]

After the closing rhetoric, Woodrow Wilson Jones reminded the jurors that after considering the evidence, they only had to answer two questions: "Did the defendants or any of them, knowingly subject the plaintiff . . . to a deprivation of Constitutional rights by depriving him (her) of his (her) liberty without due process of law, or by an unreasonable search of his (her) person, or by imposing corporal punishment upon him (her) by an assault and battery as alleged in the complaint?" Second: "Was the death of Stanley W. Altland proximately caused by the negligent or wrongful conduct of the defendants, or any of them, as alleged in the complaint?" The jurors must answer each question with a simple "yes" or "no" based on a preponderance of the evidence. Further explanation would not be necessary. Just before 4:30 on Thursday afternoon, February 13, the jury retired to deliberate.[26]

Although Jones had winnowed the seven defendants down to five and dropped three plaintiffs from the suit, Becton remained cautiously optimistic. An hour passed, then two. The longer the jury stayed out, the better for his clients, he thought.[27] It was almost dinner time when the jury returned, not to render a decision but to ask two questions. First, they wanted to know "whether it was a violation of a person's rights, not to be read his rights at the time of arrest." That might suggest that the jury believed the campers' testimony about being roughed up and taken into custody without regard for proper police procedure. That hope vanished in the wake of Jones's emphatic answer. Advising the plaintiffs of their rights, widely known as the Miranda warning, pertained "only to the competence of evidence introduced in a trial," the judge said. It had "nothing to do with the issues in this civil suit."

A Miranda warning was and is a constitutional right when one is placed under arrest, though courts disagree as to exactly when it should be issued. Moreover, the lack of a Miranda warning might well mean that Banks had placed no one under arrest at the campsite and had, as the plaintiffs insisted, taken them to Burnsville and detained them at the courthouse in violation of their constitutional rights. Jones's ruling was at best dubious, but it might make a huge difference in how the jury decided the case.

The jurors then asked "if they could find the defendants guilty of violating the plaintiffs' rights, but not award damages." That, too, indicated that the jury believed the campers. Jones told the panel that they could find any or all the defendants guilty of rights violations and award any amount or nothing at all. Then he sent the jurors home with instructions not to talk about the case, and not to read the papers or listen to news broadcasts. Becton, Adkins, and some of their clients went out to dinner that night, edgy and more concerned, but trying to stay positive.[28]

Mid-morning on Friday, February 14, the jury announced that it had reached a decision. All told, they had deliberated for just over four hours. When Adkins and Becton got the word, they called their clients together and instructed them to show absolutely no emotion in the courtroom, no matter what the jury decided. Stomachs churned and hands shook as both sides awaited the outcome. Then, in a few seconds, it was over. Had the officers violated the defendants' constitutional rights? "No." Had Kermit Banks and the deputies caused the wrongful death of Stanley Altland? "No." Jones explained that the plaintiffs would "recover nothing of the defendants" and would have to pay "the costs of this action."[29]

Crestfallen, but heedful of Becton's instructions, the Clearwater group left the courtroom in stony silence. Across the aisle, the Banks brothers, Horace Biggs, Erwin Higgins, and Larry Dean Cox broke into wide grins as they congratulated each other and their attorneys. Kermit Banks told reporters, "I think the verdict was consistent with the evidence in the trial," then added, "You can't beat a good man." If the sheriff ever expressed regret or sorrow about Altland's death, the newspapers took no notice. Erwin Higgins said that he "felt good" and was "glad it's over." Questioned about whether the issue of who fired the lethal shot had finally been settled, Higgins stood by his testimony, stating only that he "never wanted to see anyone get killed."[30]

Once outside the building, Glenn Altland told the *Asheville Citizen* that he was "very disappointed in the verdict of the jury, but we have to accept it, I guess. That's the way the United States courts go." Another of the plaintiffs said simply, "We know we're right and we know they're wrong. . . . The jury just didn't believe us." Kim Burns seemed philosophical, but defiant. "[The decision] doesn't bother me," she declared. "[Kermit Banks] knows what he did. He's got to live with it."[31] As at the Burnsville trial, some of those in attendance offered support. When Phil Lokey got outside, several spectators told him, "You all got railroaded." He also recalls a reporter saying, "This is ridiculous. The sheriff must have family on the jury." Adkins and Becton filed notice of intent to appeal but eventually decided against it.[32]

The following Sunday, the *Charlotte Observer* ran a front-page story written by Ron Alridge, whose previous reporting had favored the Clearwater group. He recounted the entire case and the conflicting accounts of what happened in Briar Bottom. His story began with tired travelers struggling to find a campsite only to settle in at Briar Bottom, where they saw a good friend die a horrible death at the hands of an overly aggressive, inexperienced sheriff. Alridge ended on the plaintive note that David Satterwhite, who might have been a key witness in the civil suit, could not testify because he had been "shot between the eyes by an elderly security guard."[33]

That was enough for the *Yancey Journal* (formerly the *Yancey Record*) to break its silence on the case with its own front-page boldfaced headline: "Yancey Sheriff Not Guilty." (Never mind that the question in civil court was one of liability, not guilt beyond a reasonable doubt.) Written by Carolyn Yuziuk, the article attacked the *Charlotte Observer* as having "really done a job" on Yancey County and its sheriff by implying that Banks and the deputies were somehow at fault. Yuziuk saw nothing wrong with denying the campers access to public campgrounds, noting that one officer "actually ran them out of Mount Mitchell State Park with a .30-.30 rifle." Even though they were unwelcome, she wrote, the hippies had camped illegally and brazenly destroyed government property (again, the No Camping sign).

Once in Briar Bottom, they had created an "awesome disturbance." Yuziuk then explained that Harold Rivers "has forgotten nearly all of the circumstances surrounding his call" to the sheriff, an odd statement considering the assistant ranger had testified in court about his role in the incident. But "others" had reported that Rivers had been afraid of the campers and told Banks, "Send all the cars you can get!"

Citing more "unsung facts," Yuziuk declared that many of the campers had criminal records, and one had violated probation by leaving Florida, a reference to Fred McNairy, who had been given permission to travel to western North Carolina but not specifically to Yancey County. She also said, without attribution, that cocaine, barbiturates, amphetamines, marijuana, and LSD had been found at the Briar Bottom campsite in a warrantless search, a legal technicality that did not bother Yuziuk. And she believed that David Satterwhite got what he deserved because he had jumped at the security guard and threatened to throw him into a "log-debarker."

The volatile diatribe suggested that Yuziuk had been fed information by someone deeply involved in the case. Perhaps the *Charlotte Observer* got close enough to the truth to prompt a reaction from one of the lawmen or their attorneys. Yuziuk's story also asserted that the SBI and FBI reports, which had never been made public but had been seen by local solicitors, showed "absolutely no evidence" of campers being struck with "gun butts" and "billy clubs." Having seen ten of the FBI interviews, I knew that statement to be patently false. Implying again that those from off (except of course the Yuziuks) could never be trusted, she concluded that anyone who knew "one or all of the law enforcement officers involved" would understand "that justice was rightly served."[34] The trials might be over, but the cultural and generational tensions underlying Stan Altland's violent death showed no signs of going away.

12

Déjà Vu

On May 1, 1975, two and a half months after the Asheville civil court decision, the Rolling Stones climbed aboard a flatbed truck parked on Fifth Avenue in New York City. As the vehicle rolled slowly down the street, the band struck up "Brown Sugar" and announced another summer tour of North America. In Clearwater, it was one more painful reminder that life would never be the same. Phil Lokey said simply, "By then we knew it was all over. We had to go on, just do the best we could."[1]

It was not quite over for me. When I started looking into the Briar Bottom killing, I had hoped to crack the case, to discover some unknown twist or new piece of evidence that would reveal a hidden truth about Stan Altland's death—the kind of thing that often pops up in heavily edited true-crime television shows. As historians know all too well, real life is unscripted, unedited, and chaotic. It turns on peculiar circumstances and snap decisions that frequently bring unintended results. After a half century of thinking about the Clearwater case and two years of living with it, I had no big "reveal." I did have what I had set out to find: an unsettling scenario for one of those sketchily explained hippie deaths and an even more disturbing explanation for why the courts held no one responsible.

According to one historian, "Violence was so deeply woven into the fabric of 1970s America" that most citizens "accepted it as part of daily life."[2] As the Rolling Stones traveled across the nation during the summer of '72, chaos followed. At nearly every venue, rebellious young fans threw bottles, set fires, or smashed arena gates. They clashed with police wielding guns, clubs, and tear gas, eager to quell every nascent riot, real or imagined. Closing every show with "Street Fighting Man," the Stones whipped their young audiences into a frenzy as Jagger defiantly sang, "My name is called Disturbance / I'll shout and scream, I'll kill the king, and rail at all his servants." Alcohol and drugs, integral parts of youth culture, fueled the violence. That a Stones tour provided context for a young person's death should come as no surprise. It had happened before. But it would be wrong to blame the killing in Briar Bottom solely on the temper of the times.

At the Bungalows, Stan and his friends had grown accustomed to doing as they pleased. They were young, with little practical experience in how to negotiate life's challenges. No one took time to investigate potential mountain campgrounds or secure a site that could easily accommodate two dozen people. As Phil Lokey now acknowledges, "We believed we could find a place somewhere off in the mountains and just do our thing."[3] Instead, they landed in Yancey County, where, as in a lot of other rural communities, law enforcement had no tolerance for long-haired kids and their antiestablishment attitudes.

Psychologists tell us that somewhere in our distant past, we developed a near pathological fear of beings different from ourselves. Our instincts told us, "That which is like me is an extension of me and therefore safe and good. That which is not like me is not an extension of me and therefore unsafe and bad."[4] Some experts believe that this "fear of the other" stems from a more fundamental anxiety about the unknown, a phobia that profoundly affects human behavior. At some point in our evolutionary development, perhaps before we became truly human, apprehension about the unknown helped protect us, and it still survives somewhere deep within the human psyche.[5] Under the right circumstances, it can quickly turn anyone we perceive as different into an enemy.

To the state park ranger at Mount Mitchell, the Clearwater kids were never just ordinary campers looking for a place to stay. Their appearance and carefree attitude immediately marked them as outsiders and troublemakers. When they questioned his right to refuse them entry to a public site, they became a threat, one the ranger met with a .30-.30 rifle. My guess is that he immediately phoned Forest Service personnel at Black Mountain Campground to tell them that a hippie caravan was on the way. Blaine Ray and others at Black Mountain made the same assumptions, but initially showed more restraint. They just tried to get the hippies to go someplace else.

Enter David Satterwhite. It is easy to understand why the Clearwater contingent took his advice over that of the rangers. Satterwhite was one of them: long-haired, laid-back, confident in his knowledge of the area, and dedicated to having a good time—just the sort of person who would have been welcome at Bungalows parties. But when he took his new friends to Briar Bottom, he unwittingly put them in harm's way. Assistant Ranger Rivers had hoped that by dusk on July 3, the longhairs would be somebody else's problem. Instead, with his boss Johnny McLain away for the night, Rivers had to deal with them. That proved critical.

After the beer run to Asheville, the campers had plenty of alcohol to fuel the night's festivities, but not all the kids were, as Kermit Banks later insisted, passed out or staggering drunk. Lokey stated under oath that he bought fifteen to seventeen six-packs of beer and a couple bottles of liquor that afternoon. Satterwhite told the FBI that he brought three six-packs to share.[6] Even if the group consumed all twenty six-packs before the sheriff arrived, that works out to about four or five beers per person over the course of four or five hours, perhaps combined with a few shots of whiskey. The Greensboro campers drank some of the beer as did Paul Brayly, the Elon student. Two or three of those present knocked back enough alcohol to pass out or hunt rattlesnakes, but others were cold sober. All of that lends credence to something Sue Cello told the FBI, that most of her friends "drank enough beer to become 'laughy' and 'joyful,'" but were not so drunk as to be incapacitated or violent.[7]

According to the North Carolina statute in effect at the time, "The purchase, transportation, and possession of malt beverages and unfortified wine by individuals 18 years of age or older for their own use are permitted without restriction or regulation."[8] No state law prohibited those of age from drinking beer in Yancey County or anywhere else. The Yancey solicitors could not prove that anyone under eighteen had anything to drink that night. Aside from Poonie Porter, no one could legally consume liquor, for which the minimum age was twenty-one. If Banks and the solicitors wanted to push illegal alcohol consumption, they had better evidence for liquor than for beer, but they charged no one with violating that age restriction.

Without question, the group ignored contemporary laws against drug possession, but from all indications the campsite festivities that ended with

Altland's death centered mostly on booze. The Stones concert was still three days away, and several campers told me that they were saving their drugs for that event, something that seems more than plausible to anyone who went to a rock show in 1972. Aside from Banks claiming in court that he smelled "burning marijuana in the air," law enforcement produced no viable evidence that anyone at the campsite *used* drugs that night.

The campers' profanity became another bone of contention. By their own admission, Sue Cello and a few others cursed Banks at some point during the raid. But at the Burnsville trial, David Satterwhite testified that Banks told him to "put that goddamn dog up" and Joel LeFebvre said that officers trying to roust the Orlando campers shouted, "Come out, you son of a bitch."[9] North Carolina's newest disorderly conduct law did not prohibit swearing in public unless the offender clearly intended to provoke violence. If Banks planned to arrest the campers under the old law that had once banned public profanity, then he and his deputies also breached the statute that night. Setting aside the drugs which, after Poonie Porter's exploits, even solicitor Clyde Roberts deemed irrelevant, the Clearwater campers were, from a legal standpoint, guilty of perhaps setting off two or three firecrackers and, in a few cases, underage liquor consumption—offenses that hardly seemed to warrant a full-blown police raid with shotguns. Something else must have been at work that night.

As anyone who spends time in public recreation areas can affirm, such sites are always shared and contested ground. Nothing is more upsetting than neighbors with different ideas about how to enjoy the outdoors. The Clearwater group took up a lot of contested space in Briar Bottom, especially in the open area where they drank beer, rode a dirt bike, played football, and listened to rock music, all perfectly legal before 10:00 p.m., and all anathema to the families staying nearby. Typically, campers who find themselves at odds with others just grit their teeth, tolerate the tension, and it resolves itself as the night wears on. In extreme cases, a word to a ranger or supervisor will bring a warning that sets things right. In keeping with that ethic, several people complained to the rangers at Briar Bottom, but that is where the normal process for resolving campground conflict broke down.

When Harold Rivers went to the Clearwater site about 9:30 that night, he could have just asked the group to show some respect for their neighbors and settle down. Or he might have threatened to call the sheriff if they did not cooperate. He did neither. He stayed ten minutes and left, allegedly because he was alone, afraid, and unarmed, and had been instructed (he never said by whom) not to enter large groups alone at night.

In fact, he could easily have enlisted help. Jack Olinger was at Black Mountain campground; the two spoke just before Rivers went to Briar Bottom. Terry Shankle stopped by Rivers's house about a half hour earlier and, like all game wardens, Shankle carried a gun. Even without their assistance, Rivers might have waited until after 10:00, when quiet hours began, to see if the noise abated. Instead, he just stood in the dark and stared, apparently working up a healthy disgust for what he saw. He did not take similar action the night before, when other drunken campers played country music at high volume and partied well into the wee hours.

Time and again, in court and to the newspapers, the sheriff and rangers justified their actions against the Clearwater group with a telltale comment: "The hippies were trying to take over the campground."[10] Rivers and Banks wanted them out of that public space, not because of anything they had done, but because of who they were. Or, as Paul Brayly put it at the Burnsville trial, "for having long hair and just being there."

The raid might have been planned or at least contemplated well in advance of the phone calls. Both Olinger and Rivers had gone to the Forest Service office in Burnsville that morning. It seems likely that Banks or someone in his office heard about the hippie caravan well before noon. Rumors that the sheriff intended to "bust the campground" had circulated in Burnsville and at Briar Bottom that afternoon. Chambers and Stein found it odd that the Banks brothers, Horace Biggs, Erwin Higgins, and Bill Arrowood all just happened be near the county courthouse late on the eve of the Fourth of July, ready to deploy at a moment's notice. A premeditated raid would also account for the ready availability of five shotguns and six cars. Once in Briar Bottom, the deputies rousted the sleeping Orlando campers, an indication that someone, perhaps the sheriff, had decreed that anyone in a vehicle with Florida plates would be fair game.

Planned or not, Rivers's calls to Burnsville turned ordinary nighttime friction between campers into something potentially deadly. Kermit Banks was thirty-two years old, had been sheriff for only three years, and at that point had little formal training in law enforcement. Having been elected by a narrow margin, he could ill afford to appear timid or indecisive in dealing with a disturbance at a popular local campground. Out-of-town hippies had invaded Briar Bottom and poisoned the atmosphere with sex, drugs, and rock and roll. The sheriff apparently had no qualms about using plenty of firepower to take back the occupied territory.

It bears repeating that, whatever Banks's motives, neither he nor anyone else set out to kill Stanley Altland. That does not absolve law enforcement of responsibility. Even after Rivers's call, the sheriff and his men could have entered the campsite carrying only holstered sidearms. Those weapons would have been emblematic of Banks's authority and not likely to discharge unless someone intentionally pulled a trigger. The sheriff might have issued a warning about the noise and booze and threatened harsher action if he had to return. Instead, according to the campers, he and his men entered the campsite racking shotguns and swinging billy clubs.

Banks's rationale for those aggressive tactics—that he feared he might encounter a violent group like a motorcycle gang—just does not ring true. Olinger, Ray, Shankle, and Rivers had seen enough of the Clearwater crowd to know that they were not Hells Angels. Only Satterwhite had a motorcycle (a dirt bike) and, as a rule, outlaw bikers do not drive Volvos, Mazdas, Plymouth Dusters, Chevy Impalas, or VW vans, all of which sat parked in the field adjacent to the campsite. Exaggerated descriptions of camp knives and deadly snake sticks notwithstanding, neither the rangers nor the lawmen saw any of the Clearwater kids with a weapon.

We may never know for certain whose shotgun fired that night. The pellets taken from Altland's body apparently never showed up at either trial, even when SBI agents testified. If that agency still has a ballistics report, they are not about to release it to me or anyone else.

Here is what we do know. In a sworn, signed statement to the FBI and in court, under oath, David Satterwhite said that the man who hit him with the gun just before it fired was not in uniform. Banks testified at the Burnsville trial that he was "in civilian clothes," and had a badge pinned to his chest.[11] The FBI interviewed the sheriff one week after the shooting and photographed him wearing an outfit like the one Satterwhite described, along with a gray sport coat. Erwin Higgins told the FBI that he was on duty and in uniform when he got the call to go to Briar Bottom. He was also shorter and stockier than the sheriff. Satterwhite described the man who hit him with the shotgun as six feet tall with a slender build. It would have been difficult for anyone, including David Satterwhite, to mistake Higgins for Banks.

Of the four officers (other than Banks) present at the campsite when the gun went off, only Higgins said in writing, under oath, that he saw Satterwhite attack the sheriff, and only Higgins said that his gun fired. Every eyewitness who spoke with me had no doubt that Banks's weapon killed Stan Altland. When I questioned Poonie Porter, he still had a clear recollection of the sheriff slashing at Satterwhite with the 12-gauge and delivering the "butt stroke" that caused the weapon to discharge. Max Johnson is certain that he saw Kermit Banks reload a smoking gun. And try as I might, I could not shake Jay Barrett from his story, never heard in court, that he "saw Banks's gun go off and Stanley just go flying."[12]

Researchers have discovered that witnessing something traumatic triggers specific neurological responses in the brain that, in effect, burn the event into one's memory for life. One of the foremost experts on the topic writes, "People remember horrific experiences all too well," and those events "rarely slip from awareness." As years pass, witnesses may not recall some peripheral information, such as the exact time or day of the week that something happened, but they can usually recount the harrowing moment in uncanny detail. The sheriff's slashing motion, the smoke from his gun as he reloaded, Altland flying backward after the shot—those are exactly the sorts of things people remember vividly and accurately.[13]

Those same criteria might be applied to the sheriff's and deputies' recollections of that night—if I had them. I have only what they told the FBI, testified to in court, or provided in writing under oath. Those stories changed as the case unfolded. Over time, some of the lawmen added self-serving details such as "smelling marijuana in the air," hearing "unusually loud hard rock music," being threatened by a vicious dog, and Higgins's eleventh-hour assertion that he and Satterwhite fell to the ground just before the gun fired. Fifty years later, it all reads like an attempt to rationalize their actions after the fact.

Finally, and perhaps most important, I see no reason for the Clearwater kids to lie about whose gun fired. They sued everyone involved, including the rangers and game warden. The group could just as easily have fingered the chief deputy or any of the others as the shooter and achieved the same result. Yet they resolutely pointed to the sheriff.

In the end, it may not matter much whose weapon discharged that night. With Altland dead, the original plan to chase the hippies out of Briar Bottom had to be abandoned and the shooting had to be justified. The sheriff and the SBI agent went back to the campsite in search of drugs or other evidence to incriminate the campers. The lawmen never found it because Banks had not left a deputy at Briar Bottom to secure the scene, an oversight perhaps born of inexperience. That allowed Poonie Porter to dispose of whatever contraband he could find.

Lacking any admissible evidence of drug use, the sheriff and solicitors turned to the nebulous charge of disorderly conduct and tacked on the common police excuse of having been assaulted by unarmed suspects resisting arrest. The county medical examiner propped up their story, initially describing the killing as a "shotgun accident." Only later did he classify it as an "apparently accidental homicide." The signature bonds offered the defendants a powerful incentive not to return for trial. If they had stayed away, Stan Altland's death might have been written off as an unfortunate mishap for which his friends were responsible.

As Poonie Porter told the *Charlotte Observer* on July 4, the kids the sheriff arrested that night were "not a bunch of greaseball hippies." Several had "parents who were millionaires," and the others came from solid middle- or upper-middle-class backgrounds.[14] Some of those parents had the wherewithal to challenge the local authorities. Emma McNairy got the FBI involved. Other parents enlisted help from Senator Lawton Chiles. Banks also underestimated the Clearwater kids' determination to seek justice for Stan. Instead of staying in Florida, they came back with good attorneys and forced the matter into the courts.

As I sorted through the details of Altland's death, I could not help but notice parallels with the two other well-documented hippie killings from the same era. Paul Green, shot on the street in Ruidoso, New Mexico, had been in jail for what the town's archaic penal code defined as "lewd cohabitation." At both of the North Carolina trials, prosecutors and the officers' attorneys essentially leveled the same charge at the Clearwater campers, continually pointing out that unmarried couples slept together. The Ruidoso policeman also swore that he did not intend to kill Green. It was only when he allegedly tried to flee that the officer fired a "warning shot" that blew a hole in the young man's skull—a story not unlike Banks's statement that the Clearwater kids kept milling around and refused to be arrested.

Guy Gaughnor, a.k.a. Deputy Dawg, drank too much and made a pest of himself, behavior that paralleled that of several campers at Briar Bottom. Gaughnor also had long hair and wore ragged clothes, just like the kids from Clearwater. In Colorado, that was enough to get him killed. When the local marshal finally confessed, he hid behind tales of a drunken hippie who tried to take his weapon, a story almost identical to Kermit Banks's insistence that inebriated campers intended to kick his ass and take his shotgun. Likewise,

Clifton Whitley told Orange County prosecutors that David Satterwhite had threatened to throw him into a woodchipper.

Too often, it seems, when hippies died at the hands of rural lawmen, officers claimed they had no choice but to point a shotgun or pull a trigger. The threat of the other might be a new topic for psychologists, but a New Mexico reporter writing of Green's death clearly understood the concept. As he explained it, the violence against hippies reflected "a fear of the young, almost a paranoia toward the new and different that resulted in overreaction and senseless death."[15] It would be difficult to find a better explanation for what happened at Briar Bottom on July 3, 1972, or, for that matter, at Mebane Lumber seven months later.

All writers, especially historians, should be careful about making direct comparisons between past and present. As I often told my students, the obvious lesson of history is that things change. To quote the Greek philosopher Heraclitus, "No man steps in the same river twice, for it is not the same river and he is not the same man." Yet, in the spring of 2020, as I began research for this book, I had an uneasy sense of déjà vu. Vietnam might be behind us, but our national political discourse had again degenerated into little more than vitriolic name-calling. Then in Minneapolis, a white policeman arrested an African American named George Floyd for passing a bogus twenty-dollar bill. The officer pressed his knee on the Black man's neck for more than nine minutes, choking the life out of him, in front of witnesses, on a busy city street. A bystander with a cell phone filmed the killing.

When the video became public, Black and white Americans, mostly young and urban, took to the streets in protest. Groups like the ACLU and Black Lives Matter reminded the nation that scores of Black people had been killed by law enforcement officers who faced no legal consequences.[16] Others, like Ahmaud Arbery, the jogger in Brunswick, Georgia, had been gunned down by civilians reacting to nothing more than a Black man's presence in a white neighborhood.

As some of the demonstrations disintegrated into looting and violence, police countered with tear gas, rubber bullets, and flash grenades. Invoking language harsher than anything in Richard Nixon's public tirades, President Donald J. Trump threatened to sic "vicious dogs" on protestors and deploy the military to "beat the fuck out of them" and "crack their skulls."[17] A large segment of Americans, generally older, rural, and white, sided with the president, urging their fellow citizens to "back the blue" and support police as they beat back challenges to the existing order. Just as in 1972, young and old, Black and white, urban and rural, cops and protesters, were at each other's throats. The pervasive fear of the other was alive and well.

Thanks to videos shot by onlookers, those responsible for killing Floyd and Arbery eventually went to court and to prison. But activists and demonstrators insisted that those convictions were exceptions to prove the rule. It all reminded me of the Briar Bottom case, where no one had ever appeared before a grand jury for shooting Stan Altland, and David Satterwhite's killer had walked away from a murder charge.

I kept telling myself that 2020 was not 1972 and, Jimi Hendrix notwithstanding, most hippies were "young, white, and middle-class." Stan Altland and David Satterwhite had never faced the kind of racism and vigilante violence that African Americans have endured for centuries. That said, hippies *were* at odds with police and the establishment, and they frequently encountered discrimination based on their appearance. When the Clearwater Police arrested Stan Altland for obstructing traffic during the bicycle protest, they suggested—based solely on his looks—that he was a violent drug pusher. Elsewhere across the country, restaurants and businesses sometimes refused service to hippies. High school principals "routinely measured hair length" and "suspended thousands who failed to meet the [local] standard." As he campaigned for governor of California, Ronald Reagan joined Nixon and Wallace in declaring that hippies "dress like Tarzan, have hair like Jane, and smell like Cheetah."[18]

That kind of suspicion, prejudice, and dehumanization of the other has long been deeply ingrained in American police culture, and it endures to this day. Most states allow cops and sheriffs to apply "whatever force they reasonably believe is necessary to make an arrest or to protect themselves." The Supreme Court affirmed that standard, adding that the "reasonableness" of police action against civilians "must be judged from the perspective" of the "officer on the scene, rather than with the 20/20 vision of hindsight." Between 2005 and 2011, police reported 2,600 "justifiable homicides" to the FBI. (Data collected by the *Washington Post* since 2015 suggests that number may be too low by half.) During that same period, only forty-one officers eventually faced murder or manslaughter charges.[19] Small wonder that a county sheriff, a Burnsville cop, five deputies, and a security guard walked away from two killings in 1972.

As the recent debate over police tactics unfolded, a particular phrase caught my attention: "contempt of cop." Essentially it means failure to acquiesce and show proper deference when confronted by an officer. It is not an actual offense for which one can be arrested and jailed, but rather an assumption embedded in police procedure, a belief that an officer's authority is absolute and must never be questioned. Talking back, inquiring about tactics, or threatening to file a complaint, all of which fall under constitutionally protected free speech, can bring violent retaliation from law enforcement.[20]

During the summer of 2020, the California ACLU issued guidelines for "Black and Brown people" speaking to local authorities. Among those rules: "Don't disrespect a police officer. Although you have a constitutional right to do so, it could lead to your arrest or physical harm."[21] Closer to home, the *Asheville Citizen-Times* reported that the city's Black residents were far more likely to be charged with "disorderly conduct and resisting arrest" than their white counterparts. Those charges frequently served as cover for "what is deemed 'contempt of cop.' The officer doesn't like the person's attitude" and "makes up a criminal offense as punishment."[22]

That, too, sounded a lot like what happened at Briar Bottom. When David Satterwhite and other campers asked about their constitutional rights, Banks and his deputies became incensed, and the violence immediately escalated. "You're animals," the lawmen declared. "Animals don't have rights."[23] Minutes later, an errant shotgun blast killed an innocent bystander, a peaceful twenty-year-old who, ironically enough, had urged his friends to cooperate with the sheriff.

The deeper I followed the Clearwater case into the justice system, the clearer the connections with Black Americans' experiences seemed to be. The best available attorneys worked for North Carolina's only Black-run law firm. Julius Chambers and Adam Stein knew exactly what to expect in the Burnsville courtroom. They had seen similar tactics used dozens of times against African American defendants. The attorneys got eighteen of their twenty clients acquitted or released for lack of evidence. Judge Gash tossed law enforcement a bone by convicting the only two campers that prosecution witnesses could identify.

As Harper Lee wrote in *To Kill a Mockingbird*, "The one place where a man ought to get a square deal is in a courtroom, be he any color of the rainbow, but people have a way of carrying their resentments right into the jury box."[24]

At the Asheville civil trial, seventeen of Stan Altland's friends, *not a single one of whom had been convicted of disorderly conduct in criminal court*, made their case to an all-white jury of local citizens over age thirty. The young people and their two Black activist attorneys, one of whom had a white mother, went before Judge Woodrow Wilson Jones, who had once been a Rutherford County prosecutor and, while in Congress, an ardent segregationist.

Though Jones was careful not to overstep, his most important rulings favored Banks and the deputies. He allowed testimony about drugs and ruled that the failure to issue a Miranda warning did not infringe on individual rights. Those decisions paved the way for the officers and their attorneys to employ the same "back the blue" defense that resonates with many white Americans today. When Garrett Bailey wrapped up his closing argument in Asheville in 1975, he told the jury, "The question is 'are we going to support our law enforcement officers?'"[25] As usual, the answer was yes.

The parallels with modern Black experience were not lost on the Clearwater campers. Linda Mancini told me that her experience with the judicial system after Stan's death "taught me a lot. Injustice really makes me mad. I had a lot of sympathy for Black Lives Matter because I know what it's like to be powerless against the police." Phil Lokey added, "Once you've been in that position, it changes your perspective on the whole thing."[26]

When I set out to investigate the Briar Bottom incident, I had no idea that I would finish by writing about African Americans and law enforcement. My subjects were about as white as they could be, and the killing took place in a county with fewer than 200 Black residents. As a historian, I should have known better. Race is always a crucial factor in American society. That it played a central role in this case is even more proof—as if we needed it—of the need to eliminate racism from law enforcement and the court system. But, as the death of a middle-class white kid like Stan Altland suggests, rooting out racist cops and judges, while vitally important, probably will not solve the problem of unwarranted police violence.

Proposals for reforming modern cop culture abound. Most plans call for hiring more women and minorities and recruiting college graduates to be trained as officers, all of which get greater emphasis now than in the 1970s. The US Department of Justice promotes "de-escalation training" for police and sheriffs to help them defuse potentially violent confrontations with suspects.[27] Still, the killings continue.

Rosa Brooks, a Georgetown law professor who also worked the streets as a cop in Washington, DC, believes that nothing will change until Americans rethink a basic premise of law enforcement work. She argues that the single biggest reason cops kill innocent people is that "everything in police training and culture" tells officers "to expect danger from every quarter" and "respond to threats instantly," because "they have a right to go home safely at the end of the day." Instead, Brooks suggests, police and sheriffs should be trained to focus more on protecting their fellow citizens, not themselves. Cops should be taught to exercise caution in all circumstances but recognize that "they are voluntarily taking a risky job and that if someone dies because of a mistake, it is better that it be a police officer who is trained and paid to take risks than a member of the public."

Such a shift in training might well result in more law enforcement fatalities but, as Brooks explains, no one tells American soldiers, also charged with protecting the US citizenry, that they have a right to go home safely. We recognize and celebrate their willingness to sacrifice their lives for our protection. When it comes to police work, that is radical thinking, but it might bring with it a court system more inclined to hold officers accountable when an innocent person dies. In turn, if police and sheriffs understand that they face swift punishment for unnecessary aggression, they might be less inclined to swing a shotgun, pull a trigger, or put a knee on a suspect's neck without cause.[28]

Those kids from Clearwater made mistakes. To use the vernacular of the seventies, they let "their freak flag fly," with little concern for the consequences. But at almost every turn, a different approach by the rangers and the sheriff, arguably the adult professionals on the scene, could have made a difference. What if Harold Rivers and Terry Shankle (with gun in holster) had gone to speak with the campers and urged them to quiet down before calling the sheriff? What if Kermit Banks had taken one or two deputies to Briar Bottom and entered the campsite carrying only sidearms? What if they had first spoken to Poonie Porter, Stan Altland, or another individual, called the campers together, and asked for compliance with local regulations and campground rules? What if Banks and Clifton Whitley had just ignored a mouthy, beer-buzzed kid instead of deciding to punish David Satterwhite for contempt of cop? What if the sheriff and his deputies had focused on protecting *everyone* in Briar Bottom, including those Florida hippies?

Given the tenor of the early seventies, perhaps that qualifies as nothing more than idle speculation, the sort of 20/20 hindsight that the Supreme

Court finds useless. As Richard Rosen, Julius Chambers's biographer, told me, "In those days, the cops always went in with overwhelming firepower and brute force. De-escalation was not part of their thinking. They figured the courts would protect them."[29] Some things in law enforcement have changed for the better since 1972, but we still live with that legacy of violence and lack of accountability every time an officer answers a call.

That is the essential lesson of the Briar Bottom case. Roger Altland put it this way: "It was bad enough that they killed Stan for no reason, but we still believed in the system. We thought if we talked to the right people and took the cops to court it would all work out."[30] Instead, they got a hard lesson in the selective application of American justice, something countless other marginalized citizens encounter every day. More than a half century later, the pain of Altland's senseless death has not gone away. As one Clearwater camper said while choking back tears during an emotional phone call, "Every time I hear a Rolling Stones song, I think of Stan."[31]

EPILOGUE

Back to Briar Bottom

On a postcard-perfect summer day, exactly fifty-one years and one week after Stan Altland died, I join another three-car caravan driving toward Mount Mitchell. No Volvos, Mazdas, VW vans, Chevy Impalas, or Plymouth Dusters this time. Roger Altland sits in the passenger seat of my Toyota. Phil Lokey, Max Johnson, and Ron Olson follow in a Jeep and a Subaru. They have come back to Yancey County one more time, hoping to make peace with the past.

After a brief stop to photograph the courthouse in Burnsville, we drive out on 19E and turn onto Highway 80. We pass through Micaville, where Kermit Banks picked up Paul Wheeler and Larry Dean Cox enroute to Briar Bottom on July 3, 1972. From there, we start up the South Toe River valley toward the Blue Ridge Parkway. For Phil, Max, and Ron, it is the first time they have driven this route since Stan's death. Roger, who was hitchhiking from Knoxville to Charlotte at the time, has never been here.

A few minutes later, we pull into the parking lot of that first country store I visited during the early stages of my research. I do not have to wait long for a reaction. "This is it," Phil Lokey says excitedly. "Man, I can't believe it. This is it. This is where we met David Satterwhite." We take note of the abandoned

Left to right: **Ron Olson, Phil Lokey, and Max Johnson
at Mount Mitchell State Park, 2023.**
Photo by the author.

original building and some ancient gas pumps that look like they might be
from the 1970s, but Phil explains, "None of these houses were here then.
This was the middle of nowhere."

The man I tried to talk with before is not in the new store today, but the
decor has not changed much. The Confederate flag is smaller now and hangs
beneath an American flag; the pool table and other paraphernalia seem the
same. We grab some bottled water for the road and talk briefly with the clerk.
Max and Ron tell her that they were here back in 1972, and she notes again that
the store has been in the same family for generations. She does not care to hear
more. We are like a thousand other people from off who stop in every summer.

We turn onto the parkway and drive sixteen miles to NC Route 128 that
winds up Mount Mitchell. I remind Roger that it was after sundown when
his brother and twenty-three friends traveled this road a half-century earlier.
Near the top, at the entrance to the small state park campground, we stop.
A sign says "Full. No Sites Available." That seems fitting, as Phil, Max, and
Ron recount the story of the ranger with the .30-.30 rifle who ran them off
on that July evening. Ron notes that it was the first time anyone had pulled
a gun on him. It would not be the last.

We drive back down the parkway to Route 80 and take Forest Service Road 472 toward Black Mountain Campground, passing a golf course and scores of luxury homes built since 1972. Once the pavement ends, I pull over not far from the campground entrance where the group stayed on July 2 before going to Briar Bottom. The fish barrier is long gone, save for a few barely distinguishable remnants that somehow survived the frequent flash floods. The area along the road is overgrown with trees and rhododendrons, and instead of "No Camping," the signs—now made of metal but still attached to wooden posts—read "No Parking Any Time."

A short path takes us through the woods to the river. After a moment or two Max says, "Yeah, I'm pretty sure I jumped or waded into the river somewhere around here that night." Phil and Ron seem less certain, but once we walk around a bit, they agree. I mention the demise of the No Camping sign. They believe they know who chopped it down. "A couple of the people on the trip . . . we didn't know them really well. It was a stupid thing to do. The rangers could have made us pay for it, but they didn't. They just kept bringing it up in court."

We drive across the bridge to Black Mountain Campground. As always at this time of year, Briar Bottom is packed. One of the group sites has the maximum fifty occupants. I ask if anything looks familiar. "A lot more trees than I remember," Phil says. The others nod. I point out the modern facilities—picnic shelters, flush toilets, charcoal grills, and well-maintained tent sites. They all look a little lost as we walk toward the old river ford. There you can still see vestiges of the open field that served as the parking area in 1972.

Ron is the first to react. "You know, I think this is it. We didn't drive far once we crossed the stream. We left our cars in the field, probably just up there, and set up camp in the trees back by the river." That area is now a thick tangle of stumps, smallish timber and rhododendron thickets, evidence of flooding and major campground renovation over the last half century. Maybe thirty yards away, a few giant oaks, poplars, and eastern hemlocks still stand around the grassy area. I think of the "witness trees," preserved on Civil War battlefields, that survived the carnage at Antietam and Gettysburg. Whether we have the exact spot or not, these trees, obviously more than fifty years old, were here the night Stan Altland died.

I hang back a little, allowing Roger and the others time to take it all in. Phil walks out of the woods and gestures to the left. "If we're close to where we camped, the sheriff and his men came from that direction. They had flashlights. I will never forget the sound of them racking those shotguns." Roger wants to know where his brother stood. The others do the best they can to re-create the scene amid all the recent forest growth.

Max recounts hearing the 12-gauge go off and seeing Banks with the smoking gun, again saying, "I saw him reload." Ron faces the open field and points to the right. "I was in my tent somewhere down there when the gun fired. Then they came and got me up." Phil shows me how David Satterwhite pushed Banks's shotgun aside several times and recalls how "freaked out" the deputies were as Stan lay on the ground bleeding out. "I was just sitting there waiting for one of them to shoot me. I remember wondering if it was going to hurt when I died."

The four of them go back into the trees around "the site." I wait alone by the campground road and contemplate what I read about human memory, that we can recall specific moments in vivid detail but find it more difficult to construct a linear narrative of those episodes. Over the last few months, as I pushed to finish my linear narrative, the events at Briar Bottom took on an abstract quality. I focused on solving conceptual problems: what should go in which chapter, how much evidence is enough to prove my point, and just today, how to deal with the uncertainty about where the group camped that night.

I am still mulling that over when the others rejoin me. They now look a bit shaken. One of them has been crying. Whether we have found the actual 1972 campsite suddenly seems a lot less important. Whatever problems it creates for me as a writer, human memory provides a powerful reminder of what brought us here in the first place: a young man's needless, violent death and the lives forever altered in its aftermath. Roger snaps me out of it. "Let's go eat lunch." Children ride by on bicycles; some preteens play Spikeball near one of the restrooms; campers walk by with their dogs. Now, as in 1972, the world keeps turning, trees keep growing, and life goes on, in Briar Bottom and everywhere else.

After the Asheville civil trial, Kermit Banks served three more terms as Yancey County sheriff until 1986, when a federal investigation uncovered voting irregularities in western North Carolina. As word spread that Banks might be a target of the FBI probe, he narrowly lost his bid for another term that November. A month later, a federal grand jury indicted him on "one count of conspiracy, five counts of mail fraud, three counts of vote-buying, and one count of offering to buy votes." If convicted on all charges, he potentially faced fifty years in prison and $35,000 in fines.[1]

The campsite at Briar Bottom, 2023.
Photo by the author.

On March 12, 1987, after deliberating for less than an hour, an Asheville jury found the ex-sheriff not guilty of mail fraud and attempting to buy votes. Afterward, the jury foreman said, "From the bottom of our hearts, we believe we came up with the right decision." Acknowledging that Banks had helped some voters fill out absentee ballots, the foreman explained that "it appeared he was helping with the ballots out of friendship and not for personal gain." Outside the courthouse, thirty or so friends and family celebrated the verdict.[2]

Banks still had to answer for conspiracy and six counts of vote buying, but this time he did not face a jury. He took an Alford plea, a legal maneuver that allowed the sheriff to proclaim innocence even as he acknowledged that the prosecution had enough evidence to convict him. In May 1987, federal prosecutors accepted the plea for one misdemeanor count of vote-buying. A judge fined Banks $1,000 and gave him a one-year prison sentence suspended for three years, during which time he could not carry or possess a gun. Robert

Long, the attorney who defended Banks during the campers' civil suit, helped negotiate the plea deal, including the three-year probationary period that ended before the next election. A sheriff's deputy from Buncombe County, who served as a character witness, told the judge, "If they ever was [*sic*] an honest sheriff, a qualified sheriff, it's Kermit Banks."[3]

Apparently, the voters of Yancey County agreed. Banks ran again in 1990 and won, amid more reports of fraudulent absentee ballots and rumors of convicted felons voting while on probation.[4] He remained in office until 2009, when he retired and appointed his son Gary Banks to fill the position. Gary won election in 2010 and held the office until January 2021, when he resigned and appointed his chief deputy, Shane Hilliard, to the post. Hilliard won election in 2022 and is currently Yancey County sheriff. According to my sources, Hilliard married into the Banks family. As far as I know, Kermit Banks still lives near Burnsville and his brother, Robert, also resides in the area. Robert's son, Seth Banks, is district attorney for the Thirty-Fifth Prosecutorial District of North Carolina. That district includes Madison, Avery, Mitchell, and Yancey counties, as well as my home county, Watauga.

Danny McIntosh, my Yancey County guide and confidant, knows the machinations of local politics and law enforcement well. He ran against Banks for sheriff in 2002 and lost. As he describes it, "They keep winning and the margins get bigger every time." Now retired from full-time public service, Danny remains active in civic causes and community promotion. As he told me more than once, he spends a lot of time thinking about "how we got here" in terms of "history, politics, religion, and education." He and his wife Sharon live in Burnsville, as they have all their lives.

I share some of what I know about the county's recent history with Roger and his friends over lunch at the house they rented for this trip. It is close to Briar Bottom, near the golf course, with a gorgeous river view. No one is sleeping on the ground this time. As talk turns to the Burnsville and Asheville trials, I note that they were represented by some of the best attorneys in North Carolina, all of whom went on to distinguished careers.

Julius Chambers became director-counsel of the NAACP Legal Defense Fund in 1984. He left that position in 1993 to serve as chancellor of North Carolina Central University, his alma mater. In 2001 he retired from the chancellorship and returned to his old law firm. He died in 2013.

Ever the legal activist, Adam Stein became well known for his work in developing North Carolina's defense services for indigent clients. He also helped found the state's Center for Death Penalty Litigation, an organization that, among other things, provides legal representation for defendants on death row. Adam lives in Chapel Hill. His son, Josh Stein, is currently attorney general of North Carolina and a Democratic candidate for Governor in 2024.

In 2005, North Carolina governor Mike Easley appointed Karl Adkins to a superior court judgeship. In May 2022, as Adkins left his house to play golf, he suffered a bad fall, and died a short while later. Charles Becton went on to become a court of appeals judge and the first African American president of the North Carolina Bar Association. He served as interim chancellor at North Carolina Central University and then at Elizabeth City State University. He lives in Durham.

Phil Lokey talks at some length about Chambers and how, when he read their written accounts of events before the first trial, he thought they had all collaborated or "cheated" because the narratives were so consistent. "That's because we were telling the truth," Max Johnson interjects, adding, "I don't trust anything anymore. That was the first time I ever heard the term 'mountain justice.' Now I know exactly what it means." I submit that it might well be called "American justice," then and now.

<hr>

They ask if I ever got to see the Rolling Stones. I did—in 1975, and again in 1978. Max remembers going to the '75 and '89 shows in Jacksonville; he's not sure how many Stones concerts he has been to over the years. Roger, Phil, and Ron have seen them several times, too. None of us can explain our enduring fascination with the band, but we agree with Phil's observation: "They just keep rockin'." Not long after I started working on this book, the Stones played in Charlotte, minus their recently deceased drummer, Charlie Watts. They released a new album of original material in October 2023 and are scheduled for yet another summer tour of the United States in 2024. Nothing, not even the relentless passage of time, stops the Stones.

As the afternoon starts to slip away, we talk about what happened to others on that ill-fated camping trip. Some faced a lot of problems that sometimes go with adult life: divorce, addiction, brief incarceration, failing mental health. How many of those difficulties stemmed from that traumatic night in Briar Bottom will forever be an open question. Poonie Porter, Sandra Drucas, Gary Graham, Fred McNairy, Jimmie Seifert, and half a dozen others are dead. No one is sure about Cathy Siebenthaler. The group eventually lost touch with her and a couple of other girls.

Jay Barrett moved about as far away from central Florida as he could get. He now lives and works in Cheyenne, Wyoming. "Stanley's death changed my life forever," he told me. "I still wish I could have testified." Kevin Shea, erstwhile rattlesnake hunter, resides near Clearwater, as do Doreen Sofarelli Ryan and Diane Cracolici.

Marty Watkins, who did not return for the Burnsville trial, jokes that she is "still a fugitive," even though Judge Gash's warrant has long since expired. Affected deeply by Stan's death, Marty earned two college degrees and became a strong advocate for criminal justice reform. She worked for more than three decades in a Pinellas County program that helps get drug and alcohol offenders sent to rehab instead of jail.

Kim Burns Newgard graduated from the University of South Florida with a degree in education and later worked for Verizon. She lives in Holiday, Florida. Linda Mancini earned an MA in sociology at the University of South Florida and worked for a time in the mental health profession. She also had a long career with Nielsen Media Research as a research director. Now retired, Linda lives in Tarpon Springs, where she volunteers at a no-kill animal shelter and with the local Democratic Party.

Sue Cello went to culinary school in New York City and enjoyed thirty years as a successful Florida restaurateur. She retired in Clearwater and spends her time working with the Humane Society and supporting a local food pantry. As spirited as ever, she says that, after what happened at Briar Bottom, she has "no time for intolerant people and [doesn't] care who knows it."[5]

I ask those around the table how they feel about the whole thing now. Max Johnson smiles. He has fond memories of those days at the Bungalows: "Best time of my life." But "after Stan got killed, things started to come apart. We all eventually moved out. That whole thing changed us. It left scars. For the first time in my life, I no longer felt safe." Max worked for several decades as an auto mechanic, a skill he learned from his father. Now he writes service for a dealership, communicating with customers, working on estimates, seeing that the right work gets done quickly. Some of his clients have been with him for years.

Ron Olson says, "I still can't believe all this could happen just because of our looks." At the two trials, he "could not believe all the untruths that came out. Going through this can change the way you perceive things in life." Ron worked for twenty-five years in risk management with Dollar Car Rental and also had a part-time job unloading UPS planes for various subcontractors. He now resides in Palm Harbor, Florida.

Roger Altland had several jobs over the last few decades, including trucking. He also worked with Home Depot, selling overstocked building materials to contractors and various other individuals. He and his wife Debbie live in Palm Harbor. "I think today brought me some closure," he notes. "I promised myself that someday I would visit the spot where my big brother died. I needed to see it."

Phil Lokey sits quietly for a moment before he says, "After all that was over, I went home, cut my hair, and went into my old man's car business. Always knew that's where I would end up. Just got there quicker than I thought." Phil soon became one of the most successful automobile dealers in central Florida. Also retired, he lives in Clearwater but travels the country and the world with his wife.

It is late. Knowing that I have the "can't get there from here" drive back to Boone ahead of me, I thank them for their time, and they walk me to my car. Just as I am about to leave, Phil says, "I told my wife that wherever we were, whatever we were doing, I was going to be here with Roger, Max, and Ron today. I feel reunited. I'm still a hippie." A few minutes later, out on Forest Service Road 472, I cue up my Rolling Stones playlist. The first strains of "Gimme Shelter" spill from the car speakers. I open all the windows and turn it up. Loud.

ACKNOWLEDGMENTS

This book is unlike any other I have written, and it required a lot of help. First and foremost, I am grateful to those surviving Clearwater campers who allowed me to tell their story. For their time and willingness to engage a meddlesome writer, I thank Kim Burns Newgard, Sue Cello, Marty Watkins, Doreen Sofarelli Ryan, Diane Cracolici, Donald "Jay" Barrett, Kevin Shea, and Mark Goodpasture. When I spoke with Donald "Poonie" Porter, his health was failing, but his razor-sharp recollections and poignant assertion that he "had waited fifty years for a phone call like this" provided both information and inspiration. I wish he had lived to see the book completed.

Max Johnson, Ron Olson, and Phil Lokey deserve special mention, not only for sharing their memories, but also for making a 1,400-mile round trip at their own expense to revisit Briar Bottom. And none of this would have been possible without Roger Altland and Linda Mancini, both of whom spent endless hours with me on the phone, helped secure illustrations, and served as travel agents and tour guides for my trip to Clearwater. Linda read the whole draft manuscript, and her keen eye saved me from countless mistakes. Roger and his wife, Debbie, arranged the reunion of campers at Lucky Dill. Roger organized and joined the excursion to western North Carolina and chased down the transcript from the Burnsville trial.

Interviews with Adam Stein, Rich Rosen, and Charles Becton helped me sort out the details of the Burnsville and Asheville trials. Despite Chip Clark's insistence that his advice was "worth every penny I was paying for it," he read all my stuff pro bono and tutored me in the basics of criminal and civil law. If I got anything wrong, it is my fault, not his. Charles Brady,

Jeff Hedrick, Jeff Young, and Hugh Stevens also provided help with legal issues.

Of all those involved with the arrest and prosecution of the campers, only Tom Rusher agreed to speak with me. I hope he knows how much I respect him for that. I would have never seen any of the FBI interviews without expert assistance from Patricia Bandy in Congresswoman Virginia Foxx's office, and Marie Maxwell at the National Archives and Records Administration. That I know anything about Yancey County is owing to Danny McIntosh's warm friendship and unflagging efforts to help someone "from off" understand the place he knows so well. I also thank the other Yancey County residents who spoke with me, on and off the record.

Any time I put my fingers to the keyboard, I depend on colleagues from the History Department at Appalachian State to keep me on track. As usual, Michael Krenn, Jim Goff, Jim Winders, Mike Wade, Judkin Browning, and Bruce Stewart made sure I stayed faithful to the historical record. Three more academic colleagues and fellow outdoorsmen—David Perry, Dan Pierce, and Richard Starnes—heard far more than they wanted to about this book, especially during the summer of 2022, as we drove cross-country to spend a week flyfishing in Yellowstone National Park. Joan Cashin, a colleague in Civil War and environmental history at The Ohio State University, read and critiqued every chapter, making my work much better in the process. Mart Stewart has long been my "intellectual roommate" and has read parts or all of everything I have written, including this book.

Joni Carter Robison, Tony Wall, and Steve Huffman kept me honest about teenage life during the early seventies. Marshall Stephenson talked with me at length about his friend, David Satterwhite. Gary Parrish, now a professional surveyor, and Mike Gilliam, both friends from my senior year in Burlington, spent an entire afternoon helping me figure out how those Clearwater kids got into Briar Bottom in 1972. Gary, along with Doug Gilliam and Rice Strange, two other camping comrades, read various parts of the manuscript, offering encouragement and advice. Fr. Andrew Hege, Rector of St. Mary of the Hills Episcopal Parish, a fine scholar and writer in his own right, took time out from his incredibly busy schedule to read my work and talk about how to improve it.

Although I knew that I would eventually write about Stan Altland's death and its aftermath, I did not know if that story could ever become a book. Fortunately, I landed in the capable hands of Lucas Church, executive editor at the University of North Carolina Press. His instincts for storytelling and savvy critiques of my prose guided me every step of the way. Lucas steered my book proposal and draft manuscript to Blake Perkins and one other anonymous reader, whose thoughtful suggestions made the finished product much better than it might have been. Thomas Bedenbaugh's assistance with illustrations and rigorous copyediting by Erin Granville and Matthew Somoroff also served me well.

Finally, I thank my family. My sister-in-law, Catherine Tribby, perused my earliest efforts and insisted that I forge ahead. Ned Taylor, my brother-in-law and a Florida native, read the whole manuscript and accompanied me on a midwinter trip to Briar Bottom to inspect the scene of the shooting. My wife Cathia, who reads more books than anyone I know, devoted considerable time to this one, offering thoughtful critiques from the perspective of a general reader and encouraging me to take the risks that this kind of work involves. Our daughter Julianna also lived through "Dad's retirement project." As always, with their grace, love, and steadfast support, I soldier on.

NOTES

ABBREVIATIONS

CE 44-1422 FBI Interviews, Florida, file no. CE 44-1422, National Archives and Record Administration, College Park, MD, secured via Freedom of Information Act, in possession of the author.

CE 44-2104 FBI Interviews, North Carolina, file no. CE 44-2014, National Archives and Records Administration, College Park, MD, secured via Freedom of Information Act, in possession of the author.

NARA National Archives and Records Administration

PROLOGUE

1. Unless otherwise noted, these and the following descriptions of the campsite, party, and events following (including direct quotations) are drawn from my telephone and in-person interviews with Phil Lokey, Ron Olson, Max Johnson, Donald "Poonie" Porter, Sue Cello, Kevin Shea, Linda Mancini, Martha "Marty" Watkins, and Kim Burns, all of whom were at the Briar Bottom campsite on July 3, 1972.

2. Allen Cowan, "A Pacifist in a Paradise . . . Then Shattering Violence," *St. Petersburg Times*, July 8, 1972, 1-B, 13-B, www.newspapers.com/image/317728898; Fred Kellander, "Eyewitnesses Tell of Pinellas Boy's Death," *Tampa Tribune*, July 7, 1972, 3, www.newspapers.com/image/332307331/.

3. "Alternative Vittles," press release, in possession of Roger Altland.

4. *Bob Dylan: Don't Look Back*, directed by D. A. Pennebaker (1967, Leacock-Pennebaker), quotation online at www.imdb.com/title/tt0061589/characters/nm0001168.

5. "Fletcher, NC, Weather History: July 3, 1972," Weather Underground (website), www.wunderground.com/history/daily/us/nc/Burnsville/KAVL/date/1972-7-3, accessed July 3, 2021.

6. Phil Lokey, telephone interview by the author, March 22, 2022.

7. The sheriff's full name is Donald Kermit Banks. He was known as Kermit in part to distinguish him from his father, who also had the first name Donald.

8. Ron Alridge, "Many Details of Night in Briar Bottom Are Still in Dispute," *Charlotte Observer*, February 16, 1975, 18-A, www.newspapers.com/image/622665812/.

9. Kim Burns, quoted in Ron Alridge and Bob Boyd, "Youthful Camper Killed in Raid," *Charlotte Observer*, July 5, 1972, 2, www.newspapers.com/image/621942077/.

10. Lokey, interview.

11. State of North Carolina v. Richard Armentrout et al., 72-CR-997-1020, Dorothy Hoover, Court Reporter, County of Yancey, District Court Division, 2 vols., October 30, November 27–28, 1972, II:14–21. (Normally transcripts are not taken in district court, but Emma McNairy secured a court reporter who completed this transcript. Fred McNairy's sons kept the transcript and turned it over to Roger Altland, who allowed me to use it.)

12. Kellander, "Eyewitnesses Tell of Pinellas Boy's Death"; Cowan, "Pacifist in a Paradise,"13-B. Sheriff Kermit Banks's account of the incident—which he gave to reporters on July 5, 1972—differs significantly from that of the campers. He denied intentionally striking Satterwhite with the gun. His story of that night is detailed in chapters 6 and 7.

13. Banks contended that another lawman, Erwin Higgins, held the gun that fired the fatal shot. The sheriff would later say that his gun had double-aught buckshot, while Higgins's gun was loaded with "duck shot." If, as the campers claim, Banks's gun fired the shot, that would mean that nine pellets, the size of .32 caliber bullets, killed Stanley Altland. See Allen Cowan, "Drug Use Is Linked to Slaying," *St. Petersburg Times*, July 7, 1972, 3-B, www .newspapers.com/image/317725973. The description of the impact as knocking Altland off his feet and sending him flying backward is more consistent with double-aught buckshot than with duck shot. I contacted Sheriff Banks on three separate occasions, asking him to tell me what he remembers about the shooting. He never answered my letters.

14. Richard Armentrout, another camper and eyewitness, told the *Tampa Tribune* that he saw Kermit Banks reload. See Kellander, "Eyewitnesses Tell of Pinellas Boy's Death."

15. Allen Cowan, "Sheriff Kills Clearwater Youth during Carolina Campsite Raid," *St. Petersburg Times*, July 5, 1972, 3-B, www.newspapers.com/image/317352273/.

CHAPTER 1

1. "Florida Youth Slain at Yancey Campsite," *Raleigh News and Observer*, July 5, 1972, 8, www.newspapers.com/image/652964900/.

2. Jennie Rothenberg Gritz, "The Death of the Hippies," *The Atlantic*, July 8, 2015, www.theatlantic.com/entertainment/archive/2015/07/the-death-of-the-hippies/397739/.

3. Christopher Andersen, *Mick: The Wild Life and Mad Genius of Jagger* (New York: Gallery Books, 2012), chap. 4, iBooks.

4. Andersen, *Mick*, chap. 4.

5. Joel Selvin, *Altamont: The Rolling Stones, The Hells Angels, and the Inside Story of Rock's Darkest Day* (New York: Harper Collins, 2016), chaps. 20, 25, iBooks; Andersen, *Mick*, chap. 6.

6. Timothy Silver, *Mount Mitchell and the Black Mountains: An Environmental History of the Highest Peaks in Eastern America* (Chapel Hill: University of North Carolina Press, 2003).

7. James Rowen, "Young Man Ran, Was Shot—Dangerous Trend Began," *Miami Herald*, March 13, 1972, 4–5C, www.newspapers.com/image/625313376/.

8. Rick Perlstein, *Nixonland: The Rise of a President and the Fracturing of America* (New York: Scribner, 2009), chap. 29, iBooks.

9. James Brooke, "Confession to '71 Killing Revives Memories," *New York Times*, October 10, 1997, www.nytimes.com/1997/10/10/us/confession-to-71-killing-revives-memories.html.

10. Brooke, "Confession to '71 Killing."

11. Brooke, "Confession to '71 Killing."

CHAPTER 2

1. "Resident Population in Yancey County, NC," *Economic Research Federal Reserve Bank of St. Louis*, https://fred.stlouisfed.org/series/NCYANC9POP, accessed February 15, 2022; "Yancey County 1970 Selected Characteristics," State Archives of North Carolina, Digital Collections, https://digital.ncdcr.gov/Documents/Detail/yancey-county-1970-selected-characteristics/382212, accessed February 20, 2022.

2. "Our Changing Population: Yancey County, North Carolina," USA Facts, https://usafacts.org/data/topics/people-society/population-and-demographics/our-changing-population/state/north-carolina/county/yancey-county/, accessed February 20, 2022.

3. Ashley Cole Brewer, "Get on Board Children: The Story of Integration in Yancey County, North Carolina" (master's thesis, Center for Appalachian Studies, Appalachian State University, 2011), https://libres.uncg.edu/ir/asu/f/Brewer,%20Ashley_2011_Thesis.pdf, accessed February 23, 2022.

4. Danny McIntosh, interview by the author, Burnsville, NC, May 22, 2022.

5. Historians call this outlook and relationship to the world a region's "mentalité." *Merriam-Webster Dictionary*, s.v. "mentalité," www.merriam-webster.com/dictionary/mentalite, accessed June 7, 2021.

6. For a concise treatment of scholars' efforts to understand and debunk stereotypes of Appalachian people as "violent hillbillies" who "acted irrationally" in the face of change, see Bruce E. Stewart's introduction to *Blood in the Hills: A History of Violence in Appalachia*, ed. Bruce E. Stewart (Lexington: University Press of Kentucky, 2012), 1–24.

7. There is now a well-developed historiography that addresses the evolution of conservatism and conservative values in Appalachia. It is beyond the scope and tenor of this work to parse it here. Most recently, scholars have argued that mountain people, like Americans everywhere, reacted to political and social change in different ways according to their own interests. As in the rest of the country, political attitudes changed over time. See J. Blake Perkins, *Hillbilly Hellraisers: Federal Power and Populist Defiance in the Ozarks* (Urbana: University of Illinois Press, 2017). On mobility in and out of Appalachian communities and the effects on politics inside and outside the region, see Max Fraser, *Hillbilly Highway: The Transappalachian Migration and the Making of a White Working Class* (Princeton, NJ: Princeton University Press, 2023). Ronald D. Eller, whose early work on Appalachia helped define the field, notes that "Appalachia's problems are not those of Appalachia alone. They will not be solved in isolation from the dilemmas facing the rest of modern society.... We are all Appalachians." Ronald D. Eller, *Uneven Ground: Appalachia since 1945* (Lexington: University Press of Kentucky, 2008), 8.

8. Our Campaigns, "NC US President," 1956 election, www.ourcampaigns.com /RaceDetail.html?RaceID=2637; 1960 election, www.ourcampaigns.com/RaceDetail .html?RaceID=2590; 1964 election, www.ourcampaigns.com/RaceDetail.html?RaceID =2501; 1968 election, www.ourcampaigns.com/RaceDetail.html?RaceID=2451; 1972 election, www.ourcampaigns.com/RaceDetail.html?RaceID=2401. Accessed November 3, 2023.

9. "From the Editor's Desk," *Yancey Record*, March 13, 1969, 1, https://newspapers .digitalnc.org/lccn/sn95072281/1969-03-13/ed-1/seq-1/.

10. Jesse Helms, "Viewpoint," *Yancey Record*, July 16, 1970, 2, https://newspapers .digitalnc.org/lccn/sn95072281/1970-07-16/ed-1/seq-2/.

11. Tom Anderson, "Straight Talk: Pornography Continues Unchecked," *Yancey Record*, December 10, 1970, 3, https://newspapers.digitalnc.org/lccn/sn95072281/1970-12-10/ed-1 /seq-3/.

12. Marilyn Manion, "The Manion Forum: Psst . . . The Gap Isn't Really There," *Yancey Record*, March 19, 1970, 2, https://newspapers.digitalnc.org/lccn/sn95072281/1970-03-19 /ed-1/seq-2/.

13. *Yancey Record*, May 27, 1971, 3, https://newspapers.digitalnc.org/lccn/sn95072281 /1971-05-27/ed-1/seq-3/.

14. "Cane River Student Gives Advice to Fellow Students," *Yancey Record*, June 1, 1972, 8, https://newspapers.digitalnc.org/lccn/sn95072283/1972-06-01/ed-1/seq-8/.

15. Michael Kruse, "Seeking Civility," *Our State*, October 1, 2018, www.ourstate.com /seeking-civility/.

16. Roy Reed, "Back-to-Land Movement Seeks Self-Sufficiency," *New York Times*, June 9, 1975, 1, www.nytimes.com/1975/06/09/archives/backtoland-movement-seeks -selfsufficiency-the-growing-backtotheland.html; Jeffrey C. Jacob, "The North American Back to the Land Movement," *Community Development Journal* 31, no. 3 (July 1996): 241–49, www.jstor.org/stable/44257280.

17. Saul Friedman, "City Folks Struggle to Find a Better Life in the Hills," *Detroit Free Press*, September 6, 1970, 1, 4, www.newspapers.com/image/98915552/.

18. Friedman, "City Folks Struggle."

19. Jared M. Phillips, *Hipbillies: Deep Revolution in the Arkansas Ozarks* (Fayetteville: University of Arkansas Press, 2019), 73.

20. Jinny A. Turman-Deal, "'We Were an Oddity': A Look at the Back-to-the-Land Movement in Appalachia," *West Virginia History* 4, no. 1 (2010): 1–32, www.jstor.org /stable/43264860, 13; Phillips, *Hipbillies*, 68–69.

21. Carolyn Yuziuk, "Hippies Elbowing Hillbillies?," *Yancey Record*, September 24, 1970, 1, 5, https://newspapers.digitalnc.org/lccn/sn95072281/1970-09-24/ed-1/seq-1/.

22. John Boyle, "Family Affair," *Asheville Citizen*, February 14, 2010, B-1, B-3, www .newspapers.com/image/199757060.

23. "Ponder Brothers, Power Brokers," North Carolina Department of Cultural Resources, November 7, 2016, www.ncdcr.gov/blog/2015/11/07/ponder-brothers -madison-powerbrokers.

24. Boyle, "Family Affair," B-1; Danny McIntosh, interview by the author, Burnsville, NC, January 11, 2022.

25. Boyle, "Family Affair," B-1; *Yancey Record*, October 29, 1970, 11, https://newspapers .digitalnc.org/lccn/sn95072281/1970-10-29/ed-1/seq-11/; "Yancey Candidates Run Tight

Race," *Yancey Record*, November 5, 1970, 1, 3, https://newspapers.digitalnc.org/lccn/sn95072281/1970-11-05/ed-1/seq-3/.

26. Reuben J. Dailey et al. v. Kermit Banks et al., Civil Action AC-74–42, US District Court for the Western District of North Carolina, Asheville, NC (1974–75), digital copy provided by NARA, Atlanta, GA, 126.

27. *Dailey v. Banks*, 132–37, 91–111.

28. *Encyclopedia Britannica*, s.v. "War on Drugs," www.britannica.com/topic/war-on-drugs, accessed June 15, 2023; Cigdem V. Sirin, "From Nixon's War on Drugs to Obama's Drug Policies Today: Presidential Progress in Addressing Racial Injustice and Disparities," *Race, Gender, and Class* 18, nos. 3–4 (2011): 82–99, www.jstor.org/stable/43496834; "Drug War Confessional," Vera (website), www.vera.org/reimagining-prison-webumentary/the-past-is-never-dead/drug-war-confessional, accessed June 15, 2023.

29. Sheriff Kermit Banks, "Parents Know the Drug Threat," September 16, 1971, 2, *Yancey Record*, https://newspapers.digitalnc.org/lccn/sn95072281/1971-09-16/ed-1/seq-2/; Banks, "Parents Know the Drug Threat," *Yancey Record*, September 23, 1971, 2, https://newspapers.digitalnc.org/lccn/sn95072281/1971-09-23/ed-1/seq-2/.

30. A woman from Clearwater who had moved to Burnsville told Linda Mancini, Phil Lokey, and Max Johnson that "Banks kicks in doors around here every weekend." Two other Burnsville sources agreed that the sheriff did not like longhairs, but those sources asked not to be identified. "Drug Raid Gets Results," *Yancey Record*, July 27, 1972, 1, https://newspapers.digitalnc.org/lccn/sn95072283/1972-07-27/ed-1/seq-1/; "No It's Not a Christmas Tree," *Yancey Record*, August 17, 1972, 1, https://newspapers.digitalnc.org/lccn/sn95072283/1972-08-17/ed-1/seq-1/.

CHAPTER 3

1. Richard Fausset, "What We Know About the Shooting Death of Ahmaud Arbery," *New York Times*, August 8, 2022, www.nytimes.com/article/ahmaud-arbery-shooting-georgia.html.

2. Josh Sidorowicz, "What's in a Name? Meet Olds, the Carmaker behind the City of Oldsmar," WTSP 10 Tampa Bay (website), October 25, 2023, www.wtsp.com.

3. "Quick Facts: Pinellas County, Florida," US Census (website), www.census.gov/quickfacts/fact/table/pinellascountyflorida/PST045221, accessed February 24, 2023.

4. "Pinellas County vs Florida, Comparative Trends Analysis: Population Growth and Change, 1969–2021," https://florida.reaproject.org/analysis/comparative-trends-analysis/population/tools/120103/120000/, accessed December 1, 2022.

5. "Philippe Park," Pinellas County (website), https://pinellas.gov/parks/philippe-park/, accessed December 6, 2022.

6. "Pier 60 at Clearwater Beach," Visit St. Pete/Clearwater (website), www.visitstpeteclearwater.com/profile/pier-60-clearwater-beach/139755, accessed March 14, 2024; Sue Cello, interview by the author, Clearwater, FL, November 16, 2022.

7. "Pier 60."

8. "Alternative Vittles," press release in possession of Roger Altland.

9. Cello, interview; Kevin Shea, telephone interview by the author, August 30, 2022; Ruth Gray, "They Offer Alternative Vittles," *Tampa Bay Times*, July 30, 1972, 79, www.newspapers.com/image/317687310/.

10. Selective Service System, "Vietnam Lotteries," www.sss.gov/history-and-records /vietnam-lotteries/, accessed November 30, 2022.

11. See information for Stan Altland's birthday, November 14, at www.sss.gov/wp -content/uploads/2020/03/1971-Vietnam-Lottery.pdf, accessed November 30, 2022; Roger Altland, interview by the author, November 15, 2022.

12. "20 USF Protesters Arrested; Gainesville, Tallahassee Calm," *St. Petersburg Times*, May 12, 1972, 1-B, 3-B, www.newspapers.com/image/317303210.

13. Cello, interview; "3 Arrested in Bicycle Protest, *Fort Lauderdale News*, May 12, 1972, 14, www.newspapers.com/image/230379765/.

14. "3 Arrested in Bicycle Protest"; Fred Kellander, "Protesters Rap Clearwater Police Following 'March,'" *Tampa Tribune*, May 13, 1972, 6, www.newspapers.com /image/332223038/.

15. Richard Pearson, "Former Gov. George C. Wallace Dies," *Washington Post*, September 14, 1998, A1, www.washingtonpost.com/wp-srv/politics/daily/sept98/wallace.htm.

16. Brian Lyman, "Stand Up for America," *Montgomery Advertiser*, August 17, 2018, www.montgomeryadvertiser.com/story/news/politics/2018/08/17/stand-up-america -george-wallaces-chaotic-prophetic-campaign/873126002/; Chris Stirewalt, "Populism, Fake News, and Racist Rhetoric—It's All Happened Before in the 1968 Presidential Campaign (excerpt from *Every Man a King: A Short, Colorful History of American Populists*), *Business Insider*, October 6, 1018, www.businessinsider.com/racism-populism-american -politics-1968-presidential-campaign-george-wallace-2018-10; "George Wallace: Settin' the Woods on Fire, 1968 Campaign," American Experience (website), PBS, www.pbs.org /wgbh/americanexperience/features/wallace-1968-campaign/, accessed February 13, 2022.

17. Milton Viorst, "Meet the People's Party Candidate," *New York Times*, June 4, 1972, https://archive.nytimes.com/www.nytimes.com/books/98/05/17/specials/spock -candidate.html; "Fourth Party Drive Opens in Orlando," *St. Petersburg Times*, March 20, 1972, 11-B, www.newspapers.com/image/320071017/; "Irregularities Charged in Pinellas-Pasco Vote," *St. Petersburg Times*, April 2, 1972, 3-B, www.newspapers.com /image/320271898/.

18. Timothy Noah, "'Acid, Amnesty, and Abortion': The Unlikely Source of a Legendary Smear," *New Republic*, October 22, 2012, https://newrepublic.com/article/108977/acid -amnesty-and-abortion-unlikely-source-legendary-smear; Rick Perlstein, *Nixonland: The Rise of a President and the Fracturing of America* (New York: Scribner, 2009), chap. 34, iBooks.

19. Gil Scott-Heron, "B-Movie," https://genius.com/Gil-scott-heron-b-movie-lyrics, accessed July 19, 2023.

20. Shea, interview.

21. Cello, interview; Phil Lokey, Max Johnson, and Ron Olson, interview by the author, November 16, 2022; Shea, interview.

22. Sue Cello, telephone interview by the author, September 1, 2021. This and the previous paragraph are also based in part on my experience as a high school student in 1971–73.

23. Phil Lokey, telephone interview by the author, March 22, 2022.

24. Lokey, Johnson, and Olson, interviews.

25. Donald Porter, telephone interview by the author, August 30, 2021.

26. Porter, interview.

27. Shea, interview.

28. "Drug Abuse: 2 to 4% of St. Petersburg is Involved, *St. Petersburg Times*, July 24, 1972, www.newspapers.com/image/317624116/; Linda Mancini, telephone interview by the author, October 12, 2021.

29. Cello, interview; Linda Mancini, telephone interview by the author, November 28, 2022.

30. Robert Greenfield, *Stones Touring Party: A Journey Through America with the Rolling Stones* (New York: E. P. Dutton, 1974), prologue, iBooks.

CHAPTER 4

1. Simon Harper, "'Tumbling Dice': The Story Behind the Rolling Stones' Classic," Udiscovermusic, October 19, 2022, www.udiscovermusic.com/stories/the-rolling-stones-tumbling-dice-feature/.

2. Joel Arambur, "Exile on Main Street at 47: The Roll of the Dice," *Rolling Stone India*, May 12, 2019, https://rollingstoneindia.com/exile-main-street-47-roll-dice.

3. John Cotter, "Hey Man, Did You Hear about the Stones," *Poughkeepsie (NY) Journal*, May 30, 1972, 19, www.newspapers.com/image/114928425/.

4. Sue Cello, telephone interview by the author, September 21, 2021.

5. Mike Jahn, "Rolling Stones Thwart Local Scalpers," *Charlotte Observer*, May 21, 1972, www.newspapers.com/image/621943539/; Robert Greenfield, *Stones Touring Party: A Journey through America with the Rolling Stones* (New York: E. P. Dutton, 1974), prologue, iBooks.

6. Greenfield, *Stones Touring Party*, prologue.

7. "Fans Jam Outlets for Rolling Stones Tickets," *Los Angeles Times*, May 15, 1972, 3, www.newspapers.com/image/379970916/.

8. Greenfield, *Stones Touring Party*, prologue.

9. Geoffrey Cannon, "The Rolling Stones Tour the US," *The Guardian*, June 28, 2016, www.theguardian.com/music/2016/jun/28/rolling-stones-us-tour-1972-archive.

10. John R. Mott III, "Stones Roll to Sellout in 7 Hours," *Nashville Tennessean*, May 24, 1972, 1, www.newspapers.com/image/112051942/; "Store Selling Rolling Stones Tickets Hit," *Winona (MN) Daily News*, May 22, 1972, 4, www.newspapers.com/image/414560617/.

11. Greenfield, *Stones Touring Party*, epilogue, prologue.

12. Greenfield, *Stones Touring Party*, prologue.

13. Allen Cowan, "A Pacifist in a Paradise . . . Then Shattering Violence," *St. Petersburg Times*, July 8, 1972, 13-B, www.newspapers.com/image/317728898.

14. Greenfield, *Stones Touring Party*, prologue, chap. 1.

15. Roger Altland, telephone interview by the author, October 30, 2021.

16. Altland, interview; James Brooke, "Confession to '71 Killing Revives Memories," *New York Times*, October 10, 1997, www.nytimes.com/1997/10/10/us/confession-to-71-killing-revives-memories.html.

17. Greenfield, *Stones Touring Party*, chap. 1; Andrew Fleming, "Archives: Cops Clash with Rolling Stones fans in Vancouver," Vancouver Is Awesome (website), June

3, 2015, www.vancouverisawesome.com/courier-archive/news/archives-cops-clash-with
-rolling-stones-fans-in-vancouver-3012242.

18. Joe Hughes, "15 Hurt, 60 Held at Arena Rock Melee," *San Diego Union-Tribune*,
June 14, 1972, 1, www.sandiegouniontribune.com/news/local-history/story/2022-06-14
/rolling-stones-1972-concert-in-san-diego-was-a-riot.

19. "Fans Riot Again at Rolling Stones Concert," *Sacramento Bee*, June 15, 1972, 36, www
.newspapers.com/image/620165601/.

20. "500 Stones Fans Left in Cold, Gas," *Minneapolis Star*, June 19, 1972, 7; Roy M.
Close, "Rolling Stones Gone; Memory of Sound, Excitement Lingers," *Minneapolis Star*,
June 19, 1972, 7, www.newspapers.com/image/190009142/.

21. "500 Stones Fans Left in Cold, Gas"; John Burks, "Jim Morrison's Indecency
Arrest: Rolling Stone's Original Coverage," *Rolling Stone*, December 10, 2010, www
.rollingstone.com/music/music-news/jim-morrisons-indecency-arrest-rolling-stones
-original-coverage-250814/; "How Janis Joplin Was Arrested in Tampa 50 Years Ago,"
Tampa Bay Times, November 14, 2019, www.tampabay.com/news/tampa/2019/11/14/how
-janis-joplin-was-arrested-in-tampa-50-years-ago/.

22. Edward Kern, "Can It Happen Here?" *Life*, October 17, 1969, 67; Todd Van Luing,
"Here Are Things You Still Don't Know about the Rolling Stones," *Huffpost*, November
20, 2015, www.huffpost.com; Greenfield, *Stones Touring Party*, chap. 5.

23. Matt Wake, "The Story behind the Rolling Stones' Angela Davis Song," Associated
Press, February 15, 2019, https://apnews.com.

24. Altland, interview; Mark Goodpasture, telephone interview by the author, August
14, 2021; Donald Porter, telephone interview by the author, August 30, 2021.

25. Greenfield, *Stones Touring Party*, chap 7.

26. Cowan, "Pacifist in a Paradise," 1-B.

27. "What Is the History of Music Festivals?" DailyHistory.org, www.dailyhistory.org
/What_is_the_history_of_music_festivals, accessed September 22, 2023.

28. Michael Childers, "The Stoneman Meadow Riots and Law Enforcement in Yosemite National Park," *Forest History Today*, Spring 2017, 28–34, quotation from 31, https://
foresthistory.org/wp-content/uploads/2017/10/Childers_Stoneman.pdf.

29. Childers, "Stoneman Meadow Riots," 32.

30. Anthony Ripley, "Peace and Religious Festival Begins in Colorado Despite Official Opposition," *New York Times*, July 2, 1972, www.nytimes.com/1972/07/02/archives
/peace-and-religious-festival-begins-in-colorado-despite-official.html.

31. Ripley, "Peace and Religious Festival."

32. Porter, interview.

33. Cowan, "Pacifist in a Paradise," 13-B.

34. Phil Lokey, telephone interview by the author, March 22, 2022; Cello, interview;
Goodpasture, interview.

35. Linda Mancini, interview by the author, November 14, 2022.

CHAPTER 5

1. Phil Lokey, telephone interview by the author, March 22, 2022; Linda Mancini, telephone interview by the author, November 8, 2021.

2. Mark Goodpasture, telephone interview by the author, August 14, 2021.

3. Lokey, interview; Max Johnson, interview by the author, Palm Harbor, FL, November 16, 2022.

4. Lokey, interview; Johnson, interview; Allen Cowan, "A Pacifist in a Paradise . . . Then Shattering Violence," *St. Petersburg Times*, July 8, 1972, 13-B, www.newspapers.com /image/317728898/.

5. Cowan, "Pacifist in a Paradise," 13-B.

6. Lokey, interview; Sue Cello, telephone interview by the author, September 1, 2021.

7. Lokey, interview; Donald Porter, telephone interview by the author, August 30, 2021.

8. Donald Jay Barrett, telephone interview by the author, August 24, 2021.

9. Johnson, interview.

10. Mancini, interview; Lokey, interview.

11. Reuben J. Dailey et al. v. Kermit Banks et al., Civil Action AC-74-42, US District Court for the Western District of North Carolina, Asheville, NC (1974–75), digital copy provided by NARA, Atlanta, 225.

12. *Dailey v. Banks*, 245–48.

13. Lokey, interview; Cello, interview.

14. *Dailey v. Banks*, 247–48; Cowan, "Pacifist in a Paradise," 13-B; Lokey, interview.

15. Lokey, interview; Cello, interview; Doreen Sofarelli, interview by the author, Palm Harbor, FL, November 16, 2022.

16. Susan Rachel Frances Cello, interview by FBI Special Agents John V. De Neale and Ernest J. Kirstein Jr., Clearwater, Florida, July 10, 1972, Tampa, FL, File no. 44-1422, NARA, College Park, MD, 27; Lokey, interview.

17. Frank Lasnick, interview by FBI Special Agent Thomas J. Brereton, Greensboro, NC, July 12, 1972, CE 44-2104, 108, 109.

18. Porter, interview; Christopher Cubbison, "Campers Call Violence Needless," *St. Petersburg Times*, July 8, 1972, 18, www.newspapers.com/image/317729071/.

19. Frank Lasnick, quoted in Fred Kellander, "FBI Questions Eyewitnesses to Death of Clearwater Boy," *Tampa Tribune*, July 14, 1972, 4, www.newspapers.com /image/332504204/; Porter, interview.

20. *Dailey v. Banks*, 236.

21. Cowan, "Pacifist in a Paradise," 13-B. Later, testimony at the Burnsville disorderly conduct trial established that Rivers told dispatcher Bill Arrowood that the group was "trying to take over the campground."

22. *Dailey v. Banks*, 121; Cowan, "Pacifist in a Paradise," 13-B.

23. Cowan, "Pacifist in a Paradise," 13-B.

24. Lasnick, FBI interview, 110, 111.

25. Ron Olson, telephone interview by the author, December 10, 2021; Ronald Baylor Olson, interview by FBI Special Agent Charles D. Vance, Clearwater, Florida, July 17, 1972, File no. TP 44-1422, NARA, College Park, MD, 78, 79.

26. Cowan, "Pacifist in a Paradise," 13-B; telephone interview with Olson; telephone interview with Lokey; telephone interview with Porter.

27. Olson, interview by the author; Kevin Shea, quoted in Kellander, "Eyewitnesses Tell of Pinellas Boy's Death"; written statement to attorneys from Ron Olson, in his possession.

28. Mancini, interview.

29. Mancini, interview; Lokey, interview.

30. Porter, interview; Cello, interview.

31. Tom Rusher, interview by the author, Boone, NC, July 30, 2021; Porter, interview.

32. Porter, interview.

33. Danny McIntosh, interview by the author, Burnsville, NC, January 11, 2022.

34. Rusher, interview.

35. Dr. W. A. Y. Sargent, in "Yancey Sheriff Accused of Killing Florida Youth," *Native Stone* (Asheville, NC), II:6, July 6, 1972, 3, Lewis W. Green Books and Papers, Box 11, Special Collections Research Center, Appalachian State University.

36. Rusher, interview; Johnson, interview. Banks told the *St. Petersburg Times*, "I don't have the facilities to detain that many people for any length of time." See Allen Cowan, "Drugs Linked to Slaying," *St. Petersburg Times*, July 8, 1972, 18, www.newspapers.com /image/317726026/.

37. Mancini, interview; Lokey, interview; Cowan, "Pacifist in a Paradise," 13-B.

38. "State of North Carolina v. Julius Stewart Sumrell, November 15, 1972," https://law .justia.com/cases/north-carolina/supreme-court/1972/53-1-4.html, accessed December 28, 2022 (emphasis in the quote added); NC State Legislature, Enacted Legislation, Statutes, www.ncleg.net/enactedlegislation/statutes/html/bysection/chapter_14/gs_14-288.4.html, accessed December 28, 2022.

39. Cowan, "Pacifist in a Paradise," 13-B; Lokey, interview; Olson, interview.

CHAPTER 6

1. Donald Jay Barrett, telephone interview by the author, August 24, 2021.

2. Fred Kellander, "FBI Questions Eyewitnesses to Death of Clearwater Boy," *Tampa Tribune*, July 14, 1972, 4, www.newspapers.com/image/332504204.

3. Roger Altland, telephone interview by the author, November 8, 2021; Ron Olson, telephone interview by the author, December 10, 2021; Sue Cello, telephone interview by the author, September 1, 2021; Ron Olson, interview by the author, Palm Harbor, FL, November 16, 2022.

4. Altland, interview; Donald Porter, telephone interview by the author, August 30, 2021; Phil Lokey, telephone interview by the author, March 22, 2022.

5. Ron Alridge and Bob Boyd, "Youthful Camper Killed in Raid," *Charlotte Observer*, July 5, 1972, www.newspapers.com/image/621942077; Linda (Putney) Mancini is quoted in the article.

6. Linda Mancini, telephone interview by the author, November 8, 2021; Cello, interview; Doreen Sofarelli, interview by the author, Palm Harbor, FL, November 16, 2022; Lokey, interview.

7. Altland, interview.

8. Olson, interview; Susan Jetton, Dean Duncan, and Nick Grabbe, "Incidents Few as Stones Roll," *Charlotte Observer*, July 7, 1972, 9–10, www.newspapers.com/image /621946594/.

9. Robert Greenfield, *Stones Touring Party: A Journey through America with the Rolling Stones* (New York: E. P. Dutton, 1974), chap. 8, iBooks; Jetton et al., "Incidents Few as Stones Roll," 10. The Stones' typical 1972 setlist is available at www.setlist.fm/stats /average-setlist/the-rolling-stones-bd6ad22.html?year=1972, accessed September 7, 2021.

10. Barrett, interview; Mancini, interview; Olson, interview.

11. Barrett, interview; Mancini, interview.

12. Jetton et al., "Incidents Few as Stones Roll," 9–10; Barrett, interview; Olson, interview; Mancini, interview; Greenfield, *Stones Touring Party*, chap. 9, 10, 11, 12.

13. Danny McIntosh, interview by the author, Burnsville, NC, January 11, 2022.

14. Kermit Banks's statement as quoted in Allen Cowan, "Sheriff Kills Clearwater Youth During Carolina Campsite Raid," *St. Petersburg Times*, July 5, 1972, 3-B, www.newspapers.com/image/317352483/.

15. "Vandalism, Plea for Help Result in Fatal Shooting," *Yancey Record*, July 6, 1972, 1, https://newspapers.digitalnc.org/lccn/sn95072283/1972-07-06/ed-1/seq-1/. Emphasis mine.

16. See, for example, "FBI Probing Clearwater Youth's Death," *Tampa Tribune*, July 15, 1972, B-2, www.newspapers.com/image/332506367/.

17. Allen Cowan, "Drugs Linked to Slaying," *St. Petersburg Times*, July 8, 1972, 18, www.newspapers.com/clip/89319131/; "Dead Youth's Friends Say Police Roughed Them Up," *Miami Herald*, July 6, 1972, 88, www.newspapers.com/image/625305613/. On Banks's demeanor during the interview, see Allen Cowan, "The Trial's Over, but Who Shot Stanley Altland?," *St. Petersburg Times*, December 3, 1972, 45, www.newspapers.com/image/317658518; Kellander, "Eyewitnesses Tell of Pinellas Boy's Death," *Tampa Bay Tribune*, July 7, 1972, 3, www.newspapers.com/image/332307331/.

18. Allen Cowan, "The Fatal Shot: Will We Ever Know?" *St. Petersburg Times*, July 6, 1972, 1-B, 3-B, www.newspapers.com/image/317722824/; Cowan, "Drugs Linked to Slaying"; Lokey, interview; Christopher Cubbison, "Campers Call Violence Needless," *St. Petersburg Times*, July 8, 1972, 4B, www.newspapers.com/image/317729071.

19. Cowan, "Drugs Linked to Slaying"; Lokey, interview.

20. Cello, interview; Mark Goodpasture, text message to the author, July 27, 2022.

21. Cello, interview; Mancini, interview; Lokey, interview; Barrett, interview.

22. Quoted in Cowan, "Fatal Shot," 8-B.

23. "Why Did He Die?," *Clearwater Sun*, July 10, 1972, 8-A, https://pinellasmemory.org/islandora/object/clearwater%3A26143.

24. Cowan, "Fatal Shot," 8-B.

25. "250 Bid Farewell to Stanley Altland," *St. Petersburg Times*, July 9, 1972, 41, www.newspapers.com/image/317731994.

26. Sam Zaitoon, "Altland's Friends Bid Him Farewell," *Clearwater Sun*, July 9, 1972, 1, https://pinellasmemory.org/islandora/object/clearwater%3A19898.

27. Mancini, interview; Cello, interview; Lokey, interview; Cowan, "Fatal Shot," 3-B; "Why Did He Die?"

28. "Times Capsules: Altland Investigation," *St. Petersburg Times*, July 6, 1972, 22, www.newspapers.com/image/317722702/; "Let's Get at the Truth," *Clearwater Sun*, July 7, 1972, 8-A, https://pinellasmemory.org/islandora/object/clearwater%3A26133.

29. "Resolution Against Death of Clearwater Boy Okayed," *Tampa Tribune*, July 11, 1972, www.newspapers.com/image/332494207/.

30. Allen Cowan, "FBI Probes Altland Slaying," *St. Petersburg Times*, July 14, 1972, 13-B, www.newspapers.com/image/317729554; "Pinellas Plea to Askew: Assure Safety of Traveling Floridians," *St. Petersburg Times*, July 8, 1972, 8, www.newspapers.com/image/317728795/; "ACLU Asks Probe of Youth's Death," *Tampa Tribune*, July 7, 1972, 3, www.newspapers.com/image/332307331; Allen Cowan, "A Pacifist in a Paradise . . . Then Shattering Violence," *St. Petersburg Times*, July 8, 1972, 3-B, 13-B, www.newspapers.com/image/317728898.

31. Robert Hooker, "Deputy's Gun Shot Altland," *St. Petersburg Times*, July 19, 1972, 2-B, www.newspapers.com/image/317340131/; Medical Examiner's Certificate of Death for Stanley William Altland, July 4, 1972, Certificate 27658, Yancey County Register of Deeds Office, Burnsville, NC; Supplemental Report of Cause of Death, August 8, 1972.

32. Supplemental Report of Cause of Death, August 8, 1972; North Carolina Office of the Chief Medical Examiner, www.ocme.dhhs.nc.gov/faq/index.shtml, accessed October 25, 2022.

CHAPTER 7

1. Tom Rusher, interview by the author, Boone, NC, July 30, 2021.

2. Robert Hooker, "Deputy's Gun Shot Altland," *St. Petersburg Times*, July 19, 1972, B-1, www.newspapers.com/image/ 317340052/.

3. Allen Cowan, "Drug Link Softened in Altland Slaying," *St. Petersburg Times*, August 18, 1972, 15-B, www.newspapers.com/image/317718758/.

4. Cowan, "Drug Link Softened."

5. Cowan, "Drug Link Softened."

6. Roger Altland, interview by the author, Palm Harbor, FL, November 16, 2022.

7. Emma D. McNairy to "Mr. Altland" [Stan Altland's father, Glenn], August 19, 1972, letter in possession of Roger Altland, Palm Harbor, FL; Allen Cowan, "FBI Probes Altland Slaying," *St. Petersburg Times*, July 14, 1972, 1-B, 13-B, www.newspapers.com/image/317728845/.

8. Stephen Siff, "The Illegalization of Marijuana: A Brief History," *Origins: Current Events in Historical Perspective*, May 2014, https://origins.osu.edu/article/illegalization -marijuana-brief-history, accessed January 19, 2022; Tim Weiner, *Enemies: A History of the FBI* (New York: Random House, 2012), chap. 34, iBooks.

9. David Satterwhite, interview by FBI Special Agent Thomas J. Brereton, July 13, 1972, CE 44-2104, 5.

10. Satterwhite, FBI interview, 8.

11. Kermit Banks, sheriff, Yancey County, interview by FBI Special Agents Austin A. Andersen and John M. Quigley, July 12, 1972, CE 44-2104, 10.

12. Banks, FBI interview, 10.

13. Banks, FBI interview, 11–12.

14. Banks, FBI interview, 12, 13, 17.

15. Banks, FBI interview, 17, 18; Sterling A. Wood, *Riot Control by the National Guard* (Harrisburg, PA: Military Service Publishing Company, 1940), 41, 42.

16. Banks, FBI interview, 20, 21, 22.

17. Erwin Higgins, chief deputy, Yancey County Sheriff's Office, interview by FBI Special Agents John S. Willis and Austin A. Andersen, July 13, 1972, CE 44-2104, 23, 24.

18. Higgins, FBI interview, 24, 25, 26, 27, 23. Later, in documents connected with a civil court proceeding, Higgins noted that he did not have a high school diploma when he went to work for the sheriff's department. See Reuben J. Dailey et al. v. Kermit Banks et al., Civil Action AC-74–42, US District Court for the Western District of North Carolina, Asheville, NC (1974), digital copy provided by NARA, Atlanta, GA, 126.

19. Horace Gene Biggs, patrolman, Burnsville, North Carolina, Police Department, interview by FBI Special Agents Austin A. Andersen and John M. Quigley, July 13, 1972, CE 44-2104, 42, 43, 44.

20. Susan Rachel Frances Cello, interview by FBI Special Agents John V. De Neale and Ernest J. Kirstein, Jr., Clearwater, Florida, July 13, 1972, CE 44-1422, 27; Ronald Baylor Olson, interview by FBI Special Agent Charles D. Vance, July 17, 1972, Clearwater, Florida, CE 44-1422, 80.

21. Max Edward Johnson, interview by FBI Special Agents Walter B. Granger and Charles D. Vance, July 13, 1972, Clearwater, Florida, CE 44-1422, NARA, College Park MD, 58; Cello, FBI interview, 27.

22. Linda Diane Putney (Mancini), interview by FBI Special Agent Charles D. Vance, July 14, 1972, Clearwater, Florida, CE 44-1422, 90, 91, 92; Johnson, FBI interview, 58, 57; Cello, FBI interview, 29; Olson, FBI interview, 78, 80.

23. Cello, FBI interview, 24; Putney, Olson, and Johnson, FBI interviews.

24. Frank Wayne Lasnick, interview by FBI Special Agent Thomas J. Brereton, July 12, 1972, Greensboro, NC, CE 44-2104; Margaret Ann Kowalski, interview by FBI Special Agent Thomas J. Brereton, July 12, 1972, Greensboro, NC, CE 44-2104.

25. Kowalski, FBI interview, 104, 105.

26. Kowalski, FBI interview, 106.

27. Kowalski, FBI interview, 106, 107.

28. Lasnick, FBI interview, 109, 110, 114.

29. Lasnick, FBI interview, 109.

30. Lasnick, FBI interview, 110.

31. Lasnick, FBI interview, 110, 111.

32. Lasnick, FBI interview, 114.

33. Cowan, "Drug Link Softened," 15-B.

34. Lawton Chiles to Mrs. Walter F. Hannaway, August 31, 1972, letter in possession of Roger Altland, Palm Harbor, FL; Emma D. McNairy to Mr. Altland, August 19, 1972, letter in possession of Roger Altland, Palm Harbor, FL; Richard A. Rosen and Joseph Mosnier, *Julius Chambers: A Life in the Legal Struggle for Civil Rights* (Chapel Hill: University of North Carolina Press, 2016), 1–5. Linda Putney Mancini, Sue Cello, and Phil Lokey all remember the Clearwater ACLU's involvement in the case and that they helped secure Chambers's help.

CHAPTER 8

1. Richard A. Rosen and Joseph Mosnier, *Julius Chambers: A Life in the Legal Struggle for Civil Rights* (Chapel Hill: University of North Carolina Press, 2016), 18–23, 31–36.

2. Rosen and Mosnier, *Julius Chambers*, 69–74.

3. Rosen and Mosnier, *Julius Chambers*, 77–83, 89–102.

4. Rosen and Mosnier, *Julius Chambers*, 123–132.

5. Rosen and Mosnier, *Julius Chambers*, 161–92, 272–74.

6. Adam Stein and Richard Rosen, Carrboro, NC, interview by the author, September 15, 2021; Richard Rosen, interview by the author, Carrboro, NC, November 3, 2022.

7. Phil Lokey, telephone interview by the author, March 22, 2022.

8. "NC Arraignment Delayed for 24 Altland Friends," *St. Petersburg Times*, October 31, 1972, 11-B, www.newspapers.com/image/317720257/.

9. General Assembly of North Carolina, Session 2021, Senate Bill 300, www.ncleg.gov/Sessions/2021/Bills/Senate/PDF/S300v7.pdf, 9, accessed April 4, 2022.

10. John Aldridge, Assistant General Counsel, North Carolina Sheriff's Association, "Officer's Use of Force: The Investigative Process," https://ncsheriffs.org/wp-content/uploads/Officers-Use-of-Force-The-Investigative-Process.pdf, 13. For an example of police policy with detailed standards and procedures, see "UNC Police: General Order 01-03R7—Officer Involved Shootings, In-custody Deaths, or Serious Injuries, 2000," https://policies.unc.edu/TDClient/2833/Portal/KB/ArticleDet.aspx?ID=132102, both accessed April 3, 2022.

11. State of North Carolina v. Richard Armentrout et al., 72-CR-997-1020, 2 vols. Dorothy P. Hoover, Court Reporter, County of Yancey (District Court Division, October 30, 1972, November 27–28, 1972), I:1–13. (Normally transcripts are not taken in district court, but Emma McNairy secured a court reporter who completed this transcript. Fred McNairy's sons kept the transcript and turned it over to Roger Altland, who allowed me to use it.)

12. Frank Wayne Lasnick, interview by FBI Special Agent Thomas J. Brereton, July 12, 1972, Greensboro, NC, CE 44-2104, 112; Fred Kellander, "FBI Questions Eyewitnesses to Death of Clearwater Boy," *Tampa Tribune*, July 14, 1972, 4, www.newspapers.com/image/332504204; Allen Cowan, "FBI Probing Altland Slaying," *St. Petersburg Times*, July 15, 1972, 4-B, www.newspapers.com/image/317732106.

13. Robert Young, quoted in Allen Cowan, "Solemn Trip into the Past to Clear Slain Friend," *St. Petersburg Times*, November 26, 1972, 3-B, www.newspapers.com/image/317652187.

14. Allen Cowan, "Friends of Slain Youth Set for Trial Monday," *St. Petersburg Times*, November 23, 1972, 16-B, www.newspapers.com/image/317688613/; "Disorderly Conduct Charges Dismissed in Burnsville Court," *Asheville Citizen*, November 28, 1972, 13, www.newspapers.com/image/195814245.

15. Glen P. Jackson, Mark A. Barkett, "A History of the Forensic Applications of Mass Spectrometry," in *The Encyclopedia of Mass Spectrometry*, vol. 9, *Historical Perspectives, Part A: The Development of Mass Spectrometry* (Elsevier Science, 2016); *NC v. Armentrout*, I:5–6.

16. "Trial For Disorderly Conduct of 23 in Altland Case Postponed," *St. Petersburg Times*, September 6, 1972, 18, www.newspapers.com/image/317615191/; "NC Arraignment Postponed for 23 Altland Friends," *St. Petersburg Times*, October 31, 1972, 11-B, www.newspapers.com/image/317720257; Allen Cowan, "Defense Wants North Carolina Incident Aired," *St. Petersburg Times*, November 27, 1972, 3-B, www.newspapers.com/image/317659663/; Allen Cowan, "Solemn Trip into the Past," 1-B, 3-B.

17. Quoted in Cowan, "Defense Wants Incident Aired," 3-B.

18. Cowan, "Defense Wants Incident Aired"; Allen Cowan, "A Pacifist in a Paradise . . . Then Shattering Violence," *St. Petersburg Times*, July 8, 1972, 3-B, www.newspapers.com/image/317728898; Tom Rusher, interview by the author, Boone, NC, July 30, 2021.

19. "Disorderly Conduct Charges Dismissed in Burnsville Court."

20. Cowan, "Solemn Trip into the Past," 3-B.

21. Lokey, interview; Stein and Rosen, interview.

22. Ron Alridge, "Suit May Follow Campers' Court Triumph," *Charlotte Observer*, December 1, 1972, 1-E, www.newspapers.com/image/622005771/; Linda Putney Mancini, telephone interview by the author, November 8, 2021. Roger Altland took a photo of the courtroom showing the flags, clock, and calendar.

23. Allen Cowan, "11 Altland Companions Are Cleared," *St. Petersburg Times*, November 28, 1972, 1-B, 11-B, www.newspapers.com/image/317662764/; *NC v. Armentrout*, I:997–1020, I:11; Rusher, interview; Stein and Rosen, interview.

24. *NC v. Armentrout*, I:16–31.

25. *NC v. Armentrout*, I:31–48.

26. *NC v. Armentrout*, I:48–63, quotations from 50, 52; Cowan, "11 Altland Companions Cleared," 11-B.

27. *NC v. Armentrout*, I:63–70, quotation from 66; "Disorderly Conduct Charges Dismissed"; Cowan, "11 Altland Companions Cleared," 11-B.

28. *NC v. Armentrout*, I:73–82, quotations from 75, 80.

29. *NC v. Armentrout*, I:78.

30. *NC v. Armentrout*, I:108, 110.

31. *NC v. Armentrout*, I:124, 125; Cowan, "11 Altland Companions Cleared," 11-B.

32. *NC v. Armentrout*, I:137, 138.

33. *NC v. Armentrout*, I:140, 141, 142.

34. *NC v. Armentrout*, I:145–69.

35. Rusher, quoted in Cowan, "11 Altland Companions Cleared," 11-B.

36. *NC v. Armentrout*, II:4.

37. *NC v. Armentrout*, II:8–14.

38. *NC v. Armentrout*, II:14–21, quotations from 20.

39. *NC v. Armentrout*, II:20–25; Alridge, "Suit May Follow," 4-B.

40. Allen Cowan, "Carolina Judge Convicts 2 for Campground Conduct," *St. Petersburg Times*, November 30, 1972," 2-B, www.newspapers.com/image/317670922/.

41. *NC v. Armentrout*, II:26–47, quotations from 28, 38; Cowan, "Carolina Judge Convicts 2."

42. *NC v. Armentrout*, II:47–76, quotations from 53, 57, 63,

43. *NC v. Armentrout*, II:76–90, quotation from 89.

44. *NC v. Armentrout*, II:91.

45. *NC v. Armentrout*, II:119–59.

46. *NC v. Armentrout*, II:156–57.

47. *NC v. Armentrout*, II:119–59.

48. *NC v. Armentrout*, II:119–20, 157–58.

49. *NC v. Armentrout*, II:165–66.

50. *NC v. Armentrout*, II:127–30, quotations from 127.

51. *NC v. Armentrout*, II:168–80, quotations from 178, 179.

52. Cowan, "Carolina Judge Convicts 2," 2-B.

53. Cowan, "Carolina Judge Convicts 2," 2-B; Allen Cowan, "The Trial's Over, But Who Shot Stanley Altland?," *St. Petersburg Times*, December 3, 1972, 1-B, 4-B, www.newspapers.com/image/317658518/.

CHAPTER 9

1. Allen Cowan, "11 Altland Companions are Cleared," *St. Petersburg Times*, November 28, 1972, 11-B, www.newspapers.com/image/317662229/; Ron Alridge, "Suit May Follow Campers' Court Triumph," *Charlotte Observer*, December 1, 1972, 1-E, 4-E, www.newspapers.com/image/622005771/; Rusher quoted in Cowan, "11 Altland Companions Cleared";

Mike Gomez, "Two Guilty in NC," *Clearwater Sun*, November 29, 1972, 1-B, https://pinellasmemory.org/islandora/object/clearwater%3A26502.

2. Allen Cowan, "The Trial's Over, But Who Shot Stanley Altland?," *St. Petersburg Times*, December 3, 1972, 1-B, 4-B, www.newspapers.com/image/317658518/; Alridge, "Suit May Follow," 1-E, 4-E; Cowan, "Trial's Over," 4-B.

3. Cowan, "Trial's Over," 1-B.

4. Cowan, "11 Altland Companions Cleared," 1-B; Gomez, "Two Guilty in NC."

5. Jody Higgins, "Trial Held in Yancey Courthouse for Florida Youth Charged with Disorderly Conduct at Campground," *Yancey Record*, November 30, 1972, 1, https://newspapers.digitalnc.org/lccn/sn95072283/1972-11-30/ed-1/seq-1/.

6. "Still No Answer in North Carolina," *St. Petersburg Times*, December 4, 1972, 24-A, www.newspapers.com/image/317668017/.

7. Gomez, "Two Guilty in NC," 1-B; Alridge, "Suit May Follow," 4-B.

8. Lawton Chiles to Beatrice Olson, December 18, 1972, letter in possession of Ron Olson; "Chiles Seeks Report on Altland Slaying," *St. Petersburg Times*, December 12, 1972, 4-B, www.newspapers.com/image/317633293/; "Updating the News, What Ever Happened To: A Federal Civil Rights Lawsuit on Behalf of 23 Clearwater Campers," *St. Petersburg Times*, December 23, 1972, 22-B, www.newspapers.com/image/332147402/.

9. J. Stanley Pottinger to Senator Lawton Chiles, March 2, 1973, letter in possession of Ron Olson.

10. Allen Cowan, "Altland Probe File Closed to Chiles," *St. Petersburg Times*, January 19, 1973, 6-B, www.newspapers.com/image/317627064/; Lawton Chiles to Beatrice Olson, March 23, 1973, letter in possession of Ron Olson.

11. Dale Edwards, "Mebane Lumber Still Building Momentum," *Mebane (NC) Enterprise*, August 17, 2022, www.mebaneenterprise.com; "Historical Population," Population.us, https://population.us/nc/mebane/, accessed January 9, 2023.

12. "Integration in Orange County," orangehistorync—Behind the Scenes at the O.C.H.M., https://orangenchistory.wordpress.com/2014/02/26/integration-in-orange-county/, accessed January 5, 2023; Jim Bissett, "The Dilemma over Moderates: School Desegregation in Alamance County, North Carolina," *Journal of Southern History* 81, no. 4 (November, 2015): 887–930, www.jstor.org/stable/43918814, accessed January 3, 2023; "1972 Presidential Election Results: North Carolina," https://uselectionatlas.org/RESULTS/, accessed January 4, 2023.

13. Marshall Stephenson, telephone interview by the author, September 9, 2022.

14. Stephenson, interview, September 9, 2022.

15. Stephenson, interview, September 9, 2022.

16. Stephenson, interview, September 9, 2022.

17. Marshall Stephenson, telephone interview by the author, December 21, 2022.

18. Stephenson, interview, December 21, 2022.

19. "Murder Charge Follows Death: Details Lacking," *Daily Times-News* (Burlington, NC), February 27, 1973, 9–10, www.newspapers.com/image/53564119/.

20. Martha Mullen, "Guard Charged," *Durham (NC) Sun*, February 26, 1973, 1, www.newspapers.com/image/786839258/; "Murder Charge Follows Death"; Stephenson, interview, September 9, 2022.

21. Barbara Horney, "Trial Set in Death Case: Plant Guard Bound Over," *Daily*

Times-News (Burlington, NC), March 14, 1973, 9–10, www.newspapers.com/image/53566938/; Stephenson, interview, September 9, 2022.

22. Horney, "Trial Set in Death Case;" Stephenson, interview, December 21, 2023.

23. "Murder Charge Follows Death."

24. Stephenson, interview, September 9, 2022.

25. Horney, "Trial Set in Death Case."

26. Mamie Dunn, "More Than Blind, Justice Is Human," *Durham (NC) Morning Herald*, December 16, 1973, 2-E, www.newspapers.com/image/787561882/.

27. Horney, "Trial Set in Death Case."

28. Allen Cowan, "Figure in Altland Slaying Is Killed In North Carolina," *St. Petersburg Times*, March 7, 1973, 13, www.newspapers.com/image/317644282/.

29. Robert L. Farb, UNC School of Government, *North Carolina Superior Court Judge's Benchbook* (September 2014), 1, https://benchbook.sog.unc.edu/sites/default/files/pdf/Grand%20Jury%20Proceedings_0.pdf, accessed January 14, 2023; Andrew D. Liepold, "Why Grand Juries Do Not (and Cannot) Protect the Accused," *Cornell Law Review* 80, no. 2 (January 1995): 266.

30. Farb, *Superior Court Judge's Benchbook*, 5; James C. McKinney and Al Baker, "Grand Jury System, With Exceptions, Favors Police," *New York Times*, December 7, 2014, www.nytimes.com/2014/12/08/nyregion/grand-juries-seldom-charge-police-officers-in-fatal-actions.html; Ben Casselman, "It's Incredibly Rare for a Grand Jury to Do What Ferguson's Just Did," *FiveThirtyEight*, November 24, 2014, https://fivethirtyeight.com/features/ferguson-michael-brown-indictment-darren-wilson/.

31. "Guard Cleared in Death Case," *Daily Times-News* (Burlington, NC), March 23, 1973, 1B, www.newspapers.com/image/53569064/.

32. Donald Jay Barrett, telephone interview by the author, August 24, 2021; Roger Altland and Sue Cello, interview by the author, Clearwater, FL, November 16, 2022.

33. "Alamance County's Matters of Public Record," *Daily Times-News* (Burlington, NC), November 1, 1971, 9B, www.newspapers.com/clip/116099187.

34. McKinney and Baker, "Grand Jury System."

35. Horney, "Trial Set in Death Case," 2B; Stephenson, interview, September 9, 2022.

36. "No Indictment Seen in Altland Pal's Death," *St. Petersburg Times*, April 8, 1973, 17-B, www.newspapers.com/image/318548033. The article misspelled Pierce's name as "Prince." Stephenson, interview, September 9, 2022.

37. Cowan, "Figure in Altland Slaying."

38. John York, "No Charges Yet in '72 Slaying," *Charlotte Observer*, July 4, 1973, 6–7, www.newspapers.com/image/622043853/.

39. York, "No Charges Yet."

40. York, "No Charges Yet."

CHAPTER 10

1. Billy Pritchard, "Yancey Sheriff, 11 Other Officers Named in $2.35 Million Lawsuit," *Asheville Citizen-Times*, May 24, 1974, 19, www.newspapers.com/image/201001632/.

2. "Karl Adkins, February 28, 1946–May 22, 2022," www.alexanderfunerals.com/obituary/karl-adkins, accessed February 17, 2023.

3. "Negro Attorney Has First Case in City Court," *Asheville Citizen*, September 21, 1951, 15, www.newspapers.com/image/197321229/; Ashley Cole Brewer, "Get on Board Children: The Story of Integration in Yancey County, North Carolina" (master's thesis, Center for Appalachian Studies, Appalachian State University, 2011), 72.

4. Allen Cowan, "Park Campers File Lawsuits over Fatal Raid," *St. Petersburg Times*, May 25, 1974, 6-B, www.newspapers.com/image/332175188/.

5. Reuben J. Dailey et al. v. Kermit Banks et al., Civil Action AC-74-42, US District Court for the Western District of North Carolina, Asheville, NC (1974), digital copy provided by NARA, Atlanta, GA, 225, 261, 262, 263.

6. "Jones, Woodrow Wilson," *Biographical Directory of the United States Congress*, https://bioguide.congress.gov/search/bio/J000263, accessed February 17, 2023; "Jones, Woodrow Wilson," History of the Federal Judiciary, Federal Judicial Center, www.fjc.gov/history/judges/jones-woodrow-wilson, accessed February 17, 2023.

7. "About Federal Courts: Civil Cases," www.uscourts.gov/about-federal-courts/types-cases/civil-cases, accessed March 13, 2023.

8. Charles Becton, telephone interview by the author, February 10, 2023.

9. *Dailey v. Banks*, 201–3, 252–55, quotations from 252, 254, 255.

10. *Dailey v. Banks*, 204–10; 211–51.

11. *Dailey v. Banks*, 138–50, quotation from 149.

12. "For Sheriff—Kermit Banks," *Yancey Journal* (Burnsville, NC), October 24, 1974, 5, Digital NC, North Carolina Newspapers, https://newspapers.digitalnc.org/lccn/sn95072283/1974-10-31/ed-1/seq-5/; "Local Unofficial Election Returns," *Yancey Journal*, November 7, 1974, 1, https://newspapers.digitalnc.org/lccn/sn95072283/1974-11-07/ed-1/seq-1/.

13. *Dailey v. Banks*, 151–73, quotation from 171.

14. *Dailey v. Banks*, 125–31, quotations from 128, 130.

15. *Dailey v. Banks*, 132–37, quotations from 134, 135, 107–11, 108, 100–105, 103, 91–95, 112–17, 114, 115, 119–24.

16. *Dailey v. Banks*, 126, 91, 112, 119.

17. *Dailey v. Banks*, 92, 101, 107, 113, 120, 127, 133.

18. Billy Pritchard, "Youths Say Sheriff Held Smoking Gun," *Asheville Citizen*, February 12, 1975, 1, www.newspapers.com/image/202678543/.

19. Charles L. Becton, interview by Pamela Foster, February 6 and 20, 1994, in the Southern Oral History Program Collection no. 4007, Southern Historical Collection, Wilson Library, University of North Carolina at Chapel Hill, https://oralhistoriesproject.law.unc.edu/oral-histories/charles-becton/, accessed March 10, 2023; Charles Becton, telephone interview by the author, February 10, 2023.

20. Phil Lokey, telephone interview by the author, March 22, 2022.

21. "About Federal Courts"; Becton, interview by the author.

22. "Historical Highlights: The Southern Manifesto of 1956, March 12, 1956," History, Art & Archives (website), United States House of Representatives, https://history.house.gov/Historical-Highlights/1951-2000/The-Southern-Manifesto-of-1956/, accessed March 3, 2023.

23. John Kyle Day, *The Southern Manifesto: Massive Resistance and the Fight to Preserve Segregation* (Jackson: University Press of Mississippi, 2014), 84–107, http://www.jstor.org/stable/j.ctt155jp9q.8, accessed March 5, 2023.

24. "An Address Made to the Lions Club, Statesville, NC, May 9, 1955, by the Reverend James P. Dees, Rector of Trinity Episcopal Church and Priest in Charge of Holy Cross Mission," and Woodrow Wilson Jones to Reverend James P. Dees, June 8, 1955, both in Basil Lee Whitener Papers, 1889–1968, Folder "Civil Rights, 1950–1956," David M. Rubenstein Rare Book and Manuscript Library, Duke University, 111–114, 105, https://archives.lib.duke.edu/catalog/whitener_aspace_ref321_tvx, 2230–68, 111–14. Italics for emphasis were included in the published version of Dess's speech.

25. Several drafts of Jones's speech against the Civil Rights Act of 1957 are included in the Whitener Papers, "Civil Rights, 1950–1956," 230–68. Adam Stein, interview by the author, Carrboro, NC, September 15, 2021.

26. *Dailey v. Banks*, 76–88.

27. Pritchard, "Youths Say Sheriff Held Smoking Gun," 7.

CHAPTER 11

1. "Police Win Civil Rights Jury Verdict," *Asheville Citizen*, February 15, 1975, 1, 5, www.newspapers.com/image/202689952/.

2. Charles Becton, telephone interview by the author, February 10, 2023.

3. Becton, interview.

4. Billy Pritchard, "Youths Say Sheriff Held Smoking Gun," *Asheville Citizen*, February 12, 1975, 7, www.newspapers.com/image/202678543/.

5. Becton, interview; Ron Alridge, "Lawmen Abused Them, 7 Testify," *Charlotte Observer*, February 12, 1975, 5, www.newspapers.com/image/622682982/.

6. Pritchard, "Youths Say Sheriff Held Smoking Gun," 1, 7; Alridge, "Lawmen Abused Them," 5, 7.

7. Pritchard, "Youths Say Sheriff Held Smoking Gun," 7.

8. Ron Olson, interview by the author, November 16, 2022; Pritchard, "Youths Say Sheriff Held Smoking Gun," 7.

9. Max Johnson, interview by the author November 16, 2022; Pritchard, "Youths Say Sheriff Held Smoking Gun," 1, 7.

10. Alridge, "Lawmen Abused Them," 7; Becton, interview.

11. Becton, interview.

12. Pritchard, "Youths Say Sheriff Held Smoking Gun," 7; Reuben J. Dailey et al. v. Kermit Banks et al., Civil Action AC-74-42, US District Court for the Western District of North Carolina, Asheville, NC (1974), digital copy provided by NARA, Atlanta, GA, 73–74.

13. Billy Pritchard, "Sheriff Denies Killing Camper," *Asheville Citizen*, February 13, 1975, 19, www.newspapers.com/image/202682322/; Ron Alridge, "Lawmen Cleared in Campers' Suit," *Charlotte Observer*, February 15, 1975, 7, www.newspapers.com/image/622687987/.

14. Linda Mancini, email message to author, March 29, 2023; Becton, interview.

15. Ron Alridge, "Deputy Says Camper Was Shot Accidentally," *Charlotte Observer*, February 13, 1975, 10, www.newspapers.com/image/622685466/; Pritchard, "Sheriff Denies Killing Camper."

16. Alridge, "Deputy Says Camper Was Shot Accidentally," 9, 10.

17. "Police Win Civil Rights Jury Verdict," 5.

18. Becton, interview.

19. Ron Alridge, "Lawmen Cleared in Campers' Suit," *Charlotte Observer*, February 15, 1975, B-1, www.newspapers.com/image/622687987.

20. Billy Pritchard, "Federal Civil Rights Jury Weighs Evidence," *Asheville Citizen*, February 14, 1975, 23, www.newspapers.com/image/202688416/.

21. *Dailey v. Banks*, 73–74; Pritchard, "Federal Civil Rights Jury Weighs Evidence."

22. Pritchard, "Federal Civil Rights Jury Weighs Evidence."

23. Alridge, "Lawmen Cleared in Campers' Suit."

24. Becton, interview.

25. Becton, interview.

26. *Dailey v. Banks*, 71.

27. Becton, interview.

28. Pritchard, "Federal Civil Rights Jury Weighs Evidence"; Becton, interview.

29. *Dailey v. Banks*, 71; "Jury Decides Raid Was No Violation of Campers' Rights," *Tampa Tribune*, February 15, 1975, 19, www.newspapers.com/image/334590100/.

30. "Jury Decides Raid Was No Violation"; Alridge, "Lawmen Cleared in Campers' Suit."

31. "Police Win Civil Rights Jury Verdict"; Alridge, "Lawmen Cleared in Campers' Suit."

32. Lokey, interview.

33. Ron Alridge, "How Summer Camping Trip Ended in Death and Lawsuit," *Charlotte Observer*, February 16, 1975, 1, 18, www.newspapers.com/image/622665428/.

34. Carolyn Yuziuk, "Yancey Sheriff Not Guilty," *Yancey Journal*, February 20, 1975, 1, 2, https://newspapers.digitalnc.org/lccn/sn95072283/1975-02-20/ed-1/seq-1/.

CHAPTER 12

1. Phil Lokey, telephone interview by the author, March 22, 2022; "Rolling Stones Gather a Crowd," *New York Daily News*, May 2, 1975, www.newspapers.com/image/464421224/.

2. Brian Burrough, *Days of Rage: America's Radical Underground, the FBI, and the Forgotten Age of Revolutionary Violence* (New York: Penguin, 2016), prologue, iBooks.

3. Lokey, interview.

4. Michael Shreiner, "Fear of the Other," *Evolution Counseling*, February 1, 2017, https://evolutioncounseling.com/fear-of-the-other/, accessed July 5, 2023.

5. R. Nicholas Carleton, "Fear of the Unknown: One Fear to Rule Them All?," *Journal of Anxiety Disorders* no. 41 (2016): 5–21, https://doi.org/10.1016/j.janxdis.2016.03.011.

6. David Satterwhite, interview by FBI Special Agent Thomas J. Brereton, July 13, 1972, Mebane, NC, CE 44-2104, 2.

7. Susan Rachel Frances Cello, interview by FBI Special Agents John V. De Neale and Ernest J. Kirstein Jr., Clearwater, FL, July 13, 1972, CE 44-1422, NARA, College Park, MD, 27.

8. North Carolina General Assembly, "An Act to Rewrite General Statutes Chapter 18, Rewrite and Transfer to Chapter 105 the Revenue Statutes Formerly in Chapter 18, and to Repeal Certain Inconsistent Sections," 1971 Session, 24.

9. State of North Carolina v. Richard Armentrout et al., 72-CR-997-1020, Dorothy P. Hoover, Court Reporter, County of Yancey, District Court Division, 2 vols., October 30, November 27–28, 1972, II: 18, 81. (Normally transcripts are not taken in district court, but Emma McNairy secured a court reporter who completed this transcript. Fred McNairy's sons kept the transcript and turned it over to Roger Altland, who allowed me to use it.)

10. Reuben J. Dailey et al. v. Kermit Banks et al., Civil Action AC-74-42, US District Court for the Western District of North Carolina, Asheville, NC (1974), digital copy provided by NARA, Atlanta, GA, 194.

11. *NC v. Armentrout*, I:120.

12. Donald Jay Barrett, telephone interview by the author, August 24, 2021.

13. Columbia University School of Engineering and Applied Science, "Why Do We Remember Emotional Events Better? Columbia Neuroscientists Identify Specific Neural Mechanism Responsible," *Sci Tech Daily*, February 24, 2023, https://scitechdaily.com /why-do-we-remember-emotional-events-better-columbia-neuroscientists-identify-specific -neural-mechanism-responsible/; Richard J. McNally, *Remembering Trauma* (Cambridge, MA: Harvard University Press, 2003), quotations from 9; Rhitu Chatterjee, "How Trauma Affects Memory: Scientists Weigh in on the Kavanaugh Hearing," Health News from NPR, September 28, 2018, www.npr.org/sections/health-shots/2018/09/28/652524372.

14. Ron Alridge, "Youthful Camper Killed in Raid/24 Campers Charged after Fatal Incident," *Charlotte Observer*, July 5, 1972, 3A, www.newspapers.com/image/621942110/, accessed December 10, 2021.

15. James Rowen, "Young Man Ran, Was Shot—Dangerous Trend Began," *Miami Herald*, March 13, 1972, 4–5C, www.newspapers.com/image/625313376/.

16. "Timeline of Events since George Floyd's Murder," Associated Press, October 23, 2022, https://apnews.com.

17. "Timeline of Events"; Michael C. Bender, *Frankly We Did Win this Election: The Inside Story of How Trump Lost* (New York: Grand Central Publishing, 2021), chap. 9, iBooks.

18. W. J. Rorabaugh, *American Hippies* (New York: Cambridge University Press, 2015), 97, 98.

19. James C. McKinney and Al Baker, "Grand Jury System, with Exceptions, Favors Police," *New York Times*, December 7, 2014, www.nytimes.com/2014/12/08/nyregion/grand -juries-seldom-charge-police-officers-in-fatal-actions.html; Mark Brennan, John Sullivan, Julie Tate, and Jennifer Jenkins, "Protests Spread over Police Shootings. Police Promised Reforms. Every Year They Still Shoot and Kill Nearly 1000 People," *Washington Post*, June 8, 2020, www.washingtonpost.com.

20. "Contempt of Cop," Academic Dictionaries and Encyclopedias (website), https:// en-academic.com/dic.nsf/enwiki/11574648. Contempt of cop surfaced as an issue in the Tyre Nichols case in Memphis, TN. See Robin Stein, Alexandria Cardia, and Natalie Reneau, "71 Commands in 13 Minutes: Officers Gave Tyre Nichols Impossible Orders," *New York Times*, January 29, 2023, www.nytimes.com/2023/01/29/us/tyre-nichols-video -assault-cops.html.

21. ACLU Northern California, "Know Your Rights: Police Interactions for Black and Brown People," September 30, 2020, www.aclunc.org/our-work/know-your-rights/know -your-rights-police-interactions-black-and-brown-people.

22. Sally Keston and John Maines, "Unequal Treatment Under the Law, *Asheville Citizen-Times*, June 27, 2020, A7, www.newspapers.com/image/669699792/.

23. Max Edward Johnson, interview by FBI Special Agents Walter B. Granger and Charles D. Vance, July 13, 1972, Clearwater, Florida, CE 44-1422, NARA, College Park, MD.

24. Harper Lee, *To Kill a Mockingbird* (New York: Harper Collins, 1960), 246.

25. Ron Alridge, "Lawmen Cleared in Campers' Suit," *Charlotte Observer*, February 15, 1975, 7, www.newspapers.com/image/622687987/.

26. Linda Mancini, telephone interview by the author, November 8, 2021; Phil Lokey, interview by the author, July 11, 2023.

27. See, for example, US Department of Justice, Office of Justice Programs, "De-escalation Training: Safer Communities and Safer Law Enforcement Officers," September 6, 2022, https://www.ojp.gov/files/archives/blogs/2022/de-escalation -training-safer-communities-and-safer-law-enforcement-officers.

28. Rosa Brooks, *Tangled Up in Blue: Policing the American City* (New York: Penguin Books, 2021), part 3, iBooks.

29. Richard Rosen, interview by the author, Carrboro, NC, November 3, 2022.

30. Roger Altland, telephone interview by the author, October 30, 2021.

31. Lokey, interview. Several other campers said something similar and had similar emotions when they spoke with me for the first time.

EPILOGUE

1. "Ex-Sheriff Indicted in Voting Probe," *Winston-Salem Journal*, December 4, 1986, 4, www.newspapers.com/image/939997282/.

2. "Kermit Banks Is Acquitted," *Asheville Times*, March 13, 1987, 28, https://www .newspapers.com/image/945127094/.

3. Paul Clark, "Ex-Yancey Sheriff Pleads Guilty to Vote-Buying," *Asheville Citizen-Times*, May 7, 1987, 1, 10, www.newspapers.com/image/198671532/.

4. Paul Clark, "SBI Vote Probe Finds Problems in Yancey," *Asheville Citizen-Times*, November 2, 1990, 1, 7, www.newspapers.com/image/200050335/.

5. Sue Cello, interview by the author, Clearwater, FL, November 16, 2022.

INDEX

acid (drug), 13, 39, 42. *See also* barbiturates; heroin; LSD; marijuana; mescaline

ACLU (American Civil Liberties Union), 54, 79, 92, 94, 126, 149, 151

Adkins, Karl, 122–28, 131–36, 138, 139, 161

African Americans: in central Florida in 1972, 38; law enforcement and, 149–52; in Mount Gilead, NC, 93; in Yancey County, NC, in 1972, 20, 25

Alamance County, NC, 111

alcohol, 13, 42, 76, 104, 142; at Briar Bottom campsite, 2, 64, 133; laws regulating and restricting, 11, 143

Altamont concert, 13, 45, 50, 51

Alternative Vittles (store), 36, 37, 55, 69, 77, 78

Altland, Roger, 16, 34–36, 39–43, 48–50, 71–73, 83, 120–21, 154–63

Altland, Stanley: at Briar Bottom, 3–5, 158, 162; death of, 6–8, 72–74, 146–48, 150–55; death certificate of, 69, 79-80; funeral of, 78; plans for Rolling Stones concert, 48, 52–53; toxicology report for, 69, 79, 134; wrongful death lawsuit, 127–28, 131–34, 138. *See also* Alternative Vittles; People's Party

American Civil Liberties Union (ACLU), 54, 79, 92, 94, 126, 149, 151

Appalachia, historians' views of, 22, 28, 171n7

Appalachian State University, 14, 22

Arbery, Ahmaud, 33, 149, 150

Arrowood, Bill, 30, 65, 67, 122, 125, 127, 135, 145

Asheville, NC, 55, 58, 122; federal civil rights trial in, 139–43, 160

Asheville (NC) Citizen, 85, 131, 139, 151

Atkins, William, 95, 98, 100, 101, 103, 104

"back to the land" movement, 27, 28

Bailey, Garrett, 124, 129, 13, 132, 136, 152

ballistic evidence, 96, 134

Banks, Kermit: account of Stan Altland's death, 75–77, 120, 170n13; author's efforts to contact, 16; campers' civil rights lawsuit against, 96, 120, 121, 123, 125–27; early life and career, 29–32, 145; FBI interview with, 85–87, 91–92; indicted in federal investigation, 158–60; named in wrongful death lawsuit, 122–23; and raid at Briar Bottom, 5–7, 65–68; testimony in disorderly conduct trial, 100–101;

191

presidential elections: in 1968, 10, 25, 44; in 1972, 10, 25, 44, 111, 109; in Yancey County, 25

profanity, at Briar Bottom campsite, 6, 7, 85, 102, 103, 105, 136, 144, 126

punitive damages, 123, 125

racism, 11, 12, 13, 150, 152. *See also* Arbery, Ahmaud; Floyd, George; law enforcement: contempt of cop; law enforcement: police brutality

Rainbow Family of Living Light, 53, 54

Raleigh (NC) News and Observer, 9, 10, 13

Raleigh, NC, 9, 10, 13, 29, 38, 44, 75, 76, 81, 83

Ray, Blaine, 59, 60, 86, 99, 122, 143

Richards, Keith, 13, 51

Rivers, Harold, 59, 60–61; at Briar Bottom, 64–66, 84, 90, 144–45; civil rights complaint against, 124–25; testimony at disorderly conduct trial, 99

roads: Forest Service Road 472, 59, 60, 61, 62, 157, 163; NC Route 80, 58, 65, 155, 157; NC Route 128, 58, 156; US 19E, 19, 58, 155

Roberts, Clyde, 75, 82, 92, 95, 110, 120, 135, 144

Rolling Stones: concert in Charlotte, 48, 52, 72–74; *Exile on Main St.*, 46, 48; "Gimme Shelter," 13, 163; North American tour, 46–50, 52, 73, 142; popularity of, 9, 12–14, 141, 161, 163; *Sticky Fingers*, 45, 46, 73; "Street Fighting Man," 12, 74, 142; "Sweet Black Angel," 45, 52; "Sweet Virginia," 46, 74; "Tumbling Dice," 45, 46

Rosen, Richard, 94, 154

Ruidoso, NM, 14, 148

Rusher, Tom, 68–69; as prosecutor in disorderly conduct trial, 99–102, 104–5, 108

Sargent, W. A. Y., 69, 79, 80

Satterwhite, David: at Briar Bottom, 3–7, 60–64, 76, 88–91; and Clearwater campers, 20–21, 60, 155–56; death of, 113–20, 139–40, 149; FBI interview with, 84, 86; interaction with Kermit Banks, 146, 151, 153; life in Mebane, 112–13; testimony at disorderly conduct trial, 97, 101–2, 106; testimony regarding, at federal civil rights trial, 124, 126, 132–36

SBI. *See* North Carolina State Bureau of Investigation

Seifert, Jimmie, 100, 103, 104

Selective Service, 36, 37, 109. *See also* draft lottery; Vietnam War

Shankle, Terry, 59–60, 64, 99, 122, 124, 125, 145, 146, 153

Shea, Kevin, at Briar Bottom, 3–6, 64, 67, 77, 87; on life in Clearwater, 40, 42; testimony at disorderly conduct trial, 102–5, 120

sheriff of Yancey County. *See* Banks, Kermit; North Carolina Sheriff's Association

Siebenthaler, Cathy, 55, 57, 63, 97, 161; testimony at disorderly conduct trial, 103–4

sign, destruction of, 59, 99, 139, 157

Sofarelli, Doreen, 43, 55, 62, 72, 73, 97, 102, 122, 133, 162

South Toe River, 1, 14, 22, 59, 61, 155

"Southern Manifesto." See *Declaration of Constitutional Principles*

Spock, Benjamin, 38–39

St. Petersburg Times, 75, 76, 82, 97, 108, 109, 117, 119

standard of proof: at federal civil rights trial, 128; at grand jury proceedings, 118

Stein, Adam: in disorderly conduct trial, 97–99, 102–3; early career, 93–94; and federal civil rights trial, 120–22; later career, 160; reaction to David Satterwhite's death, 117; on Woodrow Wilson Jones, 129

Stephenson, Marshall, 111–13, 116, 119

Sticky Fingers (Rolling Stones), 45, 46, 73

Stoneman Meadow Riot, 53–54